D0908829

Remembering
Dud Dean

Remembering Dud Dean

Arthur Macdougall's famous tales of everybody's favorite Maine guide

COMPILED AND INTRODUCED
BY WALTER M. MACDOUGALL

2   4   5   3   1

COUNTRYSPORT PRESS

an imprint of Down East Books
P. O. Box 679
Camden, Maine 04843

For orders and catalog information, visit
www.downeastbooks.com, or call (800) 685-7962

Author's note: The sketch on the title page is by Milton C. Weiler, who illustrated the Coward McCann series of Dud Dean books. The pen-and-ink sketch-
es on pages 5, 100, and 123 appeared in *If It Returns With Scars* and were drawn
by Stanley W. Greene, an angler and close friend of Arthur Macdougall.

CONTENTS

Dud Dean and His Creator

Dud said, "We have to plan on gittin' older. It goes erlong with gitten' on. But thar ain't nothin' in hell or high water to keep us from bein' good neighbors, er from livin' up to the best we know jist as long as we can tell daylight from dark. So we go a piece farther, an' a while longer."

From "Two Poachers and a Rail Fence"

THE DUD DEAN STORIES SHOULD NOT be out of print. They are too engaging, too much fun, and as the above quote indicates, too filled with meaning when it comes to life's essentials. Dud's friends, old and new, will welcome this anthology which makes available once again some of the best hunting and fishing stories ever written.

Dud Dean and his adventures first took life in what our family called the study camp. It sat perched on a steep bank above the water—as far from our family quarters on Wyman Lake as our limited property would allow. There in the camp's cozy smallness my father, Arthur Macdougall, or Mak as he was known by friends near and far, crafted these classic hunting and fishing tales. In all there were to be fifty-six Dud Dean stories, most of which were featured in *Field & Stream* magazine before being collected into a series of books. Across the country, Dud soon became for many the quintessential Maine guide and took his place among the most beloved characters of outdoor stories.

Furniture in the study camp was sparse—limited to a sizable table and a chair. A large Aladdin lamp with its incandescent mantle furnished light for those late night hours when these masterful tales took form. Writing the introduction to the last collection of the Dud Dean stories, my father imagined he was back in the study camp and seated at the table. His task set. To answer, once and for all, that question most asked: "Who served as the model for Dud Dean?" The lamp light leaves the corners of the small room in shadows and from this half light spirits of past neighbors assemble around the table. "He is all of us at our best plus his own self," they whisper.

My father knew these neighbors well. With them he had walked the trails, fished the clear waters, and sat around their fires. As pastor, he had officiated at their weddings and too often presided at their funerals. He knew their little triumphs and not a few secret despairs. My father attested that there was a depth of feeling in men who have slept out under the stars, and he used to comment that they did not have "sidewalk minds." In the pages of these stories, we meet the neighbors of the upper Kennebec as they once lived. They seem real enough for us to reach out and shake their hands. More importantly it becomes our privilege to know Dud Dean.

People constitute Dud's chief interest. Well, people and trout fishing, for as Dud tells us in his stories, it's hard to separate the two. Henry Beston, in writing an introduction to *Where Flows the Kennebec*, observed that "the best stories . . . are always about people one remembers and likes to remember." Dud's understanding of human nature comes to us woven through a penetrating combination of wit and remembering. We listen to him and are amazed by his homespun shrewdness and his perception. We come away knowing more about ourselves and why we long to be led beside the clear waters of woodland Maine.

Action swirls in these stories. We feel the tension in the straining leader. We fear we may step on a twig and warn the splendid buck. We settle back in the yellow lamp light and sense the warmth of the camp stove. At another time we can feel the cold rain dribble down our back as we fish a mist-shrouded wilderness pond. All such things we sense again; yet all the while we are aware of a deeper current.

As my father put it, Dud tramps in "a less involved and a more elementally real world." His trail leads from "small interiors into outdoor immensities." Again, it was Henry Beston who observed that one puts down a Dud Dean book refreshed. It is as if Dud offers the soul a drink of spring water on the uphill trail of life. Beyond, or rather through those descriptions that carry the reader to the edge of ponds where the mayflies are hatching from water-color copies of the sunset and beyond the hilltops silvered in the winter moonlight, there is, to borrow from the poet William Wordsworth, "something still more deeply interfused." There is in these stories, as one-time *Atlantic Monthly* editor Bliss Perry pointed out, "Mak's ability to perceive and tell the truth." My father once said that over the years he and Dud had grown together in their appreciation of an elemental strength in nature.

Speaking a fisherman's allegory Dud tells us "A man must come to love his own river." Perhaps what Dud means is that a person must come to know that river until its elemental realness flows through oneself. Ralph Waldo Emerson was saying much the same thing when he spoke of beauty stealing through one's being until one yielded to the perfect whole. But it is the reader who must find the meaning for him or herself and that finding is, after all, part of the adventure of going with Dud.

Feeling a degree of fullness may be easier to maintain when we are young and the miracle seems immediate. Dud warns us and himself about getting older. "Some men an' women don't ripen while they grow old, they jis shrink. So they come to feel that the cup of life has cracked on the bottom, an' instid of it running over, it leaks out overnight." Regardless of your age, you have to work at living. Our guide has his own advice. He admonishes us to "Go fishin' now! and then later on if you git a chance."

In writing the introduction to the anthology *Classics of American Sporting Fiction* (which contains three Dud Dean stories), Michael McIntosh seizes upon the essence of sporting fiction during the golden age of such short stories. They sought "less to tell us how we might be more efficient outdoorsmen and more to show us how we might be better human beings."

There is no doubt that Dud likes to catch fish, especially big trout, "them old sinners" as he once described them. He hates to lick a good fish, and he hates to lose them, but when Dud starts to describe trout, we know that for him angling is not simply about catching fish. Moxie trout he tells us are "almost blueish erlong the lateral line, an' spotted as red as the devil's diamonds" and those from the Kennebec's East Branch are "all silvered an' dotted 'ith the color of mayflowers that grow in the spring at the edge of the snow." Dud's advice is clear. A person "should find trout, but more than trout." Dud, like his friend Mak, "would dread to be so driven, so hurried, while angling that [he] fished on ahead of [the] ancient sounds . . . The crux of it is that when one angles for trout, he is fishing for a share of it all."

Once, a young woman who much admired Dud said to him, "I think you're wonderful, Mr. Dean."

Because she meant it, Dud was embarrassed. "Shucks. I hain't. Ask Nancy," says Dud, pointing to his wife, "She'll tell yer the truth."

"He is sometimes," said Nancy.

Far more often than not, Dud is an exceptional man. My father spoke of him as "that greatly simple man." Dud is such a person, but for all his wisdom and accomplishments he is neither infallible nor a saint. His ethical code is simple: One expects to carry his or her part and more when it's necessary; one consumes no more than his or her share and less if another's needs are greater; one respects the property of another; one does what he or she has said he would do; and when the dark becomes really black, one waits with quiet courage for the morning. That is his unspoken credo— as essential as a three-pound ax, matches in a waterproof case, and a compass are to Dud and his woods-wise friends.

I have already mentioned that Dud likes people—well, most of them. He does so because he likes life, chuckling, and good fun in general. My father wrote "Dud and I have loved fun . . . because we learned that fun is . . . a convocation of well being. We made all we could of 'fellowship' because fun is not a lonely experience."

Not everything is fun, however. Dud can get disgusted. Once our guide took several of Mak's minister friends fishing. Through no fault of the guide, the trip was a series of disasters and at the end one of the bedraggled anglers says,"Well, Mister Dean, some-day I may want to go fishing with you again, but not now." Dud informs us, "I tried to be charitable, an' all that, but the best I cu'd muster was to say, 'Some day, maybe, I'll invite you.'" Dud's wife, Nancy, said later that Dud was ashamed of himself, but he wasn't.

And Dud can get mad. When he does there comes that "steely expression" in his blue-gray eyes under those "awesome brows." A few times Dud altogether forgets his resolve to be a gentleman as he did when he took Crazy Stiller fishing. Of course, one can understand. The situation was one of those that try a man's soul.

Like all great storytellers, Dud makes a practice of being hon-est about himself. He has, for instance, known fear as when in "The Way of an Old Maid," Dud has to rescue two people from the sweeping waters of the Kennebec. "Somehow, the river scared me almost helpless," he tells us. He is acquainted with chagrin as the story "Dud Guides a Lady" discloses. Dumping your canoe and then getting saved by a young woman you didn't want to guide is not something you want in the newspapers.

I started to write that Dud was above all humble, but I am not sure that this is the case. Anyway, the reader must decide such facts for him or herself. Is it humility that he exhibits or a just respect for himself? He tells us that he has guided people who were high-hat, "but I never held that ag'inst folks . . . I've kept my respect fer myself, an' always figgered they sh'ud do the same in their own way." Perhaps to keep one's self-respect is to accomplish more than to wallow in the humbleness of saints.

No wonder so many sportsmen and sportswomen have come to the upper Kennebec hoping they might find Dud sitting on his back steps, filling his pipe and free to take them fishing or hunting. They feel Dud has gotten his life together. His direction is set in the quiet balance of his mind, and he possesses the heart to get him where he knows we humans ought to go. He is a companion for the trail—a man who understands what we can never quite express about God's great outdoors and the human journey.

Within the final story of the last Dud Dean book, there is the tale of a young soldier home on a furlough who packs his grub and goes fishing into Robinson and Lone Jack Ponds. There he forgets time. Dud recounts:

> The soldier an' his friend was on the raft that they
> had patched up. The time was early mornin'
> when the red gods haunt the wilderness, when
> countless little flowers of the day begin to open
> up, an' when the sun mixes night an' day together
> an' pours soft colors eround old conkey pines that
> stand high above the newer stuff. It was early
> mornin' and the ferever was all eround Lone Jack.
> I mean, it's good fer the saint er the sinner to go
> fishin' in the early light; good fer the genius er the
> dullard to be fishin' afore the sun comes up over
> the beloved near-at-hand. The soldier told me
> that, the best he cu'd. He felt it in his bones.

We feel Dud's wisdom in our bones, and in gratitude we celebrate Dud Dean and express our gratitude to his creator.

Dud's wisdom and his code of conduct are distilled from Arthur Macdougall's rich experience—from human beings with good in their souls, from wise minds that did not "take life as a donkey munches hay" (to use one of my father's favorite expressions), from faith and from the intimations of nature. My father discovered joy and inspiration in much of life. He found it in hard work done well, in the courage of independent men and women, in the sun's "long light" striking across the old New England hills, in the singing of the "pipers" on a spring evening, and in fishing for trout. Yet there were moments when he experienced a lingering melancholy like a cold mist after a late fall rain.

At a young age, and as the Old Testament would phrase it, my father was "acquainted with grief." Born in Enfield, Maine, on August 16, 1896, he was the son of a master carpenter who had emigrated from Scotland and, in the "new world" had been called to the evangelical ministry. His mother was Nellie Rosilla Guptill of Cherryfield, Maine, a descendant of that town's first settler, a millwright by the name of Ichabod Willey. Following my father's birth, the new family moved four times in five years. In 1901, they were in South Chelmsford, Massachusetts. It was there, in the spring of the year, that my father's mother died.

The moves continued. There were some happy memories. In the town of Granville, Massachusetts, my father caught his first trout in a winding, meadow brook. It was there, too, he discovered a wondrous realm of books in the public library.

But my father's boyhood was short. By age thirteen, he was

working for his board for a widow—the only "man" on a hillside farm in Blandford, Massachusetts. There were some excitements such as the Blandford Fair, where the widow sold maple sugar they had made to pay the taxes. But generally life was just hard. There were days when the widow and my father shared the live-stock's corn meal. My father learned that one has to find his own way through the valley of existence. He found kinship with the out-of-doors, hunted and fished when he could, and trapped for any money he possessed.

Many jobs would follow: clerking in a grocery store, working on the railroad section gang, and finally operating a paper machine at the Woronoko Mill in Russell, Massachusetts. With the money he saved he attended sessions at Mount Hermon—a school in northwestern Massachusetts that has provided opportunity for so many young men.

Returning from France and the First World War, he entered the theological seminary in Bangor, Maine. In 1923, he was called to fill the pulpit at Bingham, Maine, that village on the banks of the Kennebec so pleasantly held in the hollow of the folding hills. Wearing his only overcoat, a khaki O.D. issue, "Mak" began a thirty-six year ministry in the upper Kennebec. He never was to make much money and always claimed that the balance of his salary was paid in the form of good trout fishing.

That same year he married Leah Parks of Russell, Massachu-setts, whom he had known and admired since a boy. Any cele-bration of Dud Dean or his creator must include my mother. She and Dud's wife, Nancy, would have made good neighbors. Both possessed an admirable good sense and an unshakable propriety.

(My mother, for instance, disapproved of Dud's favorite expression, "by crotch.") It was my mother who painstakingly proofread my father's manuscripts and corrected the galley sheets. This she accomplished between mending socks, practicing the choir, doing the wash, canning garden crops, and minding the expectations of parishioners.

While my father's formal schooling was good foundation, he read and studied his way to an impressive erudition. Yet, more than education, I think I know what called the attention of great minded men to this young minister of the upper Kennebec. Once on a very dark night when he and I were following an old and nearly obliterated trail, I asked my father how he knew when we were on or off the path. "You feel the difference under your feet," he answered. My father had an intuitive ability to feel where the truth ran in the great issues of life.

As a writer, he worked to learn his craft. According to him, he had read a small library of how-to-write books. He became an expert on what he termed "plotology"—dissecting the classical plots, which he liked to say had been "incubated" in the past. He practiced the development of characters and creation of swift descriptions that can "brush-in" a setting without delaying the action. He wrote and wrote. I can hear again the tap, tapping of his typewriter punctuating the stillness of the parsonage when the rest of Bingham had been long asleep.

Those reading the Dud Dean stories for the first time may need a word of warning and explanation. The "dialect" may present difficulties, but I think only at first. The eye adjusts to the phonetic spelling, and the ear soon welcomes the easy flow of Dud's lingo.

Fannie Hardy Ekstrom, who authored *The Penobscot Man* and made a lifetime study of Maine people and their culture, was the first to observe that among the many attempts to reproduce the old Maine idiom the Dud Dean stories were the most successful. Here is a faithful recording of linguistic patterns which have as their aim an effortless articulation without a surrendering of emphasis. Dud's creator writes:

> I have noticed that Dud drops his consonants
> whenever it is euphoniously convenient; but that
> occurs in relation to his own soft, slow articula-
> tion, and Dud does not consistently avoid the
> consonants. There are times when he stresses
> them, as if he felt that in so doing he emphasized
> the part the word played.

Consonants aside, this quote makes an important point. While the Maine idiom has a common core of linguistic patterns and vocal habits, it is not a stereotypical colloquialism. Consistency is not a virtue; getting one's point across is. True Mainers like Dud Dean are individuals, speech and all. Dud is Dud, and his partic-ular articulations are a part of his message.

Dud Dean's stories are lit by language genius—his own delightful turn of phrase, his marvelous enlivenments, his similes and metaphors. One is tempted to begin a list of memorable phrases such as "the sun was stuck behind a chunk of eternity," or in referring to an awkwardly tied fly "it floated like a lump of non-sense upside down," or the description of a character as "a moun-tain of protoplasm and a molehill of virtue" or . . . One quickly realizes that such figures and descriptions in Dud's narration or Mak's storytelling are not occasional but omnipresent. It is better for the reader to discover these golden images where they exist neatly woven into the fabric of the stories. Moreover, to lay too much stress on language may lead those not acquainted with Dud astray. After all, his stories are first and foremost adventures. Through them the clear waters of the Kennebec, home of bejeweled trout and silver salmon, flow into a new millennium. We meet new neighbors upon old trails and are invited in to sit not in their Victorian parlors, but in the lamp-lit kitchen where we can feel the warmth of an old Atlantic Claridon stove.

Selecting what stories to be included in this book has proven difficult. In fact, damned difficult. I could say that I have chosen those I liked best, but that would be too easy and not quite true. Not included are wonderful yarns: funny, poignant, instructive, fine outdoor tales.

The stories selected for this anthology seem to me to best reflect Dud Dean's character and that of his better neighbors along the Kennebec. There was a nobleness in their creed that should not be forgotten.

> *Walter M. Macdougall*
> Milo, Maine

An Invitation to Dud's World

(Taken from: "My Goodness Professor")

IT WAS MAY IN MAINE. SAP WAS RUNNING. And the hills were flowing tints of yellow and red where the deciduous trees were blooming. I cut a chip from a yellow birch that the winter winds had thrown down. The sap welled into the notch, and I drank my fill of that mildly flavored liquid. The sun was in a kindly mood, and all the wilderness was wide awake.

When Dud and I had eaten lunch, I pulled an old O.D. blanket from my pack and stretched out at full length. Is there any luxury like the lazy self indulgence of a prone position beneath skies in the month of May! How good to lie there and to look up through budding trees to the white clouds, like far-off glaciers sliding down the roof of the world, while near at hand the bloodroots and violets are poking their faces through last fall's blanket of leaves!

While I was thinking about that, Dud filled his pipe and then settled his broad shoulders against an unshaven silver birch. That rite over, he squinted up into the blue through the bud-tinted branches. I watched him, lazy puffs of tobacco smoke dissolved in the golden air. Minutes passed. Then Dud turned to me.

"Y'know, Mak, whenever I git a chance to jist set an' watch white clouds goin lazy-like across the sky, my mind always starts crusin' erbout inside. Maybe it's dangerous. Fust thing I know, I come up smack ag'inst this er that which I ain't remembered for maybe years. Fer example, jist a min-it ago, I found myself thinking erbout the time I guided Professor Kelley. Did I ever tell yer erbout him?"

*Welcome friends and neighbors of Dud Dean, ease back
and let these yarns fill your senses.*

A Deal in Hounds

Dud, Mak, and another companion, identified as an architect, are bird hunting in the hills and old farm country east of Bingham, Maine. They have stopped for lunch and made tea, which Dud observes, "sh'udn't ever be boiled." The passing of a boy and his dog prompts a confession from the architect. He would give anything to be young again. Dud has reservations, which lead him to tell his companions about his early years.

One calamity after another falls upon him as he turns twenty-one. He loses money in an attempt to get rich at lumbering. His father and then his mother die. He turns to farming and has three cows and the summer's hay in the barn when lightning hits and destroys the structure. At that hour of ashes and destitution, Hosshoe, a stray hound that has attached itself to Dud, presents him with twelve pups.

"Crotch," Dud remembers, "the old saying come to me. How it never rains but somebody gits good an' wet." Only one bright spot lights the dismal moment. There are indications that the young schoolmarm is returning Dud's definite interest.

"FROM THEN ON, MY FINANCIAL SITUATION got worse. How them pups did grow. An' do yer think I c'ud give 'em away. No sir!

Even Mat Markham refused to help me by takin' some off my hands. I had to borrow money to buy a cow, becuz them pups had to have milk. Then I had to borrow more money to build a new barn fer the cow. When we got it built, it was full of half-grown hounds.

"I talked it over with the schoolmarm. She suggested that I sh'ud advertise to find the rightful owner of that hound. So I spent five dollars an' sixty cents fer ads in the old *Somerset Reporter*. The ad was so much a word. It w'ud have cost me more to mention her pups. So I didn't. We-ell, the only result that c'ud be traced to that advertisin' was a bill from the town clerk fer dog tax.

"So thar I was, a-raisin' hounds. Somehow, it didn't help my reputation. Long-headed folks begun to talk erbout how queer it was that I sh'ud turn out to be sech an impractical feller, when all my folks had been nice, sensible people. But what c'ud I do? If ever a young feller was caught in a devil of a fix, his name was Dud Dean.

"I made up my mind that I'd make a clean breast of it to the schoolteacher becuz I knew that folks was sayin' that if I had any gumption, I w'ud have drowned them pups in the Kennebec River afore they was weaned. That's jist how simple a compound situation can look to persons on the outside.

"We-ell, when I faced this situation 'ith the schoolmarm, I found out that neighborhood talk had sort of undermined her confidence in me. Yes, sir! B'crotch, when I went home that night, the moon looked as commonplace as a white doorknob, an' I felt as sad as the children of Israel when they hung their harps on the alder bushes beside the waters of Babylon. Prob'ly I was stuffed up 'ith lonely pride. Anyhow, the schoolmarm went off on a vacation.

"Summer went past. An' I was like a man with a permanent

bellyache. One day, in November, it come to me that a man might as well ride hossback if he was goin' to be hung fer a hoss thief. So I got out my double barrel gun an' bought me some number two shells. That night, I brought home a nice, prime red fox. An' I had found out sunthin' that w'ud have done my heart good if it hadn't been so bowed down 'ith other griefs. I had as true a hound as ever lifted her head in the mornin' air. She had a voice like a seraphim, which is a contralto angel.

"Wait a min-it. I don't want to sound too flippant. Actually, I ain't sure whether a seraphim sings contralto, er what. But that blue-ticked, red-speckled bitch was a masterpiece. Yes sir! I was as proud of her as a feller head-over-heels in debt, an' no schoolmarm, c'ud be.

"Yer see, by that time, I was sick of hearin' folks snicker when some idgit wanted to know how my hounds was prosperin'. An' I had it halfway through my head that the schoolteacher warn't on my side. So I didn't bother to go down town, much. I jist stuck to fox huntin'. That bitch an' me got so thin that folks c'udn't tell us apart, except that she looked the smartest.

"Come the fust of December, an' I had twenty-five fox pelts. That didn't mean a fortune, but it meant erbout $250. Folks warn't so sure that I was the biggest durn fool this side of Massachusetts. That is, they warn't so sure as they had been. Any time yer catch a person laughin' at hard cash, yer can be sure that he warn't born in Maine.

"Up to then, thar hadn't been much snow. Not much. Then we got some more. Not havin' anythin' else to do, I stuck to fox huntin'. An' I learned a lot that winter, out on the hills. It was really the most profitable part of my eddication. Gradually, it come over me that God's whole creation didn't rise an' fall along 'ith my temperature. I saw the sun rise, a good many times, from the top of windswept hills. It come up, slow an' stiddy. I saw it setting away off back of the mountains. It went down, calm an' impersonal. Yep, after a while, my troubles didn't seem to crowd heaven an' earth.

"One day, I had a big dog fox in my pack an' was satisfied, in an absent-minded sort of way. Me an' the hound was walkin' up the Solon road comin' back from the John Savage place. I hardly paid attention when she jumped inter the snow an' worked off west of the road. But purty soon, she began to sing. Thar is almost as much difference in the sound of a hound's voice as thar is in human voices. Folks who don't realize that has missed sunthin'! A man perked up his ears when that bitch began to roll her notes.

"Over where she had gone, thar was a little patch of woods. It was all west of the main road, toward the Kennebec River. I sort of hustled to look over the layout, while my hound was runnin' up in the northwest corner. An' I finally got set right where a man w'ud want to be if he was dreamin' the whole affair. I warn't thar five min-its too soon, either. That hound was rollin' hound-talk down on me when I caught sight of movement in the low brush that flanked the pines.

"I pulled the old double-barrel to my shoulder an' followed erlong on the movement till the critter sh'ud come inter the clear. My trigger finger was half squeezed, when I made out it warn't so much like a fox as a little black dog, a spaniel. We-ell, I was flabbergasted becuz I had been sure I was goin' to knock over another fox. Without thinkin', I dropped the gun on my shoulder. Then, both eyes discovered the mistake. It was a big, black fox. The realization made my heart swell up so big it nearly choked me to death. I swung and pulled, but the fox went free.

"Crotch, I felt almost as bad as I w'ud to lose a nice trout. It was jist the shake of a buck's tail, an' fox an' hound was gone like a wind in the lilacs. Gone across the County road up the ridge, an' clean out of hearin'. From then on, till dark, was a chase to remember, but I never laid eyes on that fox.

"I felt aggravated at myself, which is the most uncomfortable aggravation in all the world. That night, when I was goin' home through town, Mat Markham offered me ten dollars fer my hound. Mat always was a master at what is known as anticlimax.

"No need to say that after that red foxes looked commonplace to me, but that bitch continued to take her foxes as they come. The twenty-first of December was as mean a day as I ever saw, cold an' personal. But me an' the hound started out. It had got to be a habit. We had worked purty steady and faithful to pick up some sign of that black fox. This day, I decided that we sh'ud have another look over in the place where Hosshoe had jumped him.

"Durn my hide if he wasn't back ag'in! I saw his tracks afore

the hound found them. 'W'ud that be him?' I asks her. An' b'crotch, she seemed to know what I meant. Oh well, what if she didn't? I was excited. I reckoned that he had gone in thar fer a sleep. An' I warn't but a little behind her when she let out the yowls that said we was hot on him, which meant that I was trackin' maybe as much as a thousand dollars becuz this was the days before ranch-raised foxes had come to market.

"That far, everythin' had worked out as nice as the fust time. As yer know, foxes tend to cross at sartin p'ints, but I figger that black critter w'udn't cross where I had blazed away him no more'n ten days ago. Crotch, I tried to think of everthin' all at once. I needed to think like a genius, but I was only a hunter. At last, thar warn't time to think erbout anything.

"It's queer, but once in a hundred years a man may do a thing 'ithout thinkin' at all. Fust thing I knew, I was runnin' jist as fast as I c'ud on webs. An' I was headed west, to the river. It was jist as though I had decided that fox w'ud try to get out of the box by sneakin' south erlong the river—only a man don't decide anythin' when his mind is as blank as an attic without a floor.

"Actually, the layout was like this. Beside the river, thar's a hossback ridge that runs north an' south. Beyond the ridge, lookin' down on the water, thar's a strip of low, level land. Somehow, I was out of wind when I got up on top of that ridge. When I stopped, I heard the hound runnin', sort of puzzled-like up in the northwest.

"When I looked down at the river, I seen a dozen or more of them miserable fish ducks in the black, open water. I no more'n noticed them, then up they got, yellin' their fool heads off. It made me wonder how they knew I was thar. Then it come to me that they didn't. Thoughts come special slow when man is out of wind an' his heart is poundin' hard enough to break his ribs. But it come to me that sunthin' else had scared them mergansers. Crotch, I looked sharp, up an' down that strip below an' between me an' the Kennebec River.

"An' thar he was! runnin' erlong 'bout where the railroad is. Boys, it was a hard shot—at least it was fer a nervous man. The result surprised me, an' I reckon it s'prised the fox. Anyway, over he went in the white snow, jist a tangle of legs.

"Even now my heart dances thinkin' erbout it. Ayah. By then Hosshoe was thar. She was proud. An' so was I. That fox was to fetch me $1,100. Yer can see that luck had begun to turn fer Dud Dean. But that ain't the end.

"To save my soul from perdition, I c'udn't resist the temptation to stop in town to display my black fox. Nobudy laughed. Folks even looked like they was ready to admit that I warn't so big a fool as had been talked. And the next day, who sh'ud show up but a newspaper feller from Lewiston. He wanted to take my pitchur, an' to write erbout the black fox hunt.

"I told him that he was welcome to take all the pitchurs he wanted to make, but that he'd have to include Hosshoe an' her pups. Every man that's born is entitled to at least one stroke of genius b'fore he dies. I reckon that was mine.

"Yer see, thar we was when they printed that paper: the black fox, Hosshoe, the pups, an' me. Crotch, in twenty-four hours thar had been more fox hunters at my place than I ever dreamed thar was in the whole world! Wait a min-it, maybe that's a slight exaggeration, but anyhow they came from miles eround. So I sold $300 worth of pups. We-ell, figger it out fer yourselves. I'll be danged if the high finance warn't too much fer me. So I went down to git the schoolmarm's help."

The architect grinned and looked at Dud. "Did she straighten out your accounts?"

Dud stood up and looked down the old road where the young fox hunter had gone. His face relaxed. A slow smile grew, until the familiar chuckle came to his lips.

"Ye've met Nancy," he said.

The Way of an Old Maid

In the story entitled "Under a Willow Tree," Dud unsuccessfully—and under duress—attempts to teach Nancy's friend, an English professor at Durum College by the name of Olivet Bumpus, how to fly-fish. Now "the Bumpus" is back, and this time in the company of Atterly Dumstead. Dumstead has done very well in the making and selling of soap. He arrives with his own car, still not a common conveyance in the little village of Bingham, and his own chauffeur—a young fellow named Al.

Matrimony is hovering in the wings and it is soon obvious that fly fishing is tangled up in the whole affair. Dud likes to see Nancy happy, and to do so means he will have to take the couple fishing. They are all sitting at the dining room table—even Al at Dud's insistence—when the dreaded event is given voice by Dumstead. That next morning, as the expedition sets out, Nancy Dean gives her husband his tellings. (See Appendix II for notes on the setting.)

WHEN THE TIME COME, NEXT MORNIN', fer us to start out on Dumstead's fishin' trip, Nancy contrived not to go, jist as I had expected she w'ud.

"Now, Dudley," she says to me, "remember to be nice an kind. This is Olivet's big day. Help to make it memorable for her."

I'm afraid I warn't exactly gracious, feelin' the way I did. "All right, Nancy," says I, "I'll undertake to do my part, but if she had a big day comin' to her, why in timenation did she have to postpone it so long?"

Nancy looked disappointed with that question, so I amended it some. "Shucks," I says, "prob'ly I'm unduly pessimistic. I reckon it ain't goin' to be as bad as bein' bit by a horg."

Whether it was er not, I leave to you. Anyhow, here comes the gist of it, as I remember.

The sun was shinin' nice and bright when Al backed the doo-dad car out of my barn. Me and Al was in front, with the Bumpus and Dumstead in back. Nancy waved us off. Caesar came tearin' out of the barn an' yowled at us. An' away we goes. Al and me looked straight ahead, an' was glad to. I don't recall that we was goin' any special place, except that the general idea was to drive up the river until we sh'ud come to a stretch of water of which Dumstead approved.

Well sir, if ever thar was a couple of mortals that c'ud be described as settin' on a cloud, it was the Bumpus an' Dumstead. The danged old idgits. Anybudy c'ud see, it seemed to me, that Dumstead was mentally disrupted an' Olivet was all a-tittered.

Now an' then Al winked at me, but I meant to keep my eyes on the scenery, which don't giggle like a PhD on the backseat of an automobile.

The way Al drove made me nervous. He didn't seem to be able to run that rig at less than twenty miles an hour. After we had gone by Temple Pond an' down on Bassett Flat, I remembered sunthin' Doc Brownin' had told me a long time a-fore that. "Dud," he said, "the best medicine in all the world is relaxation. Jist relax an' ye'll live on, until dyin' is as easy as relaxing."

Poor Doc was the most unrelaxed man I ever knew. However, it seemed to me that mornin' that maybe I'd better try relaxin'. And I was almost relaxed when episode number one episoded.

Now, to appreciate it all, yer need to imagine the old Dugway Road from Bingham to Caratunk. It's gone an' fergotten now, it bein' under the new lake behind Bingham Dam. A good deal of it was dug out erlong the side of the mountain, on the east bank of the river. Thar was plenty of places so narrow that two teams c'udn't pass, and on the lefthand side, goin' up river, it was as steep down as a roof.

And it was in sech a place that we met Henry Gates, ridin' behind a little, white-nosed mare. If she had ever seen an automobile before, it had made an unfavorable impression on her. An' thar we was! smack eround a twist in the Dugway, an' no extra room fer anythin' but prayers.

On account of jist havin' relaxed, all I c'ud do was to look fer a place to jump at. As fer Hen, the one look I had at his face revealed that he felt like a man 'ith death ridin' down on him an' nothin' in hand that was adequate to stop it.

But the little mare had more sense than any of us. Somehow—I never quite figgered how—she climbed that bank an' they went by us on a down-hill cant that swung the hind wagon wheels inter the car. I said that they went by, but I only meant the mare an' the wagon. Henry had rolled out an' he lay in the ditch when we went by.

"Stop! The man is killed!" screams the Bumpus.

Al was stoppin'. He had the brakes all set of course. Then we all got out to view the remains. But before we got to them, they stood up an' gazed down the road where the mare was disappearin' like she was goin' to Massachusetts.

Henry Gates was the mildest spoken man that ever took anythin' to pieces with his bare hands. And when he turned his attention on us, I seen that sunthin' int'restin' was erbout to happen. But fer a min-it, Henry jist chewed on his mustache.

I noticed that Dumstead seemed to be all out of breath, as if his mind had raced after Henry's mare an' hadn't got back.

"My dear fellow," he says to Henry, "are you hurt?"

I knew well e-nough that Henry was as mad as Jezebel, but when he spoke, it was the same soft drawl he'd have used on a minister in good an' regular standin'.

"I have always said that if one of them autimobeels ever hit me, that I w'ud kill the driver of it. An' now, I've been hit."

That warn't exactly true. Nobudy had hit him, thanks to his smart mare, but evidently Henry warn't in a frame of mind to stick to details. I thought maybe I had better take part in the talkin'. So I says:

"How are yer, Hen? That's a smart mare ye've got."

"Yer mean," he says, "that she *was* smart, but now it w'udn't be safe fer the Apocalypse to ride behind her. She's so scared, by Jud-us, that she'll be ruined ferever. Be them folks your party, Dud?"

"In a way," I says, "they be."

Henry shook his head, mournfully. "Jist the same," he says, "I am goin' to kill that leetle, bowlegged cuss becuz he looks foolish e-nough to be responsible fer this whole business."

Dumstead back-stepped, but the Bumpus didn't. Further-more, her face didn't turn white, like Dumstead's. The reason fer that was becuz she had on enough red paint to imitate the end of day, but I reckon she felt pale behind her sunset. Nevertheless, she braced up to Henry like all the faculty of Durum College was at her back.

"Sir," she says, fixin' cold eyes on Henry, "control your misfor-tunate tongue. These are enlightened days and not the dark ages."

"Ma'am," says Henry, cuttin' her short, "I reckon I know when I've been dumped in a ditch. Yer can't ca'm me with a currycomb. An' I give yer fair warnin' that I fully intend to lick that man of yours. Ask Dud Dean if I'm a man of my word er not."

"Come, Olivet, my dear," says Dumstead, with his words trem-blin' like poplar leaves. "We'll get in our car and Alfred will proceed."

"No yer won't pro-ceed!" hollers Henry.

An' he had Dumstead by the nape of the neck, as quick as a housecat can catch a bird. It was up to me to do sunthin'.

"Hol-on, Hen," I says to him, "this is my party after all. I wish ye'd remember yer don't own this road, leastways it warn't built jist fer you. Furthermore, it seems necessary to remind yer that nobudy run inter you. Your mare run away. When she passed us, on the wrong side of the road, the hind wheel of your wagon banged inter the automobile. But, even at that, I guess Mister Dumstead w'ud be willin' to pay yer a little sunthing, if ye'll talk reasonable."

"I'm ready to settle," says Henry, "an' yer better talk fast." But he never let go of Dumstead, who was twistin' like a rabbit held up by the ears.

"Wait a min-it," says I, "ye've gone far e-nough, Hen. Let go of my man."

Henry give Dumstead a vi'lent shake, an' let go so quick the feller almost fell down.

"By the way, let me interduce yer to Mister Dumstead," I says.

"Gorsh!" says Henry, "I've already met him."

"Now," I says, "Mister Dumstead will settle any actual damage yer may've suffered."

"Sounds damned generous," says Henry, "but what way have I got of knowin' what damage has been done. All I know is that my mare an wagon has gone hellity-larrup down the road."

"Suggest a reasonable figger," says I, bein' anxious to be on our way before Hen really got fightin' mad.

The Bumpus had kept still as long as was constitutionally possible. "That is exac'ly my—" she begun, but Henry stopped her ag'in.

"Ma'am, I'd thank yer to keep your mouth out of this. It has always been my firm opinion that thar are times when a woman sh'ud be seen an' not heard. An' I don't even like your looks."

Dumstead swallowed and swallowed. I felt sorry fer him.

"I'll settle fer one hundred an' fifty dollars," says Henry. "Not a cent less, by Jud-us."

I c'udn't help laughin'. Dumstead looked at me, an' I says to him, "Offer him five dollars."

"No, yer don't!" says Henry, backin' off. "Do you fellers think I lit on my head?"

"Hen," I says, "we've been kind of patient 'ith yer. We ain't goin' to do no fool-arguin' with yer. It's five dollars now, er it's not one red cent."

Dumstead put his wallet back in his pocket. Henry looked at me as if I was his second cousin.

"Dud, I've a notion to tangle with yer, but we've always been friends. We've guided tergether."

"Yes," I says, "an' it w'ud be nice to part friends. Meantime, yer have an offer of five dollars now."

"I'll take it," he says, "but I want these folks to understand that I had rather take it out of their hides, an' by gorsh, I w'ud have but fer you Dud. Ye've always been a good e-nough feller, except when yer got inter bad comp'ny."

Dumstead handed Henry five dollars.

"Now git in an' we'll take yer back until we find your mare," I says to Henry.

"By Ju-dus! Do yer think that I'd ride in that contraption 'ith that crazy cuss steerin' it? I w'ud sooner set astride of a bag of dynamite in hell. No, thank yer!"

When we turned away, Henry saw sunthin' in Al's hand that I hadn't noticed. It was the handle he used to crank the engine.

"Say, what yer got hold of that thing fer?" asks Henry, kinda curious I 'spose.

"This?" says Al, holdin' it up at arm's length. "This? Oh, I didn't know but I'd need it. Comes in handy sometimes."

"Judus!" says Henry.

After that, I figgered that maybe Bumpus an' Dumstead w'ud suggest that we call it a day. But no sech wisdom was forthcomin', so on we went.

Of course that young Al had thoroughly enjoyed hisself, the pagan. It was written all over his optimistic map. But the other two was purty worked up. They talked erbout it as we rode erlong. Bumpus kept reiteratin' that the whole affair had been out-rageous, preposterous, an' other words that I was afraid only a smart person like Nancy c'ud understand.

As fer Dumstead, he confessed that throughout the ordeal, he had found it difficult to control his temper. An' the Bumpus said that she had realized that.

It ain't healthy to dwell on a molehill until yer think that ye're a mountain goat. So I tried to change the subject.

"Look," I says, "let's stop at the Gilroy Boom. Sometimes that's extra good fishin'."

They heard me, but w'udn't leave off rehearsin' what had hap-pened, an' hadn't. But Al allowed that he w'ud stop if I'd tell him when. So, bine-by, we come to the Gilroy. An' Al stopped.

"My soul!" says Olivet. "What is the trouble now?"

"No trouble," I explains, "but if you folks aim to do some fishin', here's a nice place."

Dumstead brightened up. "Capital!" says he.

An' we all debarked. Al and me lugged the duffle, which was, of course, mostly Dumstead's, except the lunch an' stuff that I had brought erlong.

My spirits begun to perk up, as they always have beside of runnin' waters. I took notice that it was a nice day after all, an' sech as a man might wish all his days to be. All the sky was blue and white-white, where big, tumbled clouds rolled by, an' blue where cloud an' wind seemed to be subtracted, leavin' nothing but God's old-fashioned quietness.

The old, gray boom, built of spruce an' pine logs that w'ud

have scaled five er six hundred feet a piece, stretched down the river like sunthin' tuggin' to be off an' gone. One of them little 'tis-deep sandpipers came skimmin' erlong, folded his wings, an' ran down the boom, the length of half a dozen logs. He was duckin' his head, an' repeatin', " 'Tis-deep, 'tis-deep."

"Oh! Fleur-de-lis!" says Olivet, all at once.

"What?" says Dumstead, lookin' all eround, an' puzzled.

The Bumpus p'inted at some blueflag growin' near the edge of the river.

"Oh yes, lilies. Purty," says Dumstead.

"Beautiful," croons Olivet.

Thinks I, "Maybe she ain't too old to learn." But I doubted it.

Dumstead looked at the boom. "Are those logs secure? Can we walk down on them and cast off the end?"

"We-ell," I says, "they're hitched, if that's what yer mean. But them logs ain't reliable. Don't experiment becuz the water out thar is deep an' strong."

Dumstead looked disappointed. "Looks to me as if the best of the water was, or were, whichever, out off those logs," he says.

"To be truthful, it is," says I, "but I reckon we can pick up all the fish we want by wadin' out a bit off this shore."

Dumstead seemed sorry to do it, but more er less resigned. So I strung up his rod. When he had waded out, chipper as a boy, I begun to rig up that little beauty of a rod that he had given to the Bumpus. The Lord fergive me, as Mahitable Tutle said when she hit her mother-in-law over the head with an ax, but I know well e-nough that I warn't thinkin' kind thoughts while I was stringin' up that rod. It was too nice an instrument fer hands like hers to beat up. An' I had to shut my eyes at the pitchur of what she'd do 'ith it if she hooked a salmon.

But a man can think like the devil, hisself, an' still keep his mouth shut. When I had it all ready—a nice reel, by Hardy, an' a line to match—I reached it out to the Bumpus. But dummed if she didn't shake her head.

"The water is very cold," says she, "and I dislike getting wet."

"We-ell, in that case," says I—thinkin' that I better take the rod down ag'in.

"In that case," says she, "you use it. It is a nice fishing rod, don't you think?"

Crotch, I doubted my ears! On top of the words, she was actually smilin' in a friendly way. That is, I felt sure it was intended fer a friendly smile.

"Marm?" I says, like a phonograph on a parlor table. "Marm?"

"I wish to botanize and to watch Mr. Dumstead. Have you noticed his flawless technique?"

"Yes'um," I says, lookin' at the little rod in my hand, which, to tell the facts, I was itchin' to try with a fly.

"I dare say that you cannot match Mr. Dumstead's art," says the Bumpus.

That sounded more like what the Almighty expected of her, it seemed to me. An' it per-voked me a mite, "If I had my own rod here," says I, "yer might be surprised."

Damnation if she warn't laughin' at me. I put on a Cow Dung, thinkin' erbout salmon. That was a bad mistake, as Dumstead soon demonstrated 'ith three nice trout. Thar didn't seem to be any salmon in thar at all.

We-ell, who don't like the Kennebec when she's in a trout mood? I switched to a nice, slim Párm Belle. An' I hooked a trout that was a half pound bigger'n any Dumstead had found, but the Bumpus paid no attention to that. Instead, everytime he re-membered to look in her direction, she waved at him as if he was a fust class descendant of old Izaak Walton hisself.

I thought to myself that she was puttin' on a purty good show fer a greenhorn, but somehow that left my mind after them trout begun to hit. Kennebec trout, native, wild, river trout—they're trim, slim, an as purty as mayflowers on the lap of spring!

But bine-by, the sun come up too bright an' warm. The trout stopped risin'. Dumstead kept on fishin', but now an' then he'd stop to look out toward the boom. Now, as ye've reason to know, Mak, our river booms have a way of lookin' as stidy an' safe as a sidewalk hitched on both ends. But that is deception.

Bine-by, Dumstead reeled up his line. He had an air erbout him of the man who has made a decision, so I said jist as quick as I c'ud, "Well, got enough fer dinner, er do yer want to try it up the river a piece?"

"No," he says. "I am going to fish off that string of logs because I have seen a nice fish rising, repeatedly, out in that fast water, off the fifth log down."

"I wish yer w'udn't," I says, "becuz Nancy'd be worried to death."

The Bumpus was hoverin' nearby. "The very idea!" she says to me. "Mr. Dumstead is an experienced angler. Remember that his fishing experience is not limited to one river."

Thar she was, shootin' off her mouth ag'in! It seemed to me that she was the most opinionated person that had ever contradicted me.

"But booms——" I begins.

"Fiddlesticks!" says the Bumpus.

By that time, the three of us had walked up the bank a few rods. Olivet an' me a-followin' Dumstead, who warn't payin' attention to either of us. I felt the need of support, an' my eyes lit on Al, the chauffeur, but he jist sot thar on a rock 'ith an unbaptized grin on his face. So all I c'ud see that might be done warn't goin' to stop Dumstead.

I picked up my long-handled net an' followed after that little bowlegged, pig-headed soap-maker. It's pervokin' to have your good advice ignored. I did say to the Bumpus, who acted like she was coming too:

"Now don't git any ideas in your head that you're goin' out, becuz it hain't safe!"

When she jist sniffed at me, Al stood up off his rock an' turned his back. I c'ud see that he was laughin'.

"Laugh," I says to him, "but don't fergit that this can turn out crotchly serious. An' don't underestimate it!"

He turned eround with his face straightened out. "My sympathies are on your side," he says. "But after all, these folks are of age."

"Not mentally," I snaps back at him. "Mentally, they're as simple as a wart on the end of an idgit's nose. I can tell yer one thing, if he falls in, he can drown fer all of me. I w'udn't wet a foot to haul out a person that won't listen to hoss sense."

"He's already on the boom," says Al.

And, by gosh, he was! Now the fust two er three logs in a boom are stidy e-nough. It's when ye've gone out where the current sets ag'inst them, that the pesky nature of each log shows up.

I knew every log in that boom. Thar was some that was always dunkin' one end er the other, an' those wet places git as slippery as anythin' a mortal ever set foot on. Then, some logs have their own peecular yanks an' twists. So a man can't tell, until he's tried 'em, which way they're goin' to roll 'ith him. All he can be sure erbout is that whatever happens will take place quick as a weasel. Besides, thar's then an' now an old log that sh'ud have been cut out of the string, becuz it hardly floats at all. Sech a log sinks 'bout a foot under a man's weight, an' the devil's to pay fer it. Add to that the way the water sometimes looks as if it was rushin' up river, in reverse. Let a man watch hisself when that takes place!

Of course, a man gits used to all that. He knows that no log can roll all the way over—the chains and fin logs prevent that. So he can keep his eyes on the footin' ahead, an' ignore the river as much as is practical. But thar never was a beginner unused to river ways, that warn't more er less handicapped.

Fer all that, Dumstead walked down the boom like a man led on by a single purpose, until he come to one of them spruce logs that rolls like a cat on his back. He was a busy man fer a few min-its. His knees went up as high as his chin, an' his free arm went 'round and 'round like a windmill. Then he lost all resemblance of balance an' landed astride the log like a man on hoss back, weavin' one side to t'other, till it didn't seem possible he c'ud ride it out. But bine-by the log settled down, like a discouraged pony. An' Dumstead had won his fust heat. He was safe fer the time being, but gittin' back on his feet was goin' to be sunthin' else. The water was suckin' at his legs an' snarlin' all eround his coat tail. If it seems to yer that this situation warn't complicated, I have teetotally failed to paint the pitchur.

When I undertook to walk down the log to git at him, it rolled so that we both w'ud have gone in all over. The only way out of it was fer him to hitch forward until he c'ud reach the butt of the next, where the two was chained together. At that p'int, the footin' w'ud be reasonably stidy an' I c'ud give him a lift.

Thar was admirable things erbout this Dumstead. Through it all, he hung to his rod, an' I guess that he w'ud have chosen to drown rather than let go of it. I felt like takin' my hat off to him. Maybe his mental processes never got beyond the makin' of soap, but that's sunthin'!

When I got down thar, where I c'ud git a grip under his arms, he looked back over his shoulder. "Take my rod," he says. "Take it back on dry land. It's the best I ever owned."

We-ell, I approved. Thar's no room to lay down a rod on a rollin' boom log. So I took it back an' handed it to Olivet, who was treadin' eround at the head of the boom like a scared heifer. It's likely that all the time she had been treadin' between hysteria an' a widder's fate.

When I got back to Dumstead, I lifted him to his feet. It was a ticklish stunt an' I expected we'd both git a duckin'. But we managed. Once on his feet, Dumstead dripped like that lady god who came up outer the sea, but he took it like it was all in the day's fishing.

"Now," he says, "bring back my rod, if you'll be so kind." I argued that it warn't good sense to ask fer more, but he was as pig-headed as some of the rest of us. So, ag'inst my best jedgement, I fetched his rod an' he begun all over ag'in.

Then come the Bumpus, who sartinly was born to upset even the balance of nature. I was concentrated on Dumstead an' his fishing, so her voice, so near at hand, jumped me.

"I am joining you men," says she, jist as if we was havin' so much fun that she c'udn't bear to miss it. Now, what c'ud yer do 'ith a person like that? Verily!

Dumstead had been through enough, by that time, to be scared when he saw her trippin' down the boom.

"My dear Dr. Bumpus," he says, "you mustn't. It positively isn't safe out here. These logs are as slippery as cheap soap in a bathtub."

Holy crotch, she begun to pout. It was a sight. A pie-eyed crane, standin' on a dictionary, c'udn't have looked more rediculous. Thar she stood, swayin' from east to west, an' poutin' like a sixteen-year-old girl. An' she's forty years old, if— Wait a min-it, who am I to estimate the Age of Reason?

Anyhow, I didn't utter a word becuz I suspected that if I did, she w'ud begin to act like an irregular verb instead of like an adjective er sunthin'.

Dumstead looked purty doubtful an' scared. "Well," he says, "if you'll be very, very careful. But I urge you to come no farther because these logs are treacherous."

I knew one thing, if nothin' else, which was that she sartinly w'udn't git by me. The Kennebec ain't no flow-gently-sweet-Afton. An' it will drown one idgit as quick as another.

Dumstead went back to his fishin'. He had on the longest gut leader I had ever seen—as much as w'ud have lasted me all summer in those days. His fly was a neat pattern of the old Silver Doctor. He cast up across current an' fished his fly on the down swing. That was an old trick, but at the end of the fly's run he c'ud lift his arm, swing his wrist so as to cart-wheel the fly back over the river a piece. Later on, I heard folks call that "mending," but it was new to me that day. In fact, the feller was so good 'ith a rod that it was natural to fergit erbout the Bumpus, although I don't think Nancy ever come to understand how I c'ud. One thing that helped was that she was keepin' her mouth shut, which was a miracle.

After erbout ten min-its, I seen a nice fish, which I guessed was a salmon, take sunthin' off the surface. It happened behind Dumstead's range of vision. When he begun to cast up an' across all over ag'in, I was as int'rested as a small boy that had set a trap fer a woodchuck.

In a second, thar was a big swirl beneath the fly an' Dumstead grunted under his mustache. Danged if yer c'ud have spit before that salmon erupted like a squirt of red-hot silver. An' it was as nice a fish as I had ever seen in the Kennebec.

"Oh!" squeals Olivet.

Thar was a look on Dumstead's face, like the price of soap had doubled. His line was straightened out, west, an' a-runnin' off the reel as if it had been conscripted. In another second that salmon had leaped ag'in—silver an' gold in the sunshine, an' wonderfully alive.

"Great!" says Dumstead, puffin' out his lips an' blowin' his mustache a-tilt all over his face. "Great!"

Then the fish tailed-it down the river.

"Snub him if yer can!" I yells.

"If I can!" echoes Dumstead, an' he lifted his rod until it bent like a gray birch.

Up goes that salmon, four feet clear of the water, and this time hardly an arm's length from the boom. An' he let hisself fall flat. That's an old trick, born in every good-sized salmon yer ever see.

If they manage to fall on a taut leader, the fly is ripped out of their mouths. But that flop warn't timed jist right, so he tried it all over ag'in—three times in a dizzy row, slashin' up the river as he jumped. I hope that I have made the p'int clear that this Dumstead c'ud handle a rod an' line.

Well, sir, when that salmon went by Olivet, danged if it didn't leap ag'in, splatterin' water as if somebudy had thrown a handful of jewels in the river.

"Eee-eee!" goes the Bumpus, an' she durn near fell off the log, but didn't.

Of course I was enjoyin' the excitement, but it per-voked me to think that the Bumpus might spoil the chance to catch this nice old timer.

"By crotch," I says to her, "you go back on dry land! Do yer want to spoil Mister Dumstead's chance to land this fish!"

An' maybe I did shake the net in her face. Yes, I guess I did. But thar was no time to mind de-tails becuz that salmon was plowin' down the river all over ag'in.

"Watch him!" I yells at Dumstead. "He's goin' to try to git under the boom."

Dumstead seemed to be as calm as a forefather.

"I expect that he will Dud. This fish tops anything I ever hooked on a light rod. Won't he ever tire?"

"Yes," says I, "that's the sad part of it. They wear 'emselves out, arter a while."

"Dashed noble!" says Dumstead through his mustache.

An' then I knew thar was good stuff under his bald head. An' I liked him.

We-ell, we had come to the peak of it all, when that fish made a fight fer the boom, becuz it's mighty seldom that a leader will stand sech punishment. Dumstead an' me had moved down the log, followin' after the fish—him a-fightin' that fish, inch by inch, an' me a-grippin' my net handle in both hands. Everythin' was runnin' fast, an' the pitch was high C.

The Bumpus picked that min-it, out of all eternity, to fall in head over teakettle. Or, maybe it was me a-treadin' erbout on the log that upset her. Anyhow, thar was a tremendous splash, as if an imported cow had fell off a gangplank. Dumstead twisted around, eyes off his fish.

"Lord!" he gasps out, "Olivet has gone."

Crotch, the most helpless feelin' took hold of me. I felt like a caribou on glare ice. Fer a min-it thar was no evidence where she was. Then, down by Dumstead, her arms shot up in the air, both of them, like two ladies of the lake, only no swords that I c'ud see. But the Bumpus seen the boom, which was providentially within her reach, an' she laid hold of it 'ith a will, erbout ten feet below the p'int where Dumstead stood beseechin' Providence not to be too danged practical.

Ayah. She made a vain attempt to ride the boom. The log only rolled her way, which started Dumstead performin' a dance to maintain his balance. It was a sight! If a bull calf sh'ud undertake to do the light fantastic, I guess the results w'ud be similar. His arms an' feet went up an' down like the spirit of dawn stung by automatic hornets. At last, he had one foot in the air while t'other was doin' little hip-hops. Then, in he goes!

It was a de-lemma! If both of them folks drowned it might seem poetic, but I knew Nancy w'ud be awful upset. I had to do sun-thing, but fer the life of me I c'udn't think what sh'ud be done fust.

Up comes Dumstead like a jil-poked log. The fast water rolled over him. An' his head almost bumped the boom.

"Grab it!" yells the Bumpus.

He did. An' thar they was, almost opposite each other, with a boom log between 'em an' eternity lookin' them in the face. The long hair that Dumstead used to comb across his bald head was all askew which made it look like a big egg in tall, wet grass. We-ell, I c'ud imagine the shock he got when he laid eyes on Olivet, becuz the red paint she had worn on her face was runnin' down her neck an' drippin' off her chin.

Somehow, the river scared me almost helpless. Thar it was, snarlin' at them folks, suckin' at them, threatening every min-it to close out the deal. I've seen a few folks drowned in my time, but the Kennebec had never seemed so fateful to me as it did that min-it. It stretched off fer half a mile of fast, angry water.

The Bumpus begun talkin' to Dumstead. It was like they was all alone in the middle of an ocean.

"I can't hang on much longer," she says to him. "It's no use. The water is pulling me so that my arms are screaming with pain."

"Nonsense," says he, trying to git a grip on her shoulders. "Nonsense, you must hang on until Dud can figure a way to get us out of this predicament."

I let out a beller to Al, who'd gone up to the car er somewheres.

"Will you be quiet!" says Olivet through a pair of lips that was stretched as tight as a snubbin' rope. "I have something to say to Atterly."

"Yes, my dear, but hang on now. I promise you we shall soon be out of this predicament!"

"Atterly, listen. It was your fortune, at first. I was ambitious to secure a large endowment for our college. Our position was insecure. Funds were lower than the public could guess. I deceived you. I lured you. I pretended that I was interested in soap; that I was an eager angler, although I knew nothing about fishing and cared less."

"Hang on," begged Dumstead.

"Listen, Atterly. That was in the beginning. The end, the outcome, Atterly, was love of you. I love you. Good-bye."

We-ell, blast it all, thar I stood an' heard it all! When she started to let go, I got hold of her shirt, but it tore in my hands an' the Bumpus went out of sight. I dove but she warn't thar. The current was even worse'n I had guessed. Then I caught sight of her, rollin over an' over, as it seemed to me. I reached out an' catched hold of her. Fer what seemed like a half hour, I thought that I w'ud drown myself. But bine-by I got my head above the water. An' I was a long time, it seemed, draggin' her weight 'ith me until my knee bumped on a rock an' I st'imbled ashore. Al was thar. He had heard my call an' had come a-runnin'. I was never so glad to see anybudy, I reckon. Between us, we hung her over a log that had catched on the gravels. She was purty wet, inside as out, but when she come to her thoughts the fust thing she whispered was:

"Atterly. Atterly."

B'crotch, Nancy had been right, as usual. I felt so durned ashamed that I apologized to myself.

Come to think of it, we had lost track of Dumstead. So I legged it up to the head of the boom an' ran down it until I reached him. Fust thing I done was to git a grip on his shirt, which warn't made of sech foolishness as Olivet's.

"Let go!" he says. "Where's Olivet?"

"Safe ashore," I says.

The next question he asked sounded perfectly natural in my ears. "What happened to my rod?"

I don't intend to blaspheme, but I c'udn't help it. "Damnation 'ith the rod," I says. "Ye've got to git out of this fix."

Al appeared on the scene, stripped down to what, as I recollect, was called BVDs. He hadn't bothered to come by way of the boom, but had swum down. It was a relief to find a man that c'ud swim, I can tell yer. My heart stidied down to sunthin' like a hopeful tune.

"How we goin' to git this feller on?" I says.

"Simple as rollin' off," he says. "We'll put him up there by bull strength and ignorance."

So we laid hold. We got him up thar, but the blarsted log rolled an' the three of us went in together.

"That settles it," says Al when we got hold of the boom ag'in. "No more foolishness. We'll take him ashore same as you towed the old lady. Dummy, let go of that boom."

But Dumstead warn't lettin' go until he heard erbout sunthin' better to hang on. "What's your plan? I'm willing to co-operate, but I can't swim you know."

"The plan is as simple as making soap out of fat, and other waste products" says Al. "You lay over on your back, as though you were goin' to float."

"But I don't float," objects Dumstead.

We didn't pay any attention to that, but when he let go of the boom, we durn near lost him. Makin' all that short, we made a fetch of it. Dumstead c'ud cough, puff, an' spit out water, which I took to be evidence he'd still be in shape to make soap where folks need it. Olivet came a-runnin' down to us like a duck on frozen feet.

A pale, green grin spread all over Dumstead's face. Al and me walked away. I've read in the Book that love is stronger than death, an' it must be.

"It has been quite a day," says Al, grinnin' at me. "I must say that you fellers up in Maine do things up brown when you go fishing."

I sot down on a comfortable rock, near by where I had left the tea pail an' the nice lunch Nancy had put up fer us. All at once, I felt as tired as a man who had hoed corn all day. Bein' so dog-tired set heavy on my spirits.

Prob'ly I had sot thar ten min-its when I felt a hand on my shoulder. When I looked up thar stood Atterly an' Olivet. They looked like drowned cats, but not so hopeless.

"We have just decided," says the Bumpus, "that you're to be our best man."

"Huh?" I says.

"And," says she, ignorin' my thickheadedness, "I want to apologize for past ah, ah, rudeness. I now fully comprehend why Nancy Dean has always been so happy-hearted and contented. You are like Great Heart, in John Bunyan's book."

Shucks, I know well e-nough that my face was as red as an empty kettle on a hot fire. An' I felt as foolish as a rabbit in a bird cage. An' I said the most pod auger remark that was possible.

"Pshaw," I says, "it warn't nothin'."

The old Bumpus w'ud have picked me up on that, quick as a cat, but she only stood thar an' smiled at me. Her face looked like sunthin' that had returned from the wars, but the smile was kind an' well intended.

They actually seemed to be bashful. When they'd walked away, I filled my lungs 'ith good Kennebec air until they w'udn't hold no more. Everythin' seemed to swing eround inter its fittin' place. An' when I looked at the river, it was blue. Blue fer re-membrance, as Nancy always says.

Another of them little spotted sandpipers, er maybe it was the same one I had seen when we came down in the morning, scaled down an' lit on the old boom. Down he run, bobbin' his head an' cheepin', " 'Tis deep, 'tis deep!"

Crotch! I put my head between my knees where I sot an' laughed, an' laughed. An' I says out loud to that little 'piper:

"Ye're danged right it's deep! An' the ways of a river are strange, but not so strange as the way of an old maid 'ith a man!"

We Made It Eight
An' a Half

In this story we meet another true Maine character, Mat Markham. Mat regularly frequents the Dud Dean stories. In several, he is the protagonist. For Mat "fishing is durn serious business," and so is the rest of life. Mat wouldn't be the least surprised to run up against supernatural forces created just to bother human beings. He is taciturn and even melancholy at times. But there are redeeming qualities like his unflinching honesty—and his biscuits that come out of the reflector oven as if Mat had rediscovered the recipe for ambrosia. He can also tell a story when he is in the mood or is forced to spin a yarn. In one story Dud remarks, "Mat ain't company, he's a burden," but obviously the trails of mutual friendship run deeply into their souls. Dud tells this story to another dear friend, Mak. (For setting, see appendix.)

"THAR ARE MORE LOST PONDS IN MAINE than game wardens," said Dud Dean. "Up on Fletcher Mountain thar is a little pond that shares the honors. As I remember, it's labeled 'Young's Pond' on the topographic, but its local nom de plume is 'Lost Pond.' Yer might say that Young's Pond is lost.

"Anyhow, it's a minx of a pond. Thar is a three mile walk, which apes a climb over the Alps. An' the average catch of trout does the trick up brownly, in fact, scorchingly. Most of the fishermen I ever talked with round here has been thar once. They gen'rally emphasize the once, when they tell yer erbout it. An' the implication seems to be that once is e-nough. Fer my own part, I'd been thar two er three times. But I didn't plan on goin' up thar ag'in, right off, until one mornin' Mat Markham knocked on my front door. Yer might say it was a front-door occasion becuz when I answered the knock, Mat dangled a chunky, red-spotted trout right in front of my eyes. Also, he grinned like a ten-year-old kid, although I knew Mat had seen bigger trout than that 'un. Still, he acted awful proud fer some reason. An' a man that feels like Mat looked is apt to bust if someone don't tap him. So I says, 'Hello Mat. Where'd yer git that little feller?'

"The question warn't none too carefully conceived, becuz I was somewhat int'rested. Mat's trout weighed six er seven pounds. But what int'rested me was that the finned critter, dead as he was, had an unmistakable cast of personality erbout him. His under jaw was Napoleonic, an' like I've heard you say Mak, the spots on his side was like jewels inlaid in oil-washed silver.

"Mat got both feet under him an' says, 'W'udn't yer like to know where I got that trout though!'

"'Um,' I says, 'I c'ud guess purty near. Yer caught him in Spruce Pond, er Decker Pond, er, er—'

"'Ayah,' says Mat, 'them is all close guesses.'

"'We-ell,' I says, 'he don't look like a Pierce Pond fish.'

"'Don't does he.' says Mat.

"'But he must weigh close to five pounds at that,' I goes on.

"'He weighs six pounds an' seven an a half ounces,' says Mat, 'but when I took him—'

"'Up at—' I says, tryin' to help him yer see.

"'Ayah. He weighed more'n that.'

"I see that I'd got to change flies. 'Have a cigar,' I says. 'Danged if it ain't a nice trout. The nicest trout I've seen this year. I'll bet he jist swallowed that gob of worms.'

"'Not much!' says Mat. 'This here trout was took scientific. He larruped a little Montreal fly—smacked it like an Injun comin' home from his wars. Gol-durn it, I never see sech a trout! He run away from me like a bull hitched to a spool of thread. An' he never stopped till he'd got 'way across the pond. Um—nice ceegar, hain't it?'

"Now in them days, Mat was a notorious worm fisherman. But he was a hand to keep his game laws. So I figgered I had two p'ints on him. The pond was a small one, an' it was most likely closed to everythin' but fly fishin'. Them was purty foggy p'ints, to be sure, but I was makin' some headway maybe.

"'So he put up a real fight, did he?' says I. 'Well, that's what makes fishin' different. It's sartin that he's one of them old natives. Personally, I've always claimed that an old native is a stronger fighter'n the stocked fish, but Mak says—'

"'He does, does he?' says Mat. 'We-ell, I hain't neither kind, an' I ain't swallowin' your bait neither. See here, it's plain as the nose on your face that ye'd like to know where this trout come from.'

"'I sartinly w'ud, Mat.'

"'Whyn't yer come out like a man an' say so? We-ell, I hain't goin' to tell ye!'

"Maybe my mouth dropped, as some writers tell when they're describin' disapp'inted folks. Mat laughed, in that humorless way of his'n. Then he looked at his cigar and said, 'But I'll take yer Dud.'

" 'Fine!' I says. 'When?'

" 'Thar's no use to go until after dinnertime. Best fishin' is in the evenin' this time of year.'

" 'That's right,' I says. 'After dinner then?'

" 'Termorrow,' says Mat.

" 'Check,' says I.

"But I was bothered, a little. Mat has got funny ideas of a joke. In fact, he ain't got any ideas on that subject. His story indicated a nearby pond. I c'udn't quite pitchur that trout Mat had as anythin' but an accident in any of the nearby ponds. But he had offered to swear on the Bible that this trout was only a sample, an' not the last survivor of the days when trout was trout. Finally, I settled my notions to my own satisfaction. I concluded, thinkin' it all over, that Mat had got his trout in Beane Pond. Doc Brownin' useter say that it was remarkable the way an array of ill-sorted facts w'ud dip their lances to a hypothesis. Once I had hit on Beane Pond, it became perfectly clear to me that Mat's trout had come from thar. So I got my mind made up that we was goin' to Beane Pond.

"So I warn't surprised when Mat informed me after dinner the next day, that we w'ud cross the bridge an' take the Pleasant Ridge road. But I tried to act that way becuz it was Mat's party. Mat only grinned when I stopped at Floyd Hunnewell's. The Beane Pond trail runs up the mountain from Floyd's, yer remember.

" 'Keep on keepin' on,' says Mat. 'We hain't goin' to Beane Pond.'

"That upset the apple cart an' lowered my blood presure. In fact, I was so much disapp'inted that I felt as though Mat had thrown a pail of cold water at me. 'Where be yer goin'?' I says.

"'Lost Pond,' says Mat.

"'Crotch,' I says. 'It can't be that yer mean Lost Pond, Mat.'

"'Nothin' else,' says Mat. 'I got that squaretail an' three more that was almost as good in thar.'

"Imagine how I felt. So perish rosy dreams in a world full of durn fools. Fer a min-it, I didn't know but I'd punch Mat, fer all his gray hair. But somehow I'm geared 'ithout breaks. Once I'm started on a fishin' trip, I ain't apt to stop unless sunthin' happens like a snow. Of course it was possible that we'd git a pan fish er two. But it never occurred to me that Mat might be tellin' the truth. It looked like Mat had set up nights an' figgered out one to pull on me. But why? It was hard to make sense of that. I've guided off an' on with Mat. Maybe, in an off-hand moment, I've bothered him jist a little, but I never betrayed no trust er confidence. Then too, thar's easier ways to even up old scores than to walk up a mountain as steep as it is on the Lost Pond trail.

"Usually, Mat is erbout as talkative as a hawk-owl, which is jist what he looks like. So we climbed in silence. Mat seemed to be enjoyin' the walk. Once, when I turned 'round, I thought he had been grinnin', but thar is sech a slight change in Mat's face even when he laughs out loud, that I c'udn't be sure. I needed to save my wind anyway.

"Mat spoke twice in three miles, which was a big average fer him considerin' that he warn't urged none. The fust time he says, 'Big trout is pee-culiar creeters.'

"I didn't make no comment on that. Thar are folks who claim that all yer need to do when things don't look very int'restin' er satisfactory is to begin thinkin' happy thoughts. I sort of tried that. I needed to try it. Thar I was. But an hour b'fore, I'd set out as I s'posed fer some haven of joy. An' look how it had turned out! I knowed danged well that I knew as much erbout Lost Pond as Mat. So I begun to look round fer spots on the trail that w'ud remind me of happy thoughts. I rediscovered places where I'd shot pa'tridges. Then, all of a sudden, I remembered one time when some of us went in to Lost Pond duck huntin'. Somebudy had come out 'ith a report that thar was a gang of black ducks in thar. We-ell, my spirits begun to pick up. I begun to feel like myself.

"We had gone another mile when Mat finished up what he'd started to say erbout pee-culiar big trout. 'Sometimes they bite, an' then ag'in they won't,' he says. An' havin' got that brilliant observation off his chest, he didn't say no more. Maybe he'd have offered some explanation if we had been goin' eight er ten miles farther, but I doubt it.

"Bine-by, yer c'ud see a flash of water through the hardwoods. 'Thar she be,' says Mat.

"Well, thar's nothin' strikin' erbout Lost Pond. It's jist another nice little, spring-fed pond, that's all. It's tucked in the hills, like a small handkerchief in a pair of overalls. It was four o'clock when we got thar. The little camp thar is privately owned.

"'Damnation,' I says, 'this place is locked tighter than the Bank of England.'

"You know what a boat means in a place like that. Unless yer can git out on the pond, thar's no chance to fly fish becuz the shores is so heavily wooded, right down't the water.

"Mat jist grinned. It was his idea of a funny matter. 'Now ain't it a sight?' he says.

"'Don't tell me,' I says, 'that boathouse door was wide open when yer was here, day 'fore yesterday.'

"'No. No it warn't. An' fer that reason I looked round fer the key. Took me quite a spell. Now, Matthew, I says to myself, if yer was hidin' the key to that door, where w'ud yer put it? An' where d'yer think I found it?'

"'In your pocket,' I says.

"'Naw. Jist go an' look in that tomato can that's hid under this plank walk.'

"'Git it yourself,' I says, 'it hadn't oughter take so long.'

"So Mat triumphantly produced the key. Somehow, my faith begun to revive—like a weak chicken pickin' out of his shell.

"Now, as you know right well, thar is times on Maine lakes when a feller can pick up trout any time of day. At such times, weather don't seem to count. But day after day, on the average water, early mornin' an' evenin' are the hours to bank on. An' although I've caught my best trout under the fog of early mornin', I like the sunset an' twilight the best.

"In general, thar are two food conditions. Thar's times when flyin' insects are skiddin' an hoverin' over the water, actin' like crazy. Then the trout feed 'ithout much regard fer time er taxes. An' a flight of insects, like mayflies, off the shores at swarmin' time, produces the best of fishin' I've ever seen, if ye're equipped.

"An' then thar's the movement of insects from beneath the surface like a hatch. The water will be a-boilin' with feeding fish at sech times. An' the stage seems all set fer a full house. But the fish don't strike, as a rule, until the developin' insect begins to move his wings. A feller fishin' with wet flies expects plenty of action on the end of his line, after watching the trout durin' a hatch. An' it seems to be natural to go on expectin' until the bitter end. Prob'ly, I've fished through a hundred sech experiences, an' I can't remember one time when the trout w'ud strike at a wet pattern.

"In fact, I'd say it was a rule that trout never strike a wet fly durin' sech doings. Sometimes, a quick cast fly, placed right in a boil, will hook a fish, but it don't work often enough to pay fer rememberin'. An' I've seen times when it w'udn't work at all.

"Thar ain't much of an argument, as I see it. Dry flies is the only rig durin' a hatch sech as we have on our ponds. An' I begun fishin' with dry flies when it was generally understood that they had to be cast up a stream er kept in your pocket. The funny part of a hatch is that the trout seem to be out to eat up all of one kind of insect. An' they seldom look at anythin' else.

"We-ell, Mat an' me paddled right into sech a miracle. Thar was a big hatch, er maybe several hatches, of mayflies that night. If them trout had been all common run, I hope that I c'ud have changed flies an' offered them until Sunday mornin' without gittin' excited. But they warn't. Some of 'em was old basters. So after a while, I was in a mood to kick a hole in the bottom of that canoe. I tried all the flies I had—wet er dry. Mat done the same. But Mat jist sot an' whistled, like it was high noon an' lemonade.

"Thar was the trout, jist as Mat had promised—big jokers that acted like dynamite. Sometimes, they stuck their noses out of the water an' winked at Mat an' me. But I done no winkin' back. Crotch, ain't it funny how serious a man will git when he's fishin' without any luck?

"Finally, I guess Mat begun to catch it from me. 'Gol-dang-it!' he says. Gol-dang it! If this hain't a sight. D'yer s'pose if a feller had a leetle contraption that waggled its wings when it lit, that them trout w'ud break at it?'

"'Contraption be condemned,' I says. 'All a feller needs is a set of flies that look like mayflies—tied natural an' right. I've sworn, every year, that I'd never git caught out on a pond 'ithout some.'

"'No,' says Mat, shakin' his head, like he was sorry that I warn't born no smarter, 'them w'udn't work either. Ye've got to have sunthin' that waggles its wings. That w'ud fool 'em, maybe. Jist watch one of them gaddis flies (Mat always calls mayflies that) when it begins to warm up its wings. Right then, a trout'll nail it where it sets.'

"Somehow, I happened to look at Mat's hat, an' I caught sight of a tuft of feathers stickin' out of the hatband. 'What's that in your hat?' I says.

"'Must be my head. I d'know what else.'

"'Let me have those feathers,' I says.

"'What fer? They was got legal,'

"'I doubt it,' I says, 'but let's see'

"Mat handed his hat to me. The feathers had 'parently been pulled out an owl's breast. I had a spool of silk in my pocket that I'd bought, plannin' to wind a rod. I manufactured a fly right then an' thar. Of course it was a mess. Jist the same, I hitched it on an' cast it out. After a while, it lost all its backbone an' sunk.

I fished erbout fer my little bottle of gas an' wax. B'crotch, if I hadn't spilled it all. So I dipped that crazy rig into my fly dope, which was concocted of linseed oil fer a base, an' several other oils fer perfume.

"'Gol-dang-it,' says Mat. 'I never heard of—'

"'If this works,' I says, 'I'll make yer one.'

"'That w'ud be askin' too much,' says Mat. 'Nobudy c'ud make another rig like that.'

"Here's the funny part of it, Mak. It did work. I saw a trout miss a natural on the take off. He was mad, an' swirled around. My fly lit right in his path. An' he took it!

"'Crotch,' says Mat, 'it must be that fly dope.' An' he reached fer his paddle.

"'If yer move this canoe before I ask yer to,' I says, 'I won't promise to control myself. This leader I've got on is as thin as a guess an' a maybe. I can't drag that fish an inch.'

"'Like enough the citronella will kill him,' says Mat, filling up his pipe.

"'If he gits away,' says I, 'give me a dose. Look out!'

"By crotch, that trout turned on a slack line and dove straight at us. I pulled in line, an' put a strain on him that turned him around my end of the canoe.

"'He's a lazy cuss,' says Mat. 'Believes in short cuts.'

"I think that it was for the sheer joy of what he was doing to me that the squaretail plowed along the surface of the pond at fifty miles an hour. But if yer was to insist that no trout ever swam that fast, I c'ud only say that it looked faster. He took erbout all the line I had at hand anyway. Mat shot the canoe after him.

"'Keep her nose on,' I says, fergittin' that Mat had traveled after as many fish as I had.

"'Crotch, yer act like a volunteer fireman,' says Mat. 'Keep your shirt on an' leave the canoe to me.'

"When that trout see that he c'udn't beat us on the level, he begun to sound; shakin' his head like a blind buck. An' he was draggin' the line down in short splurges. I began to figger that trout was erbout done. All of a sudden, a-fore I c'ud spit, he was under the canoe. Then he wallered on the other side. Many a leader has busted like a banjo string under such circumstances.

"'Thar he goes!' I says, feelin' consid'able desperate.

"'Sure he has,' says Mat, lookin' mighty solemn. 'Thar warn't no more up here to stop him than thar was down thar.'

"Becuz Mat was handy 'ith a paddle, we got straightened 'round in a second, an' so that emergency was side-stepped. Fact is, I'm not sure that a canoe in quiet water is fair play. Sartinly a flat-bottomed boat er a raft must look advantageous from a trout's p'int of view.

"'Durn his hide,' says Mat, 'here he comes, back for more!'

"But Mat was wrong. That trout had jist erbout pulled his last stunt—brave old cuss that he was. He dug fer bottom, which is a tactic all trout have in common. I've been surprised over an' over ag'in at the stayin' powers of a trout on a light rig. They ain't got the rare an' tear of a salmon er bass, but few of 'em throw up the sponge until their bag of tricks is empty.

"Fer five min-its that old cuss laid in twenty feet of water an' defied me to budge him. I tried rappin' with my pipe on the butt of the rod, but shucks that jist impresses the lookers-on an' don't impress an' old stager. Bine-by, by puttin' on all the lift I dared, I got that old superintendent of spawnin' beds to swirlin' erbout an' plungin'. An' at last, to the tune of Mat's whistlin' through his teeth, I brought my fish to the boat.

"An' the old hero rolled over on his side. Go ahead an' laugh at me, but fer a second it seemed to me that the gold an' pink tints on him was stainin' the water where he lay. Mat reached fer a landin' net. With a steady hand, he guided it under that dead-beaten fish.

"'How big is he?' I says.

"'Seven pounds, an' maybe a leetle more,' says Mat.

"'Eight,' says I, 'an' we let him go.'

"'Eight she is until death do us part!' says Mat. An' to the trout he says, 'Go on yer durn measly cuss!'

"The big trout jist lay thar a few min-its. After several tries, he got righted an' p'inted his head down. That was the last we seen of him. The feathers was gone on the fly, an' the silk thread trailed behind, purty much unraveled.

"Over on the other side of the pond, a big bullfrog grunted out, 'Be doggoned!' An' it was still as a snowstorm.

"Thar was a tiny flame of softish light, as Mat relit his pipe.

"'Blinkity blank an' gol-dang-it,' says he. 'If I hain't often felt almost converted on nights like this. When it's so still a budy can hear hisself think, he kinda wishes he c'ud trade in his thoughts fer a new set.'

"'Eight pounds,' I says.

"'Gol-dang-it,' says Mat, 'let's make it eight an' a half.'"

Soliloquy in the Woodshed

Superstitions and the supernatural aren't given much room in the Dud Dean stories. When they do figure, Dud's usually recounting secondhand. Dud's personal world is wonderfully natural. With his magnifying glass he finds magic in a bit of lichen. He senses mystery in the morning mist fingering through the branches of an ancient pine. Yet he observes that there is a vein of superstition in us all. For many of Dud's neighbors living along the upper Kennebec, the vein was deep and wide. Stories abounded: strange animals seen in the twilight, a cry heard in a blizzard-crazed night up in Enchanted Township, and the ghost of a man murdered along the old Canada Road. There was an arsenal of cures and cautions that sometimes kept uneasy associations with Christian faiths, but they mostly kept their own company, fed by occult aquifers as old as the race and seemingly as at home in the upper Kennebec as in the forest.

To be fair, Mat Markham, who we find featured in this story, is not especially superstitious. However, he wouldn't be surprised to run into the supernatural nor to find it bent on making life that much more troublesome for humans. It makes sense not to tempt the inexplicable, and, besides, everybody knows that shooting a white deer can bring on bad luck.

Anyway, if you haven't sat in a lamp's twilight or around a shadow-casting campfire and shared stories of things that aren't natural, then you've missed a part of living.

"I NEVER MET A MAN," SAID DUD DEAN, "who didn't have a vein of the superstitious in him. Doc Brownin' useter call it the Irish twilight. Now, take Mat Markham. Mat's got his shortcomings, but he's as matter-of-fact as a cabbage.

"Or take them two sports that hired Mat to guide them up in the Moxie Lake country. One was a doctor—a specialist at deductin' anatomy. After watchin' him, yer w'ud have thought him so calm that he c'ud have taken a man's pulse in the stock exchange durin' the 1929 flurry. As fer the other feller, I w'ud have bet my best hat—which ain't the one I wear Sundays—that he was so two-and-two-is-four that he w'udn't have blinked an eye under one of them shower baths. Matter of fact, he was a famous authority on the explodability of an atom. A man who can monkey 'ith atoms ain't apt to lose his head in a figgerative sense. Them atomists don't deal with facts, as the run of us know facts, but they go erbout their business 'ith erbout as much fluster as a man sproutin' potatoes.

"Anyhow, if ye'd tried to tell any one of 'em that sunthin' was goin' to happen on that huntin' trip that w'ud make the hair on their heads stand up straight, they'd have laughed at yer like the cat did at the country feller who proposed to the queen. They was calm men, whose only purpose was to shoot daylight out of some of them deer up Moxie way.

"Things went off sunthin' like this. They got into camp erbout four o'clock on a Friday, October 21st. It was too late in the day to start out huntin', so Mat left his sporters discussin' sunthin' er other an' went off hisself, to scout fer deer signs an' maybe shoot a pa'tridge er two fer supper. After he'd walked 'bout two miles, he come out in a little swamp-meander of bog grass. The ground was a mite wet, but it was shorter to go through than eround, so Mat barged ahead.

"Erbout halfway through the bog, Mat saw some of the most pee-culiar tracks he'd ever set his eyes on. Fust off, he thought they was moose tracks. But a closer look disproved that. In fact, Mat decided that the critter which made them tracks warn't nothin' he'd ever seen in the woods.

"'Crotch!' says Mat to hisself. An' he got down on his hands an' knees. Mat warn't in the habit of sech a position, an' it reminded him of the time Jed Sperry lost his compass.

"As a matter of fact, Jed was lost hisself, although he always told it as if he'd been jist turned eround. Anyhow, it had come dark an' Jed was still in the woods. So he got out his compass, which he sh'ud have consulted b'fore that. When he lit a match an' held the flame over the compass, it was p'inted straight at Jed's rifle, which was tucked under his arm.

"Says Jed to hisself, 'This hain't never goin' to do.'

"So he set the compass down on what seemed to be a convenient stump, an' looked eround fer a tree to lean his rifle ag'inst. When he went back to the stump to git his compass, the rig warn't there. In fact, the stump warn't.

"'The devil take that compass,' says Jed. 'I never did take any truck in them things anyway.'

"So he walked back to the tree, where he'd left his rifle. An' the rifle was gone. We-ell, as Di'mond Beane said the time he stepped in a b'ar trap, Jed was in an uncomfortable fix. It was good an' dark by that time. Thar didn't seem to be nothin' to do but to git down on his knees an' then start a systematic search. He did that, after one more nip of o-be-joyful. After a while, his head bumped into sunthin' that felt like a stump. Further investigation proved it was a stump. An' sure e-nough, thar was his compass. After that, an idea come to Jed's head.

"Says he, to his compass, 'Now, by Judas, let's see if ye're any good at all to a man. A few min-its ago, yer was bound an' determined to p'int at my gun, when I knew where it was. Let's see yer p'int at it now.'

"Yes sir, all that come to Mat while he was down on his hands an' knees, a-lookin' at them queer tracks. But no solution suggested itself to Mat. He was plumb puzzled. He had hunted that country since before the caribou left it, an' he knew fer sartin that he had seen every track made by any critter thereabouts. An' yit, thar was them strange tracks, right under his nose. Thar they was, plain in the mud. An' thar ain't nothin' more matter of fact than mud.

"The whole business upset Mat sunthin' terrible. He figgered that maybe his eyes was goin' back on him. But even when he ran his fingers eround the outlines of them tracks, they felt jist like they looked. It produced an unearthly feelin', and Mat got up on his feet an' looked over both shoulders, by turn. Thar ain't no doubt but that Mat more'n half expected to see some of them prehistoric critters that was all drowned becuz Noah w'udn't let 'em in his ark.

"But all that Mat c'ud see was jist as natural as hisself. The sky was overhead. The wind was northwest. An' thar was a reassurin' view of Bald Mountain.

"'Crotch!' says Mat an' started fer camp a bit quicker than was his habit to walk.

"On the way back to the camp, which was jist a lumber camp that Mat had tidied up, he decided that maybe it w'udn't be wise to tell his customers erbout them strange tracks. But the bad feelin' they had inspired stayed 'ith Mat after he got back. Somehow he c'udn't git the business out of his mind.

"After supper, the professor of atoms got out his razor an' shaved his face like an ordinary mortal. Then the doctor borrowed some of Mat's terbacca, which added to the sense of the common-place. Then Mat washed the supper dishes, which is regulation. All in all, he almost got rid of the disturbed feelin' the tracks had set up in his mind.

"The night was jist sharp enough to make the fire in the old heater feel invitin' and companionable. An' the yeller light from the old oil lamp splashed erbout the camp in a homey way. An' so they gathered eround the stove, an' filled their pipes fer an after supper chat.

"Some evil imp must have prompted the professor to say, while Mat was pullin' off his boots, 'I understand that many of your Maine woodsmen are superstitious about shooting a white deer.'

"Of course, that was jist bait to set Mat a-talkin'. In the older days, most folks did hold that it was positive bad luck to shoot a white buck, as a matter of fact. Personally, I don't believe a word of it, an' yit, becuz I've heard it said since I was knee-high to an affidavit, I know that thar'd be no pleasure fer me in shootin' at a white deer. It w'ud be the same 'ith Mat. He might allow the idea was foolishness, but his inside mind w'ud make some reservations, I reckon.

"At any rate, Mat told them fellers, who was frankly curious an' theoretically amused, that thar was some queer things in this world. Fer instance, he mentioned the Black Buck of Chase Stream Township. Now, that black buck got blacker every time folks mentioned him. An' he assumed damp, eerie attributes, as Doc Brownin' said one time when he was talkin' erbout a bootlegger.

"Actually, the black buck was jist one of them old-timers that goes on livin' longer than most deer becuz his wits is as sharp as his hoofs. Accordin' to Mat—an' I've heard him tell the yarn more'n once—him an' three other fellers figgered that they had a water-tight plan to outwit that old buck on his own stampin' grounds. The plan was simple—in more ways than one.

"Yer see, that buck had a provokin' habit of goin' up on some little nubble of a hill. Thar, he was placed so that no matter how a lone hunter went up at him, he c'ud go down the opposite side. Mat an' his friends figgered that they'd track the old cuss until he went up a nubble. Then they was goin' to surround him—movin' in slow an' careful. When they got set, one of 'em was goin' up to start the buck. That way, they'd have him covered, yer see.

"We-ell, they done that. Mat even saw the buck go up the nubble an' watched him until he was hidden. Thar was erbout eight er ten inches of snow to help 'em.

" 'Now, by Ju-dus,' says Mat, 'let's see him escape!'

"So the feller who was to do the drivin' did his part. An' it fell to Mat to do the shootin'. Mat is, by the way, a sartin kind of a shooter. Thar was a crashin' of bushes, comin' Mat's way. The rest of the gang heard Mat's rifle. Crack! Then thar was silence fer erbout twenty seconds. Then they heard two more shots, as fast as a man c'ud work a bolt on a .30-.30. They started on the run to help Mat dress off the black buck. But when they had catched up with the details, it seemed that what had come down Mat's side of the hill warn't a buck deer but a thunderin' big b'ar.

"Thar ain't a doubt but that ordinarily Mat w'ud have knocked that b'ar fer a row of pie-eyed cranes. But, yer see, Mat's whole anatomy was organized to shoot a buck. An' danged if he c'ud reverse the machinery. When that b'ar loomed up, Mat c'ud no more pull the trigger than he c'ud have shot a soprano singer where the bill called fer a bass. But the confounded b'ar was awful scared. He was puttin' his hind feet alongside his ears at every jump. An' he was so aimed fer the foot of the nubble that Mat was goin' to git stepped on. So he made up his mind that he'd have to shoot to save his hair.

"Mat always swore that, after the fust shot, the b'ar galloped right over his laid out body, but I reckon thar warn't no scratches to prove it. He also declared that he fired right into the critter's open mouth. It seemed that yer was supposed to believe that the fust bullet traveled right down the b'ar's digestive track. So that the next two shots, which was fired at the rear view of the critter, collided with the fust. Anyhow, all hands testified that Mat sartinly did some fancy shootin' which 'parently went to naught.

"However, the p'int yer are supposed to keep in mind is that what went up the nubble, a black buck, came down a black b'ar. All hands measured the b'ar tracks in the snow. When Mat fust told that story, up to my house, Nancy said, 'Matthew, why didn't you go back and follow that buck deer's track? If you had done so, I am sure that the whole mystery, as you term it, would have been solved.'

"Mat looked like he'd never thought of that. An' it took him several min-its to come back with the information that they didn't do it becuz thar warn't no sense in it. The buck went up a buck an' come down a b'ar, an' that was all thar was to it. As a matter of fact, them fellers was upset. In fact, they was scared. The legend of the black buck had licked them. That's all.

"Mat ain't much of a talker, so when he does tell a yarn it's becuz he can't help it. The result is awful soberin'. But I don't doubt that them two sports winked at each other the night Mat retold his story. However, we all know that it's perfectly possible to carry a joke too far. An' I assure yer that Mat warn't jokin' anyway.

"Ayah. Each of them fellers told a story of his own. Prob'ly they'd read 'em in a book. So they had that advantage over Mat.

"'One night,' says the doctor, 'when I was doin' general practice, a young man came to my office at half-past midnight. I was reading a new book on anatomy that had come in the evening mail. The young fellow was in a most disturbed state of mind. His mother was dangerously sick, and he implored me to visit her at once. I wrote down the street and number, which, incidentally, was nearby.

"'I hurried to the address. Sure enough there was a very sick woman at the house, but when I informed them that her son had requested me to call, I learned that her only son had been killed in Chateau-Thierry.'

"Mat looked from man to man an' figgered they had doubted his buck story. 'I don't b'lieve a condemned word of that,' says Mat to the doctor. But he had to reach up an' pat his hair back down jist the same.

"Then the professor cleared his throat, like a man will when he wants to git down to brass tacks. 'I remember a similar case,' says he. 'It occurred a number of years ago, when I was working long into the nights on an involved experiment.

"'One night, at about one o'clock, I looked up from my work to see Professor Burkley standing before me. I was astonished, for so far as I knew the professor was in Europe. I stood up to shake hands with him, but he motioned me back to my work. If you will do so and so, he said to me, you will arrive at the solution. And then he turned and walked out of the laboratory, as though he were in a hurry to go home.

"'I went to work, as he had directed, and, by the shades of Francis Bacon, I got the predicted result. The next afternoon, while on my way to the lab, I saw the professor's daughter coming out of the Western Union. I hailed her and told her how surprised I had been to see her father. And I was about to add that I wished she would inform him that the work had turned out as he predicted, when I noticed that her face was very white, and that she was leaning against the doorway.

"'Father,' she said, 'died last night in Paris. The cable was delivered this morning.'

"We-ell, gor-ry, Mat can't tell a joke from a joker. He didn't know jist what to do. Finally, he says to the professor, 'You fellers must have been bad drinkers in your younger days.' But he had to push the top of his hair down where it belonged.

"As luck w'ud have it, he noticed that the fire had burned low, an' that the wood was all gone. 'Guess I'd better lug in some wood,' he says, glad to have a familiar chore to do.

"But when he started to pull on his boots, the professor says, 'Man, don't bother. I'll get an armful of wood.' So he takes Mat's lantern an' goes out in the dingle fer the wood. He was gone a min-it er so, an' Mat was fillin' his pipe 'ith Everyday Smoke. He'd got the bowl of his pipe whittled down, so it c'ud be held in one place without a block an' tackle, when there broke loose in the dingle the most devilish noise that a white man ever heard. It was awful beyond description. An' it was so devilishly real that thar was no doubtin' it. Mat's pipe fell out of his hand, an' when he reached over, automatically, to pick it up, his fingers w'udn't work.

"'Great Jehovah!' says the doctor, jumpin' to his feet, 'What in the world is that?'

"Mat's mouth w'udn't say a sound. So the doctor grabbed fer his rifle, which laid on a top bunk. While he loaded it, droppin' more shells than he got in the magazine, Mat staggered to the table an' held up the lamp. When they got the door opened, thar was the professor, standin' like a stone image—only swingin' what was left of Mat's lantern in his right hand. Nobudy said anythin' fer a few min-its. Then the professor cleared his throat like a man at the bottom of a well.

"'I am afraid,' says he to Mat, 'that I have broken your lantern.'

"Fer a second, Mat felt relieved becuz it seemed possible the professor had only fallen down on the lantern. But then it come to him that even a schoolteacher an' a scientist c'udn't make a noise like that had been. Furthermore, the professor was standin' thar all of a tremble, like a man hesitatin' beside a hole in the ice on a Saturday night.

"The doctor got hisself together fer practical purposes. 'What was that damnation noise?' says he. 'Surely it wasn't the lantern exploding! Was it?'

"'No, it wasn't the lantern,' says the professor, like a man who was sure of one thing, and that of no importance.

"'Go on,' says the doctor.

"'I came out here, as you know, to get an armful of wood. I walked over there, where the wood is piled. I knelt down on my left knee, after carefully settin' the lantern to one side. I had started to carefully pile the sticks in my arms when suddenly the place was rent with a screaming I am at a loss to describe. An infernal—'

"'We heard it,' says Mat, lookin' as solemn as a spruce pa'tridge on the tip end of a witchhazel bush. 'Skip it.'

"The professor looked grateful at Mat an' went on 'ith his report. 'The creature—or creature-like thing—rushed past me, kicking with all four feet at once.'

"'Kicking?' gasps the doctor. 'Did you say it was kicking?'

"'I assure you,' says the professor, 'that I am endeavoring to render the account with due precision, although I confess that my critical faculties are somewhat shaken. To continue, without due consideration, I picked up the lantern and struck the creature over the haunches. I regret that I—'

"'Did you say haunches?' puts in Mat, feelin' as nervous as a setter pup p'intin' at a bull moose.

"'Well, haunches, or whatever,' says the professor.

"Mat looked at the doctor fer his comments, but the doctor looked like all the sponges was missin'.

"Then the professor concluded his remarks. 'Whatever it was,' he says, 'it has gone out. For which, thank Deity.'

"'Do yer reckon it c'ud have been a b'ar?' says Mat, beginnin' to git his mind in its usual order.

"'I do not think it was a bear. It had hoofs on all four feet, with which it kicked me. In fact, I think that both my legs are broken.'

"'C'udn't have been a b'ar,' says Mat, 'becuz they don't kick, that I ever heard of. An' they sartinly don't have hoofs.'

"Then the doctor come to life. The professor's legs was sunthin' real to think erbout. 'Come inside,' says he, 'and let me examine your legs.'

"By tryin' it, the professor found out that his legs was still able to walk. They went inside, leavin' the door open becuz Mat still had the lamp in his hand. Nobudy seemed to think erbout that. Jist as a matter of habit, Mat looked eround in the dingle fer sign of tracks. What he found was as plain as a billboard. The tracks was the same as them he had seen in the swaley place that afternoon. Mat was jumped, but he managed to swallow an' spit.

"'Git hold of yourself, Matthew Markham,' says he. 'Thar's a nice, natural explanation o' this, if yer keep ca'm an' collected. What has come in, has gone out, leavin' tracks in both instances. An' although they hain't like any tracks ever made by a livin' critter in these parts, it is possible that sunthin' from other parts has.'

"That was as far as reason an' Mat got 'ith the subject, becuz sunthin' that was jist outside the dingle an' was too evidently bent on comin' under cover ag'in, let go a blast of noise through its nose—that is, blew, brayed, howled, an' whatever. After which, it departed with a clatter of hoofs on the new frozen ground.

"So did Mat. An' he didn't bother to take any wood 'ith him either. But he kept in mind that he must act cool an' unafraid when he entered the camp, which he did purty good except that he shut the door like the Injuns was after him. Then he turned erbout, an' faced his sporters.

"'Good evenin',' he says.

"But the faces on them men w'ud have been jist what an artist needed if he was illustratin' folks in Dante's outer hell.

"'Did you see it?' demands the professor.

"'Nope,' says Mat, slow an' careful, 'I didn't.'

"'It kicked me,' says the professor, sort of wanderin' back over the course of events.

"'You will appreciate the fact that, aside from bruises, the professor's legs are not seriously affected,' says the doctor.

"I guess Mat was in a frame of mind to appreciate a good set of legs, but to do him justice, he made up his mind that sunthin' had carried on too far to be tolerated.

"Mat always says that he made up his mind he'd be a Tuttle an' a Brown if he didn't take a crack at it 'ith his old .30-06. An' jist then, they all heard the thing a-walkin' eround in the dingle, bold as all git-out.

"Mat recognized the time had come—maybe his time. 'Look,' says Mat, 'I am goin' to find out what that is, if it's the last thing I ever do on God's footstool. I am goin' to git out of that winder. Then I'll sneak eround to the dingle door. When I let a yell out of me, one of yer pull open the door out into the dingle. T'other one of yer hold the lamp up good an' high, so I can see what I'm shootin' at, becuz I'm a-goin' to shoot by Ju-dus priest!'

"So they got the winder open at the other end of the camp. Mat climbed out an' they passed him his rifle. Then they waited at the door. The doctor had his own gun in his left hand, an' the professor had the lamp. Bine-by, Mat let out sech a hell-awful shout that the professor almost dropped the lamp on the floor. The doctor pulled open the door, an' the wind it made blew the lamp out.

"Crotch a'mighty, it was a terrible commotion, but nothin' moved in the dingle.

"'Whatever yer be,' says Mat's voice, 'don't try to cut up no capers becuz I'm armed.'

"Meantime, the professor burned his hand on the lamp's hot chimney, an' the doctor c'udn't find a place to scratch a match on. In fact, he had a devil of a time tryin' to find a match. But after erbout five min-its of that, they got the lamp lit ag'in.

"At fust they didn't see anythin' out thar in the dingle. Then their eyes got adjusted, somewhat, an' they made out a common donkey critter over in one corner—a mean lookin' little burro. The little cuss had e-nough of sech doings an' wheeled erbout to make its escape. Yer can bet that Mat stood aside when it charged.

"Yer see, Mat hadn't known that the folks who ran the Trout-dale Camps had bought two of them critters to tote baggage an' sech. This one was so mean an' lazy that when he run off, nobudy bothered to go git him. So he had gone half wild. His hoofs had grown out long in front—as much as five er six inches. So it was no wonder that Mat c'udn't identify the tracks.

"We-ell, laughter is God's medicine fer all situations, an' we sh'ud practice it more. Of course, Mat was taken back sunthin' awful. Fer a min-it he c'udn't look them fellers in the eyes. Then, when he had recovered his balance, he looked up as solemn as a rabbit.

"'We-ell,' he says, 'thar's only three of us now. The other jack-ass has gone outside ag'in.

The Sun Stood Still

Chronologically, this is the twentieth Dud Dean story. It was first sold to Field & Stream *in November 1933 and became the title story for the second Dud Dean book, published in 1939.*

Every angler remembers or at least dreams of a magic day when the fish are there. Dud takes us to his river, the Kennebec, and the fish we find are, as Dud emphasizes, trout.

Now submerged under Wyman Lake, the setting for this story is some seven miles above the village of Bingham, where the river once flowed around islands and past interval farms in a valley-world walled on east and west by long, steep hills.

IT WAS PAST SUNDOWN, and a moment to twilight. A spell of lazy light moved over the lake, while a distilling tint of yellow passed in the west.

The sense of well-being that follows the satisfaction of hunger possessed me. If the calm on Dud Dean's lean and kindly face was evidence, the same sense of tranquillity dwelt in him. And as for our guest, Dick Lord, he had been unrestrained the livelong day in declaring his continual pleasure. The cup—the angler's cup—was full to the brim. I stood up to light a lamp. Its yellow light softly invaded the log camp. And outside, the ancient quiet of the night possessed the world.

Dick Lord slid down a bit in the chair he occupied and wiggled the toes inside the sock on his right foot. "I presume," he said, "that each of us has some eventful fishing trip that stands out in his memory, a day—to borrow from the King James Version—when the sun stood still. I hope that I shall not sound like a schoolteacher assigning topics for discussion, but I do wish that Dud would tell us about the day's fishing that comes back to him most often in memory."

Dud smiled. "That's a big order, young feller. 'Fraid my memory ain't that selective. I've done consid'able fishin' in my time, fust an' last. When I begun, we useter hoss 'em in on a stiff pole. The idea was to git as many as yer c'ud as quick as possible. The trout was as plentiful as good wishes at a wedding. That's all I remember erbout the fishin' in them days—the bounty of the wilderness.

"Since them days, I have fished more waters than I can rec'lect offhand. I've caught, an' seen catched, some really big trout. The best one was a 'leven-pounder who had lived a long time on the fat of the land. I've been elated, an' I've been pooched. I have been blessed, and I've been practically frozen to death. I have hooked an' netted three trout at the cast. I mean that I had 'em on from start to finish, an' that they struck so near at a time that I c'udn't have told which was fust. An' I have lost trout so large that I never fergot them, an' the pervokin' sense of defeat is with me yit.

"And now yer want me to name the top day out of all these years! We-ell, b'crotch, I'll go yer. The day an' its fishin' took place no more'n eight miles above our town on the old Kennebec. I was born beside it, an' I love it above all the rivers God uses to fill the sea. This partic'lar day, I know that I never did see more trout, size fer size, in one place.

"Tell the good truth, the trout fishin' is only so-so on the Kennebec becuz the log drives plow an' scoured the life out of one of the best trout rivers in the world. How it happens that thar are any trout left I d'know, unless we have the hundreds of lakes, ponds, bogs, an' streams that feed it to thank.

"Anyhow, the time I'm thinkin' erbout was jist before an' durin' a thunderstorm. Now Mak is beginnin' to rec'lect. At least, I sh'ud be surprised if he has fergotten that afternoon."

"Do you mean above the Gut, below the Ed Berry place?" I asked.

Dud nodded. "That's it. An' I mean that I never saw anythin' to beat that show in all my life. When I got home that night, I told Nancy that I bet heaven an' hell was one an' the same place. Nancy said fer me to go on bettin', and I'd be apt to find that thar was a clean-cut distinction. Anyhow, if Mak an' me sh'ud fish until we're a hundred, we w'ud never see the beat of that ag'in."

"How many fish did you get?" asked Dick.

"They was trout," replied Dud. "I can't remember jist how many we caught."

"Five," I said, for the whole event was coming back to me.

"Did we?" asked Dud, indifferently. "I c'udn't have told you to save a winter's pay, but I know that it all happened quick, an' that lightnin' struck twice—once up on Pleasant Ridge an' ag'in over in back of us. Say, Mak, what ever did become of that feller, what's his name?"

"But there's something I don't get," interrupted Dick. "It has always been my experience that fish will not rise in a thunderstorm."

Dud chuckled. "Thunder an' lightnin' usually bother," he conceded. "I've seen the time when they was comin' good, an' a little bluff of a storm w'ud blow up to ruin the fishin' fer the rest of the day. Most always a low glass is thumbs down on a fisherman. But I have known exceptions among thunderstorms. To tell the truth, if I knew all erbout fishin' fer trout, I w'ud give it up and tackle sunthin' more int'resting.

"And my advice w'ud be that if yer happened to be fishin' when Gabriel blows his horn, to keep right on fishing. The trout might begin to rise that very min-it. But why don't yer git Mak to tell erbout this special fishing? He'll remember it, becuz that was the time he busted off short the best rod he ever owned."

"How? Big trout?" asked Dick.

"No. He stepped on it hisself. Say, Mak, the more I think on it, the more I want to tell this yarn myself. So a man's motto sh'ud be: Go fishin' now! An' then go later on, if yer git the chance. Let's see, what was that feller's name, Mak?"

"McComick."

"Ayah, that was his name. Seems as how he was a friend of Mak's, he was prob'ly a Scot."

"He was not."

"No? Crotch, this yarn starts uphill, don't it? We-ell, this man McComick come up to visit Mak. It was in August, becuz I 'member that I warned 'em that at sech a season thar warn't much use to go fishin' anywhere, an' less in the river. However, I finally agreed to go. But by crotch, when I met Mrs. McComick, I felt like backin' out. Anybudy c'ud see that she didn't favor fishin' much.

THE SUN STOOD STILL

"They had a brand new car that was almost as long as a string of hoss sheds, an' she was seated in front.

"'How d'yer do?' she asks me, when she was interduced.

"'Fair to middlin',' I says, but of course I knew she didn't care a durn. Her face showed that she was one of them persons who don't take no int'rest in anythin' but their own comforts.

"When Mak started to climb in the back seat, she took one look at his old boots an' britches an' says, 'Spread that robe out over the cushion.'

"'Thanks,' says Mak, 'but we won't need it in this weather.'

"She ignored that. 'Spread it out on the seat,' she says. 'It's the one we use for the dog.'

"Maybe yer don't know it, Dick, but this feller Mak can be danged perverse, if he feels that way. So he c'udn't understand. 'Where is the dog?' he says, lookin' over the back of the front seat. I took the robe an' spread it out over the cushion.

"Then we told McComick where to drive, an' started out. In them days, the old road ran close to the Kennebec. If a man didn't have better manners, he c'ud lean over an' spit in the river in some places. Now that road is under Wyman Lake. The Dugway, as we called it, give Mrs. McComick the jitters. But I think she was the sort of person who w'ud kick erbout the road to Glory—and w'ud have turned back, most likely.

"Her husband was built like an elephant. His neck was wide an' short. Thar was three upholstered rolls on it, an' they got redder'n redder as his wife talked. After a while he said a few words that was as red as his neck, but the lady never wavered. If thar is anythin' in all the world that's more uncomfortable than listenin' to somebudy else's family row, I'm glad that I have missed it, so far.

"Bine-by we drew up opposite the Gut. Thar was a little field next to the road, where folks landed logs sometimes. The Gut was a run of water off the main river, eround an island. It ran shallow an' fast by a p'int of intervale land an' then swung down to the river ag'in, like a kid that had run away from home an' was glad to git back. Once in a while we useter git some nice trout in the Gut. An' once I got a nice mess on the other side of the island in the main river. But it was off the p'int, in the main river, where we usually had the best fishing. On an' off, I've seen some nice trout thar.

"When we got out of McComick's car, we agreed that him an' Mak w'ud try the Gut, an' then wade over to the p'int, while I was to go up to the Berry place, which was erbout a fourth of a mile up the road. I was to fish down the river until I met them at the p'int.

"McComick suggested that his wife w'ud drive me up thar, but I said not to bother—an' she didn't. When I was leaving, she spoke up an' said that it was surely goin' to rain. An' although Mak said sunthin' optimistic, I agreed with the lady. It was goin' to rain.

"However, the water in the river was jist right. Thar had been a head earlier in the day, but the river was back to a normal pitch. I started out 'ith wet flies, but somehow they didn't raise a trout. Thar was a queer run of natural flies on the water. They was erbout number sixteen, an' all of a reddish brown. The strangest part was that they all seemed to be dead. An' they was floatin' high and dry. I was puzzled becuz I c'udn't figger where they all come from. Evidently from up the river somewheres. Near as I observed, thar warn't a single fish all the way down to the p'int that paid attention to the naturals. An' nary a one did I raise to my flies.

"Consequently, I warn't long goin' from the Berry place to the p'int. Now, remember that fer a ways above the p'int thar was several oak trees. At the head of that stretch, at 'bout the fust oak, the water ran fast over some big rocks an' through a couple of turn-in-and-out pools. Right thar them brownish flies was uncommon plentiful. They was comin' down at a fast clip. An' it was thar that I noticed the fust signs of trout. In fact I hooked two little fellers erbout ten inches long.

"Thinks I to myself, 'Might's well keep them becuz it is goin' to be scant fishing,' as Doc Brownin' said, the time a fella offered him a bunch of skunk skins fer services rendered. An' it was while I was bent over unhookin' the second trout that one of them wide-open blasts of thunder let go, like a crack of doom. I warn't exactly surprised becuz it had been grumblin' up on Pleasant Ridge fer ten minits er more. But I was taken 'back when that woman of McComick's opened up. The river makes a lot of noise in a place like that, but the yell she let out of her carried like the report of a ten-gauge gun.

"'Harry! Har-ry!' she screams.

"Crotch, yer w'ud have thought she had been hit, until it come to yer that she c'udn't make so much noise if she had been struck. I looked down the river an' see McComick drop his duffle an' dust out of thar as fast as a man wearin' rubber boots c'ud run. I reeled up an' went down thar becuz I figgered we'd prob'ly be leaving, if we went back to town 'ith the McComicks. But Mak was castin' as if thar hadn't been any thunder er commotion.

"'Guess the lady was scared,' I says to Mak.

"Mak looked up, an' it was the fust notice he'd taken of me

bein' thar. 'Dud,' he says, 'this river is full of trout, old codgers!' And then he went back to castin' ag'in, like mad.

"Crotch, when I looked at the water erlong thar, I see that it was full of feedin' trout. It's likely thar warn't a million, but they was thick as hens on a roost. An' big fellers. They laid thar in two er three feet of water, takin' them brown flies as they come down to them.

"Jerusalum! It really looked like all the trout in the Kennebec had congregated in that place. Fust ye'd see a big, flat-sided cuss roll up. Then Mak w'ud cast in the boil. Next, maybe twenty feet up, er out, another w'ud rise, an' Mak w'ud switch to him. By jumpin' hornpout, it was some performance! An' I was jist so long as it took me to wade out erbout gittin' in on it myself.

"I fergot all erbout the McComicks. An' Mak had never remembered them at all. But it didn't do me any good to join the party. A man might jist as well have been castin' in a haymow. Them trout simply w'udn't look at a wet fly. But don't think that we stopped trying!

"Purty soon a trout that was five pounds old sprung up out the water and says, 'Hello, hayseeds!' And I reckon that was too much fer Mak, becuz he reeled in his line an' stumbled ashore.

Out of the corner of my eye, I see him goin' through that old ducks-back huntin' coat of his'n that holds half a ton of stuff. After he had pulled out a fistful of last year's shotgun shells, a tin cup, and an old felt hat—in fact, erbout everythin' but a prayer book—he hauled out a little box erbout four inches square.

"'Dud,' he shouts, 'come in here.'

"When I got thar, he says to me, 'Now pick out a dry fly that looks like those naturals.'

"All the time we was gittin' fixed up 'ith lighter leaders an' them dry flies, the thunder got louder an' the sky blacker. When we begun to fish ag'in, the rain come. It come at us in a straight wall, like ye've seen it sometimes. An it come at us so evenly that yer w'ud have thought the devil hisself was drivin' a sprinklin' cart at us. At a hundred feet away, the river was a-pelt with big drops, but thar warn't a sprinkle touchin' us. Then it hit. At sech times a man knows that all this talk erbout controllin' nature is nothin' but danged foolishness.

"I had made a few casts b'fore the rain hit us. When it got thar, it sunk that fly like a stick of pulp in white water. I was disapp'inted, but when I started to lift the line, I felt a big, wide trout take that fly from underneath. Crotch, one of them size sixteen hooks gits lost in a real trout's mouth. I don't use number eight shot fer ducks, and I don't plan to use number sixteen hooks fer really big trout—not when I'm doin' the choosin'. But of course, jist at that moment thar warn't nothin' as per my specifications.

"When I set that hook, it took hold good, an' that trout rolled over as mad as a skunk at a tea party. So I let him run until he had taken practically all my line out inter the river, an' then I tried to turn him while he was rollin' crossways of the current. We-ell, thar's some things we jist can't do, although it may be up to a man to try.

"That give me a chance to git the rain water out of my eyes. I made out that Mak was also fast to a heavy trout. His line was slicin' the water like a knife drawn through a sour-milk cheese. Up an' down it went until finally Mak got him back in near shore where I c'ud git the landin' net under him. That trout was mighty beautiful in that wild half-light. A trout is purty in any light. An' they're firm an' pink-meated inside, which gives the lie to that old sayin' that beauty is only skin deep.

"We-ell, what a spell of weather we had after that! When the wind an' the rain had passed over us, it looked like it might clear up, so we waded out ag'in. But that was jist a lull before the decks was cleared fer action, an' in a min-it the heavens turned loose a broadside that rumbled an' roared an' exploded like all hell was on a drunk. Once thar was a crack of white-hot light, as wide as a door, that run from the top of the universe to the bottom. An' either I had some wet matches in my pockets, er I actually smelled brimstone.

"Three er four times it looked like a hand that we c'udn't see had cut a slit a hundred miles long in the black sky. An' them slits let through the most uncomfortable yeller light a man ever see. Then streaks of lightnin' w'ud go dodgin' down the sky like a three-legged rabbit in front of a bowlegged hound."

Dud paused. And Dick asked, "Do you mean to say that the trout were rising in all that inferno?"

"No, no. I don't say that. I really don't know what them trout was doin' jist then. Y'see, fer the fust time in my whole life I had lost all int'rest in fishin' fer trout. Mak an' me was lyin' down flat. That storm was a little too much fer a man to stand up under. The wind w'ud blow like a cyclone, an' then the rain w'ud come on by spells. An' the thunder never missed a cue, b'crotch!

We-ell, that sort of passed. So we raised up an' begin to wonder erbout them trout. We fixed on some more flies an' was goin' out and at it when McComick appeared. He was as wet as we was.

"'My wife insists on going home,' he says.

"'I don't blame her a bit,' says Mak, an' he waded out inter the river ag'in.

"Then, by crotch a-mighty, it came! A flash of light as white as a frog's belly. I can remember jist how Mak looked, out thar in the river up to his knees. I can remember jist how everythin' looked, an' I thought I was lookin' at it fer the last time. That crash beat anythin' that ever happened, I guess. It hit a big pine up on the hill, on our side of the river.

"Now a quarter of a mile is a quarter of a mile, but when it's that near to a charge of lightnin' like that 'un, it's only a hair. McComick had jist picked up his own rod and basket, preparatory to leaving, but they fell out of his hands like sunthin' he w'ud never need ag'in. An' his face looked as if his soul had left him an' was already six miles down the road. But almost always in a time like that, sunthin' earthly happens to bring a man eround. An' it did then.

"'Har-ry!'

"'That's my wife,' says McComick, lickin' his lips.

"It's funny how differently we react to this an' that. Mak had his arm comin' up to make a cast when that crack came. Guess it scared him so that he paralyzed right in the act. When it was over, an' his senses come back, nothin' c'ud be more natural than he sh'ud finish the cast."

Dud broke off, turning to me. "You tell this feller what happened after that cast was completed. He'll never believe me."

"A trout hit it," I said.

"A trout hit it," reiterated Dud, with his heavy eyebrows drawn down and his gray eyes daring Dick to question the statement.

Dick didn't indicate belief or disbelief. And Dud went on with the story.

"Now I wish yer c'ud believe that I had been all prepared to go home like a gentleman when Mak made that automatic cast. But thar he was, fast to a trout ag'in. An' at that very second, I seen another boil within ten feet of the shore. McComick seen it too, but he jist moaned, 'My wife insists—'

"I'm askin' yer ag'in. What c'ud I do? C'ud I leave Mak in sech a perilous situation? 'By crotch,' thinks I, 'she's your wife, not mine.'

"And I waded out with the landin' net. We got that fish. But thar was signs of some more. I dropped erbout forty feet of line up the river an' watched my fly—er tried to watch it. Blub! she goes. An' the fun was on. That felt like the best fish yit. That is, that's what I thought until I discovered it was better'n that. It run clean to the end of my line, but it warn't two min-its after that till I was pullin' slack line—so much of it that it got out of my left hand an' trailed down the river. Jericho! That trout had it in his head to visit more places than a president's secretary c'ud keep track of. Yer understand that all this was goin' on in fairly quick water, an' at the end of a guess-and-by-gosh leader. We-ell, thar's an end to all important things—one end or another— an' at last, I got that trout so licked it didn't care how it looked floatin' eround.

"Mak got hold of his landin' net. When he tried to git that trout inside, two thirds of it hung over. I mean that the small half was inside. An' that's the way we started fer the shore. An' we got along fine until Mak slipped. He didn't go down but pitched for-wards, an' kept goin' that way. That's how it come erbout that he walked on his nice rod, which he had left on the bank when he got ready to net my trout.

"But we got that old-timer where he c'ud only flop a little. An' then danged if the sun didn't try to come out. Yer might say, Dick, that it had been standin' still. But it c'udn't seem to make a full go of shinin' through them clouds. Everythin' looked like a circus grounds after the circus has gone.

"We admired that trout. Then, all of a sudden, Mak remembered his McComicks. 'Dud,' he says, 'how are we ever going to face that woman?'

"Crotch, it did look like we was up ag'inst sunthin' worse than the storm. But it had to be faced. So we went eround the p'int, waded across the little brook that come down the intervale, an' then climbed up the bank to the car—but thar warn't no car.

"An' thar sot McComick on a rock. 'She's gone,' he says, 'with the car.'

"'Man, man,' says Mak, 'we're sorry about this. Why didn't you go with her?'

"And then McComick begun to laugh. An' how he laughed. 'She must have left,' he says, 'jist after the last crack.'

"Gosh, we felt purty mean, but jist then I see a car comin' down the road an' I waved my arms as a sign of distress. The driver was Albert Clark, an' he took us in."

"You haven't finished that story," I said. "Why don't you tell Dick what you did with that big trout?"

"Ayah! I weighed him. That's what I done, b'crotch. Nine pounds an' two ounces!"

"And then?" I prodded.

"And then, like a danged fool, I sent him to that Mrs. McComick erlong with my apologies fer the thunderstorm, an' all thunderstorms past an' future. Sunthin' had to be done—didn't it? I never did blame her a mite, except . . . well, crotch! She —Well, thar was them trout a-jumping!"

Dick gave way to a hilarious reaction, as though he could stand it no longer.

"Did she, ha, ha, did she ever forgive you fellows?"

"Ayah. She had sense enough to see I was in bad comp'ny. She sent me a nice little note of thanks writ on paper that smelled like them Lotus Islands, which Nancy says is a wicked place."

Dead Water Doings

This story first appeared in the third Dud Dean book, If It Returns With Scars *and was reprinted later in* Where Flows the Kennebec. *When the story begins we are at Dead Water, once a gateway to a land of spruce and pine. Though now a place of alders, it still remains on the threshold of a cut-over wilderness. As the brief description indicates, Dead Water was once a busy sawmill settlement on the Somerset Railroad, which became a part of the Maine Central. When the rails and ties were pulled in 1939, the road bed continued to convey logging trucks. At the time of this story some trains are still running, but Dud and Mak have walked up the seven-mile grade from Bingham.*

As the name of this settlement implies, Austin Stream lies quiet for several miles above Dead Water before it receives the contribution of Heald Stream and turns eastward into big country. Beyond Edgely Dam, the scene of combat in this story, the stream splits. The north branch drains Bald Mountain and Austin Ponds; the south branch wanders far into the Township of Mayfield. On this June day, perhaps seventy years ago, history lingers in the remains of logging dams and memories clung to such names as Weeks Basin and Palmer Flowage. The Depression is ravaging the outside world, but here in the quiet realm of Dead Water there are gorgeous trout in Heald and Austin streams.

Several of the Dud Dean stories feature an unlikely looking fellow who proves he is a man and can handle a fly rod and himself in a country where even a gentleman sometimes needs his fists. None of these stories do it more dramatically than "Dead Water Doings."

DEAD WATER HAS ITS UPS AND DOWNS, though it was never more than a row of shanties and a company store on the ridge above the Kineo BranchWash in that dirty water! Are not Abana an' Pharpar purtier rivers than all the waters of Israel?" Jumpin' horn pout, Scripture is generally too much fer me, but I c'ud have read that to the bottom when I was knee-high to a pie-eyed crane. Naaman k Water.

In 1930 the town was deserted, dreaming back to wilderness in the midst of a lull since broken by the saws. Coburn heirs maintained a storekeeper there. He had little to sell and no customers. And so he was glad to have company and happy to converse.

Dud Dean and I stopped there one day, after a seven-mile walk from Bingham.

"Howdy Bert," said Dud.

"Well, by gorry di'monds, how be yer Dud? Glad to see yer, by gorry. Set down and rest yer."

"Bert w'ud be glad to see a delegate from Topheth," Dud said to me. "He prob'ly ain't seen a livin' soul fer ten days."

Bert laughed after carefully spitting tobacco juice in a pail full of wood ashes.

"That's whar ye're wrong, Dud, becuz I've got a boarder-feller that got off the train last night."

"Y'don't say? Who'd he be?"

"Wa-al, I know his name and consid'able else, an' yit, b'gorry, I d'know's I can rightly answer your question. His name's Bart M. Latcher. Bart is short fer Bartholomew. I found that out. An' he lives down't Lynn, Mass'chusetts. In fact, he's a shippin' clerk in a shoe fact'ry. He ain't married, but he's got an old mother an' a cripple sister to look after. He says that she was an awful purty girl, till erbout sixteen when she was took with infanteel paralysis. She's all bent up now, but cheerful. Don't seem possible, does it? Anyhow, so he never got married. Not that he wanted to, er so he says.

"Lookin' him over, ye'd guess that maybe he warn't much of a temptation fer womenfolks, although sometimes they marry most anything. He's six feet four er maybe five inches tall, I bet. But ain't much wider 'n a sheetpolk. His neck's almost as long as a cubit. Peculiar lookin' cuss. Yep. He makes twenty-three dollars a week. Useter make twenty-seven fifty. He don't know how come the extra fifty cents. I asked him. But he 'lows that he's lucky to git that much, in these times. Can't git ahead much, er he claims. Rent an' all.

"This is the fust time he's ever been in Maine. Been savin' up to make sech a trip fer years. Don't smoke. Don't drink liquor. Don't even chew. He told me how he hired an older, married sister while he was away on this trip. All he's got to pay her is five dollars fer the week. Hellation, don't it beat all how some relatives break out all over with geniosity?

"But, still, he acts as happy as folks with more brains. I ast him, 'How in jippypop did yer happen to git off the train at this place?'

"'Well,' he says, 'it figgered out right. I had jist money enough to come this far an' git back home ag'in. So here I be.'

"'Damned if yer ain't,' I says.

"Well, hellation, a man has to be kerful these days. So I didn't warm up very fast. Folks has been murdered by strangers, b'gorry, even if it ain't common. But mostly they're robbed. What in tarnel is thar to steal eround here? Thinks I, 'Yer might fool Bert McMaster in your own stampin' grounds, but yer hain't smart enough to put over anythin' in my own atmosphere.'

"Yep. Don't think I warn't cautious. Bine-by, I see that he was one of them mortals that never dried off behind his ears. Sort of a big kid. Smart enough to earn a livin' but ga'nt of grown-up ways. Fer instance, nothin' to do a-fore he started out, but that I had to go down't the pond to pass jedgment on his fishin'.

"'Hellation,' I says, 'what I don't know 'bout fly-fishin' w'ud fill a geography. When I fish, I fish fer breakfast.' Nevertheless, nothin' to do but I must go down. Dud, that cuss c'ud cast a fly line 'bout two hundred feet, durn near! Yes, sir! An' he can drop a fly on any-thin' ye're a mind to pick out. Jippypop! I hain't ever seen his match, not even you, Dud. An' all the time, he was so anxious erbout how he was doin' that his for'head wrinkled right inter his hair.

"'Gorry di'monds,' I says, 'thar hain't no more sense in yer askin' me to criticize your fishin' than thar'd be in the minister' comin' up here fer help of me 'bout writin' his sermon.'

"Wa-al sir, he hooked a chub on a Brown Hackle fly. It was a big cuss of a chub that w'ud go a pound, maybe. Corndemned if that feller didn't git all in a sweat, an' he netted that chub as kerful as I'd catch an angel fish, if one bit my hook.

"'What species is this?' he says to me, all puzzled an' his hands shakin'. 'Is it a white fish?'

"'Shucks,' I says, 'jist look at the mouth on it. It's nothin' but a dadblasted chub. This dead water is full of 'em most of the time. An' no self-respectin' cat w'ud eat one, unless he'd gone blind.'

"Then b'gorry di'monds, he was goin' to put it back in the water.

"'Don't do that!' I says. 'Them cussed things is unreasonable competition fer good fish. They're jist like fleas on a rabbit, meaner'n the devil an' twice as pop'latin'.'

"So I took it an' throwed it to hell-and-gone inter the alders. An' we went up to the store.

"'Look over my flies,' he says, 'and tell me if I have the necessary patterns fer Maine trout.' And mark yer, he was as anxious as a bride gittin' married fer the fust time.

"'Look,' I says, 'if I had took it inter my head to name my kids arter the flies I know by sight, five of 'em w'ud have been what's-a-names. Thar w'ud have been Parma Cheenee, Silver Doctor, an' old Cow Dung, an' that's all. An' the only reason I recognize them by name is becuz a Parma Cheenee is all right to fish 'ith, if yer can't find no worms, er grasshoppers, er crickets, er nothin' else; an' a Silver Doctor don't look no more like a doctor than an Eskimo; an' a Cow Dung ain't real polite anyways. Don't ask me 'bout flies, unless yer mean black flies, corndem them.'

"But fer all I said, I had to look 'em all over while he picked 'em out of a little box with weezers. How he rattled off the names: Beaverkill, Evenin' Done, March Round, Olive Pill, Pro-fessor, Grizzly King, B'ar's Ear, Paddis, Empty Bottle, Hell Cat, Hell's-a-poppin'—shucks I can't begin to remember.

"He says that he has been buyin' them, one at a time, fer weeks an' years. The whole show made me kinda suspicious.

"'Look,' I says to him, an' lookin' him right in the eyes, 'do yer mean to tell me that yer didn't know that fish was a chub?'

"Jippypop, he 'lowed that he seen it warn't a trout becuz he had seen trout in fish markets an' in pictures. B'gorry, either he's a corndemned liar er he never saw a real trout in his life! He's catched bass—what in hellation is a bass anyway? An' yeller perch, white perch—he's catched lots of them. An' he mentioned a fish by the name of punkinseed, but I reckon thar hain't no sech fish as that. Anyhow, no trout. An' no salmon! What d'yer know 'bout that! No trout! Thar hain't any in the city water-works where he lives.

"Gorry di'monds, I c'udn't catch on what he meant by 'city waterworks,' until I questioned eround. It's jist a made pond. That's all it is—with them bass, pickerel, perch, an' sech stuff in it. But jist think of a man that never catched a trout! Ain't it a sight?"

Bert paused to expectorate.

"Crotch," exclaimed Dud Dean, "have yer run down, er jist stopped while your tongue cools off? Where'd that remarkable specimen take hisself off to?"

"Went up the track. I told him not to dare leave sight of the Austin Stream. 'Whatever yer do,' I says, 'don't fergit that water can be relied on to run downhill. When yer git ready to come home, foller it back.'

"Hellation, if it had only been a rainy day, I w'ud have gone 'ith him. Fact, I'd give a day's pay to see him hook inter a good trout. But somebudy has to stay here to answer the telephone, case of forest fire, so I c'udn't leave."

Dud looked at me whimsically.

"We-ell, Mak, I reckon that leaves us Heald Stream to fish. We don't want to compete with no sech Izaak Walton as Bert describes. Two-hundred-foot casts! Crotch, Bert, that's a medium long cast. How much w'ud yer discount that if Saint Peter had yer by the nape of the neck?"

"Not one dadblasted inch! It w'udn't be necessary."

"No? We-ell, I sartinly hope we'll meet up 'ith this seventh son of a son of a gun. Meantime, me an' Mak has got to git goin', if we are to catch a few trout fer dinner."

Bert called after us, "If yer don't meet him, he'll be back here tonight. That is, if the cuss don't git lost. I told him he c'ud stay here. 'It won't cost yer a cent,' I says. But he had a suitcase packed full of grub anyway—as much as two men c'ud eat. His mother baked it fer him a-fore he left home. Say! 'Fore I fergit it, have you fellers got plenty of worms?"

I am afraid that we walked away while Bert was still talking. As Dud had said, we had to catch trout for our dinner. We walked up the track to Dimmick Siding, where Heald Stream slips out of the tangle of wild land from upcountry at the foot of Moxie Mountain. There, where the steam flows under the track, we rigged up our rods.

When two or more are setting out to fish the Heald, or any stream, there is a bothersome moment. Who should fish ahead? There are anglers whom that question does not trouble, so long as they fish first. I never discovered the slightest evidence that Dud Dean desired to fish ahead. He prefers to fish in the rear. This should simplify the problem, but for the fact that I long ago decided that Dud's magnanimity isn't good for my soul. Therefore, I have insisted on the ancient rite of the flipped coin. Dud lost. In other words, "heads" said that he was to fish ahead of me.

Now from Dimmick Siding to the spot where, with a spurt, Heald ceases to be, and the larger Austin Stream carries on to the Kennebec at Bingham, may be a mile. It may be less than that. I have fished that stretch a score of times but haven't considered the distance. If a mile, it is a pleasant mile of pools and half primal, half despoiled, and yet wilderness water, cold, and tangy of the forest.

Dud and I were using long leaders, rather longer than I like. The water was summer-clear. We were, of course, fishing wet flies; using the old patterns that seldom disappoint one up in Maine: Parm' Belle, Montreals, Brown Hackle, and the like.

I sat and waited a while until Dud had fished along—so that I would not be fishing over nervous trout. The day was sweet with sunshine. Small birds filled the friendly air with their busy songs. A doe, big-eyed and cautious, poked her head out of the alders near the bridge. Two lambs, as Dud would call them, impatiently minced into the brook, and thrust their yellow muzzles in the cool water. I waited until they had gone, not wanting to disturb their sense of tranquillity. Time enough for fright and alarm when November comes, when harsh experiences are in keeping with the cosmic mood.

When the doe and her twins had gone, I tied on a Light Montreal. I anticipated that many of the trout that might rise to the number ten would be short fish, for those cold brooks are breeder streams, worth more in the aggregate than all the hatcheries and rearing pools the state can support. For fishing in such waters there is only one hook. Therefore, I do not hesitate to name it. It is the Bill Jameson barbless—the hook with the cleverly contrived hump. Why it is not more usually employed in waters where the trout are not uniformly large, I can't comprehend. The carefully devised point hooks the striking fish easily and securely. I am not a crank, but I do appreciate fair, square angling, and the barbless hooks make it possible to liberate small trout with a modicum of serious wounds.

Anyhow, I thoroughly enjoyed that stretch of clean, flowing water. Certainly I am not one of those folks who sentimentally attribute qualities and abilities that belong only to animate things, to trees and waters. Brooks do not "sing," so far as I am concerned. Pines trees do not "sigh." But the welcome sounds are, to me, a music of the elemental forces in tune with a harmony other than that which men make or birds sing. I would dread to be so driven, so hurried, while angling that I fished on ahead of these ancient sounds. That sort of sport would be so much loss to me. Before I had fished two hundred yards, I knew that Dud had skipped some pools and ripples. So I was able to save eight trout ten inches long or over. And at the ripples hurrying past the big gray boulder, just above the long abandoned sawmill boiler, I hooked a half-pounder that slashed out at a little Dusty Miller armed with the humped hook. It was only an incident that while I netted that gold-washed, brightly spotted trout, a white-crowned sparrow spilled his own joys across the little breeze that blessed us both— only an incident, but one doesn't forget those moments.

Then I was sure that I had taken my share of trout from the Heald and I reeled the line, removed the leader, and hurried along to overtake Dud Dean.

I found him at the mouth of the Heald. He had kindled a little fire on the gravel bar. Clear water bubbled in the tea pail. Trout, rolled in corn meal, were waiting, crisp and hot, in his small frying pan.

The old, slow grin welcomed me.

"Look, Mak, what size of a boot is a good 'eal bigger'n a number twelve? Jist take a look at them tracks headed up the Austin! Danged if it don't seem as though the toes on a foot like that w'ud be unable to remember the heel. An' think what a bother it would be to wash both of them feet on the same Saturday night!"

"Must be the fellow Bert told about," I ventured to guess.

"Anyhow, them must be his tracks," said Dud. "An' do yer know that I had kinda figgered on fishin' up the Austin a ways. What say? Will we glean after that feller, even if common sense suggests that it w'ud be foolish to follow arter a plague of locusts?"

"Why not?" I asked. "Surely he can't catch all the trout."

"Um, think so? Remember that he can cast a hundred feet of ord'nary fish line."

"Bert said two hundred feet."

"Did he? Gosh, some folks recognize that human language ain't sufficient—don't they? We-ell, I w'ud like a chance to watch this human object of Bert's enthusiasms, although, hard as Bert seems to take it, this feller ain't the only man I ever heard of who had never catched a trout. I even risk the guess that we've had some presidents who never went trout fishin'."

Austin Stream, above the crossing, is a slow, meandering little river. The north branch makes out of Austin Pond, and it elbows its way through what is now a tangle of burn, blow-downs, and new growth in thousands of acres of wild land. The south branch placidly twists about through wild meadows that are a paradise for muskrats, mink, otter, and beaver.

It is a short walk upstream to the relic of Edgely Dam, of which only a few logs remain and part of the lower apron. On the left, the full flow of the stream pushes by and into the pool below the dam.

If a man has it in him to enjoy wild pastures teeming with life, from tiny warblers to an occasional moose, he enjoys the Austin and happily survives the rough and rugged footing along its winding banks and the black flies that abound in June.

Dud walked ahead as we approached Edgely Dam. He held up a hand for quiet. I looked ahead, and there, on the flat, plank apron, stood an angler who surely illustrated Bert's report. He was softly casting into the pool below, where sunlight shadows lay like a patchwork.

Dud and I sat down. A bunch of white birches, six feet tall screened us and our inquisitiveness. Bert's exaggeration concerning the man's ability to cast a fly was pardonable. The chap was an artist. And his artistry betrayed hours of painstaking practice

"He's middlin' good," whispered Dud, indulging that Yankee understatement that is compliment enough. "Look how nice an' soft that line settled on the water. An' he's got the trick of delayin' the cast so the fly an' leader lands before the line. Crotch, he's a loose-j'inted feller."

The stranger turned quickly, watching something swimming in the race of the water at his right. Then we saw a half-grown mink swimming across the pool. It ran along the rocks on the shore and disappeared.

Dud chuckled softly. "This is a great country fer mink," he

whispered. "Wonder if this Bart knows what it was? Prob'ly. A man can learn most anythin' out of books, if he's really int'rested. But the real pleasure comes 'ith checkin' the books on livin' samples."

The stranger changed flies. A trout, a nice trout, rose half-heartedly, swirled, and went down. The stranger cast again. There was no response. He sat down. When he had filled and lighted a pipe, he wrote in a small notebook.

"Good on his head," whispered Dud to me. "He's restin' his fish. Sometimes one cast, now an' then, over a fish that acts like that 'un is better than twenty. 'N fact, it's generally smarter."

The fellow stood up to cast again. There was a much more vigorous response, and a trout that had been a trout a long time tumbled over itself on the surface.

Dud whistled. "Hope he remembers his books now!"

My eyes caught movement around the ragged ends of the logs in the old dam. Someone else appeared.

"Look, who's that newcomer?" I asked Dud, forgetting that we were in hiding, and speaking aloud.

"Hump," grunted Dud. "That hunk of cheese? Crotch, don't you rec'nize him? You know him."

I did, after all. It was Bill X, whom I particularly disliked because of his habitually mean poaching.

The stranger's trout shot down the pool, tugging out line. Bill X stepped in front of the stranger, flexed his cheap telescope bait pole, and shot a lump of worms out in the pool.

"Just a minute!" protested the stranger. "I have a beautiful trout on my hook. Our lines will tangle."

"Yah? Well, I've fished this stream fer years, and I hain't never seen no fish marked with your name on them. You outlanders come up here actin' like yer owned the whole country. But it's a free country, by darn it. Hain't it?"

Dud made a precautionary sign for silence, filled his lungs with the forenoon air, and blew it out with abandon.

The stranger was obliged to play his trout from one side. And the fish was cutting back and forth at the foot of the pool. But the stranger also found time to reply to Bill X.

"Yes," he said, "this is a free country, but unless I am mistaken, your kind have mighty little to do with maintaining its freedom.

"Is that so, Professor?"

"Yes, I think it is so!"

Whatever Bill might have replied was lost in that moment, for something took his bait. Bill reacted true to form. He tried to "horse" his fish out of the pool. His line and rod were obviously chosen for just such performance, but although he achieved a floundering commotion on the surface of the pool, he could not force his fish to heel in to the apron.

"Geeprus Nettie!" he howled. "Look! Look a-that!"

Dud stood up, eyes shining, but sat down again.

"Sometimes," he whispered to me, "a few of them nice fish run up here from the dead water. It's what I had in mind."

"You had better give that trout more line, or something is going to break," said the stranger.

"Think so, do yer? Well! Let me tell yer that it won't be my riggin' that breaks. When I fish, I use stuff that'll hold. Who in hell asked yer fer advice, anyhow? You don't look to me like a feller who c'ud tell a trout from a togue."

The stranger ignored Bill X. He began to work his way cautiously down the right-hand bank. And he stepped on a round rock about the shape and size of a number one McIntosh apple. He caught his balance, but the rock splashed into the pool.

Both fish seemed to awaken from halfheartedness to wide-awake defensiveness. The stranger's trout charged headlong up the pool, slacking the taut line. Bill X's fish shot from side to side, held by Bill's heavy hand from further action.

"Crotch," said Dud, "now watch what happens. It's a-going to be turrible, as Mary Smithee said the time her man set a b'ar trap under his daughter's winder when somebudy told him she was goin' to elope."

For some reason that wasn't self-evident, the stranger raced back to the apron, from which, apparently, he hoped to manage this new turn of events.

"Don't come up here!" bellowed Bill X. "Lead your fish downstream! Git him outer this pool!"

"But I am afraid that I'll lose him down there in the shallow water," said the stranger.

"See if I care. Git him out, d'yer hear me!"

"I heard you," said the stranger, in a tone of voice that Bill X seemed to ignore.

Dud scrambled to his feet.

"Git up quick, Mak. View's better up here. I can smell a climax."

"Thar!" shouted Bill X. "Yer damned, blarsted, white-livered fool! What did I tell yer! Now we're all tangled to hell."

"Permit me to remind you," said the stranger, "that I was here first. And so was my trout."

Apparently the stranger's fish was straight across the pool, resting for a plunge up the shoot of water to the left. And Bill's fish, frantically thrashing about, had hopelessly tangled the lines. Bill X was a seasoned campaigner. He interpreted the situation calling for swift action. Somehow, he opened a huge jackknife, jumped, and caught the stranger's nice line.

A moving-picture camera would have caught all this as a series of acts, but to me it seemed one swift event without many separated parts. The stranger moved with astonishing swiftness and purpose. His large foot caught Bill where he obtruded, as he bent to slash the line; and Bill slid into the pool headfirst. The water was not deep—not deep enough to drown a man who couldn't swim a few strokes. Bill stumbled ashore near Dud and me. Brushing the wet hair out of his eyes, he said:

"Hello, Dud! Watch me kill sunthin'."

And having delivered himself of that, he roared up the shore, splashed across the fast water at the foot of the sluice, and— went into the pool again, neatly assisted by a resounding smash on the chin. Bill is a stout fellow, and I presume that he went to the bottom that time.

There was a wondering light in his eyes when he fumbled ashore. In fact, he looked like a wet bull walrus, and as intelligent. Dud was laughing as I had never heard him laugh—not quietly but uproariously.

"Whatinhell is so funny?" bellowed Bill X.

And then he began to search for a rock. The search was frantic, and he rolled over several in the mad attempt to locate one suitable for a missile. At last he laid hold of one large enough to have killed an ox, providing it could have been directed so as to hit an ox. For a moment, I feared that he would throw it at Dud or me, but I could not stop laughing. At that point, Bill made his third mistake. He ran forward to shorten the distance between himself and the adversary. When he hurled, he missed his mark. The target did not wait for Bill to find another stone. The stranger came on the run. The events were too swift and confused to be seen in detail, but Bill was lifted from his feet and dangled in the air. Then he was tossed into the pool. The bottom there was bumpy.

The stranger met Bill as he crawled to the bank.

"Are you wet enough, or do you choose to drown?" demanded a shrill voice.

Bill pawed for another rock. A painful kick in the wrist upset that maneuver. And Bill decided to appeal for intervention.

"Dud," he howled, "are yer goin' to stand thar an' let this crazy orphan (that was not Bill's word) carry on like this?"

The stranger grabbed Bill by the shirt front. Bill's arms flayed out like a rabbit's hind legs, but the stranger continued shaking Bill with a slow intensity that seemed to loosen every joint in the victim's body.

"Answer me!" yelled the stranger. "Have you had enough, or must I smack the nose off your miserable face?"

Dud stepped down to the level of action.

"Stranger," he said, "I reckon Bill's had enough. Don't think I'd interfere, though, if I didn't think more was a waste of your time an' strength."

"Very well," said the stranger, loosening his grip so abruptly that Bill fell a-sprawl in the shallow water.

Regaining his feet, Bill made his painful way back to the apron, where he picked up his rod and basket and went off down the opposite bank. Evidently the hook was gone from his line, for he permitted it to drag.

"Someday," he promised, "you an' me is goin' to meet ag'in, then what I'll do to yer won't be fit to print in any papers."

The stranger made a gesture with his hand as though dismissing a naughty child.

"My name's Dud Dean, an' this is my friend Arthur Macdougall. Reckon your name w'ud be Bart Latcher. Glad to meet yer" said Dud.

"If you will excuse me a moment, I want to look at my rod and I'll be back, sir."

We walked along behind him. He picked up his rod, which he had wedged, reel down, between the planks. Slowly, carefully, the man reeled in the line.

"The leader broke," he said.

"Crotch, kinda too bad," said Dud.

"Oh, aside from the provoking circumstances, I do not mind. I have two nice trout."

"That so? Let's have a look at 'em."

From the shadow of the dam, the stranger produced a trim willow creel. And there, sitting on a bed of dagger ferns, were two fine looking fish, as the stranger had said.

"Guess either w'ud go a little strong on two pounds," said Dud. "I guessed the fish yer had on was a five-pounder."

A grin spread across the man's homely face. "I guessed," he said, "that the other fellow's fish was much larger."

"Then I guess, maybe, I better cut down my estimate. Never see anythin' up this way that went better'n five pounds. That's rare, too, yer know."

"How did you know my name was Latcher?"

"Bert told us," replied Dud.

"Yes? A charming gentleman!"

"Ye're prob'ly right, but I never heard him classified that way a-fore. By the way, I'm jist a little curious. What was yer writin' down in that little book?"

"Oh, that? That's Sis's book. I write down observations. Sis knows all the birds that come near our house. Up here, I have seen several species that we do not find down home."

"Had the idee," said Dud, "that yer was keepin' fishin' notes."

"No. The notebook is for Sis. I heard a pewee in that birch tree over there."

"We-ell, how erbout some hot tea? I see that ye've got a lunch. Mak an' me c'ud spare some pan trout, if ye'd like a few fried."

So we initiated the stranger from Lynn. He drank Dud's tea and ate five of my trout.

"This is royal good of you fellows," he said.

"Um. I hope it squares us up. Y'know, we didn't have time to buy ringside tickets."

An embarrassed grin appeared on the stranger's face. "I owe you my apologies," he said. "If you had not come along as you did, it might have been a most regrettable episode."

"Maybe that will occur to Bill," said Dud.

"Do you think that, ah, fellow will bother me again? That is, will he come back here looking for more trouble?"

The man's face was a mask of seriousness. I saw Dud struggle to smooth out his own face, which, of course, was of a mind to laugh. When his face was as grave as the stranger's, he said:

"We-ell, I'll tell yer, Bart, I sh'ud say that it is extremely unlikely that ye'd ever set eyes on Bill ag'in, but if yer do, I hope that ye'll use some discretion, but not too much."

And the Deal Was Off

All the Dud Dean stories are about life and living, but this story is human through and through. Once Dud told Mak that he ought to write about fishing in the rain, and write it so the reader could feel the chill run down his or her back. It does in this story. It is a chill that gets deep down into the bone and the better nature of a person, leaving no room for foolish enthusiasm. The story ends, however, in an extraordinary encounter with a trout, a fishing lesson, and an affirmation.

The setting of this story is important both in terms of time and place. Today a good gravel road with many lesser branches crosses the "wilderness" area of ponds, streams, swamps and mountain that lie between Indian Pond (part of the East Branch of the Kennebec) and Route 201. When this story was written, an angler took the train to Indian Pond Station and walked the miles into the Chase Stream country, or the so-named Ten Thousand Acre Tract. There was only one way back to the rails and home, and that was to put one foot in front of the other.

THE MAN FROM NEW YORK and Dud Dean were playing checkers. Rain beat upon the cedar splits above our heads. The wind seemed to be marching the downpour in company fronts across the camp roof.

"Hear it rain," said the man from New York.

"Puts me in mind of the time Mak swore off trout fishin' fer-ever," said Dud.

"The provocation must have been extreme," said the man from New York.

"We-ell, the weather had been kinda provoking. In fact, it rained every min-it fer three days an' nights. An' the fishin' been as flat as an Injun's feet. Anybudy w'ud have thought the sun was stuck behind a chunk of eternity. The wind was cold. Maybe ye've noticed that when the seat of a man's breeches is wet, he's wet an' cold all over.

"Danged if we didn't have to give it up. We was at Island Pond, Ten Thousand Acres, an' so we had an eight er ten mile walk to Injun Pond station. All the way out, the ground felt like a man was steppin' on a sponge. Most of the way the trail wanders under hardwoods as tall as a fable an' as old as Nokomis. As we was walkin' under them trees, it seemed like all the world was leakin' on us—sput, spat, splash. My leather-top boots felt like I was walkin' in a pair of ten-gallon coffeepots. An' to save my soul, I c'udn't think of a reason that w'ud have passed muster in Hell Huddle fer gittin' inter sech a situation. Yes, sir! I'd had e-nough of it, as Dan'l Bean said when somebudy asked him if he cal-lated to git married ag'in after his wife had run away 'ith a tin peddler.

"But the weather was only part of the trouble. We had a feller 'ith us who had got hisself lost amongst Saul's father's jackasses. Now wait a min-it, becuz I reckon he was a good-intentioned feller. But as the twig is bent, the tree inclines, and the flatteries this world had bent that chap clean eround a delusion. Actually, I don't mean to be hard on him. Charity is all the clothin' the angels wear in heaven, I figger.

"But gosh-all-hemlock, this feller was a specialist at gittin' under a man's shirt! He knew most everythin'. He felt as smart as a schoolteacher on hossback. An' to frost it all off, it was like he had taken a correspondence course, er sunthin', on how to cheer folks up. So the harder it rained, and the more the wind blowed, the oftener he told us to buck up.

"Crotch, if only he'd been able to keep his mouth shut so brains c'ud function where thar warn't sech a draft, it might have occurred to him that Mak an' me had been out in the rain a-fore this partic'lar time, an' that we had managed to survive without his help. His everlastin' talk was like Sam Smith's poplar boards. Sam said that they was all sawed jist twelve inches wide when he used them to board up the back end of his barn, but that they kept shrinkin' an inch every year fer thirteen years, when thar warn't hardly anythin' left of 'em.

"Cheerfulness is a durned fine thing. It's a triumph of spirit over matter, but thar are times fer talkin' and times fer jist puttin' one foot in front of t'other, until a feller reaches a place where he ain't when he starts out, as Solomon told the Queen of Sheba. Not that thar w'ud have been any sense in tellin' this feller that becuz he w'ud have thought that Solomon was a bunch of islands. We-ell, come to think of it, maybe that w'udn't be sech a bad notion becuz I've known times, arter I'd made a partic'lar mess of sunthin', when it seemed to me that the famous wise man must have been a sort of island in hist'ry entirely surrounded by a sea of durn fools.

"Ayah. We-ell, that was on the way home. We was comin'

down the ridge from Hoss-shoe Pond an' had got almost as far as Chase Stream. Our Cheerio was still a-talkin' with his mouth. An' Mak's face looked almost as dark as the sky. If I c'ud read signs, Mak was erbout to start talkin' hisself. An' I figgered it warn't likely that he'd pick out a text to comfort the widders an' orphans in their afflictions.

"Bine-by, we was goin' down the last pitch before yer reach Chase Stream. Cheerio stepped on a streak of clay. Now, maybe Almighty made sunthin' slipperier than wet clay in the beginnin' of things, but it warn't necessary. Down goes Cheerio. An' blessed if he didn't stop talkin' fer a half min-it, er so. All of a sudden it was as still as the Day of Jedgment in a rainstorm.

"The situation was Mak's opportunity to git in a word. 'Dud,' he says, 'don't ever mention trout fishin' to me, except in a derogatory manner.'

"'Dee-rogatory?' I says, kinda puzzled.

"'Yes;' says Mak. 'To heck with it!'

"We-ell, crotch, I jist stood thar an' wiggled my toes like goldfish in a bowl of cold water. Finally, I says, 'Yer w'udn't go so far as to say, "To hell with it," w'ud yer?'

"'I certainly w'ud,' says Mak, 'becuz trout fishin' is getting worse every year. To get any, a man has to walk farther an' further, until sometime he's bound to die a thousand miles away from a graveyard, which, incidently, w'ud serve some folks right.'

"The tail end of that seemed to be aimed at Cheerio, who was rubbin' the clay off the back end of his britches, with the sort of a look on his face that is preliminary to cussin'. I c'ud see that it was a struggle, but somehow his better parts rose to the occasion.

"'Look,' he says to Mak, 'don't be that way! Remember that we have to take the bitter with the sweet.'

"'So I am beginnin' to suspect,' says Mak.

"I guess Cheerio didn't like that none too well becuz he looked at Mak like the parson was sunthin' it w'ud have been a pleasure to hit between the eyes.

"'Look,' he says, 'did you mean that talk about bein' done with trout fishin' ferever?'

"'I certainly did,' says Mak, lookin' at our Cheerio as if he hoped the feller w'ud jist try to hit him.

"'Then you won't need that nice rod. So I'll buy it. An' to indicate the kind of honest feller I am, I'll give you twenty-five dollars, spot cash.'

"Mak looked, all at once, like a man who'd lost his politics. 'Guess I don't want to sell this rod,' he says.

"'But,' says Cheerio, 'you'll not be needin' it. Come on. Just to show you that I'm no piker, I'll give you thirty dollars for it—that's a nice price for an old rod. But maybe you were only talkin' when you swore off trout fishin' forever.'

"Mak scowled at Cheerio as if the feller looked like a bow-legged pismire. 'Mister,' he says, 'you've bought something. Here's the rod, reel, an' line.'

"We-ell, Cheerio was took 'back. 'I'll have to give you a check when we get out to the car,' he says.

"'I'll even accept that, if you'll hold those porcelain teeth together until it stops raining.'

"Crotch, it seemed to me that maybe things was gittin' too personal, so I says, 'We better be movin' erlong.'

"And we did, until we come to a little patch of blueberry bushes where thar had been a log landin'. Them bushes was loaded 'ith big, ripe berries. By that time, Cheerio had got hold of his fust principles fer bein' the life of the party.

"'Well, well,' he says, 'let's enjoy life as we go along! How about some blueberries, à la aqua H_2O? What do you say?'

"'I say that it's too bad they didn't permit you to finish grammar school,' says Mak.

"But them blueberries did look good—nice an' clean an' cool in the rain. So when Cheerio waded out of the trail and inter the bushes, I followed him.

"'Yum, yum,' says Cheerio, tippin' back his head an' rollin' a handful inter his mouth. 'Come on, Mak, don't be a wet plaster—'

"That was as far as he got becuz he had planted both feet on a hornet's nest. Gosh, I doubt if Mrs. Post c'ud have maintained any decorum in sech a position. Anyhow, this Cheerio went out of thar like a rabbit 'ith six legs. I warn't only a moment sizin' up the sit-

uation myself. Durin' that pause in my mental processes, I noticed that Mak already had a lead on Cheerio.

"We made good time, until them hornets got discouraged. Cheerio and me stopped runnin' when we come to the west bank of Chase Stream, but Mak splashed through like a troop of cavalry. An' thar's no doubt but that he w'ud have kept right on if I hadn't yelled at him that the danger was over.

"One of my eyes didn't function good, but a man 'ith half an eye c'ud see that Cheerio was a sad pitchur. But Mak had escaped without a scar. Cheerio an' me had borne the brunt of the battle, an' Mak looked like a member of the Quartermasters to me.

"Anyhow, Cheerio an' me sot down beside the stream an anointed our stings with mud. Mud is great stuff fer hornet stings when yer can't find nothin' better. Thar was plenty of it, thank God, an' after a while we felt easier.

"'Where's Mak?' says Cheerio.

"Sure e-nough. Mak warn't nowhere in sight of us. 'Looks like he has wandered off,' I says to Cheerio. 'You hunt him up, while I rig up a fire to make some hot coffee. Tell him what I'm doing— if I can find anythin' that will burn in this hindquarters of the world. I reckon that a cup of b'ilin' coffee'll smell good to him.'

"All that happened on the seventh day of September," Dud explained to the man from New York, "but up to that time it hadn't snowed none. But erbout the min-it Cheerio started out in search of Mak, big, damp flakes begun to spin an' churn in the air. That made the departin' Cheerio look like a Eskimo ghost that had lost its igloo.

"'Where do you suppose the crazy cuss went to?' he yells back at me.

"'We-ell,' I says, 'of course I don't know, but maybe he went down the flowage a piece to try a few casts.'

"'Casts?' says Cheerio. 'I thought he said that he was all done with trout fishing.'

"'Guess he did make some sech talk, but a man might take inter his head to make a few last casts,' I says.

"So Cheerio went off down the stream, an' sure enough found Mak's tracks on the east side of the flowage—I mean old Number Ten Flowage that Walter Robinson made a good many years ago. By that time, snow squall an' all, Cheerio was erbout lost. So he begun to shout. When Mak answered him, his voice sounded as pee-culiar to Cheerio as a frog talkin' French.

"'Where be you?' yells Cheerio.

"'Out here,' grunts Mak.

"'What, in the water?'

"'No. You lunkhead—on the water, of course.'

"'How do you mean?' says Cheerio in a nervous voice, becuz he warn't prepared to believe that Mak c'ud walk on water, I s'pose.

"Mak unbent e-nough to explain that he was on a raft. Then the flurry of snow petered out an' the air looked almost yellowish. An' Cheerio c'ud see Mak all plain.

"'Look, Mak,' he says, 'you may as well give it up. Trout will not rise in a storm like this. Heck, man, the barometer must be down around hurricane, I bet.'

"But Mak w'udn't answer him. He jist kept on to his fishin'. So Cheerio tried another tack. 'Dud told me to tell you that he was making a pot of hot coffee.'

"Still Mak warn't int'rested.

"'And there's some canned milk left for it,' adds Cheerio.

"But he had to give it up. When he got back, I had a nice little fire burnin'.

"'Find him?' I says.

"'I found him,' says Cheerio, 'but the crazy cuss is fishin' again; and he won't come in.'

"'Is he doin' any business?' says I.

"'Of course he isn't. Haven't we demonstrated the futility of that for the last three days. The glass is probably—'

"'Never mind the glass,' I says. 'Let's go on down an' have a look at the situation.'

"So we went down. Thar was Mak, jist as Cheerio had said. Now he was changin' flies.

"'How they biting?' says I.

"Mak reached down by his feet. When he straightened up ag'in, he was holdin' three trout that w'ud go erbout a pound a piece.

"'Dud,' he says, 'there's a tremendous trout out here.' Then went to castin' ag'in.

"'I w'ud like to know when he caught those trout,' whispers Cheerio in my ear.

"'What yer got on fer a fly?' I asks Mak.

"'Welch Rabbit streamer,' he says, not botherin' to look at us. 'I need a big hook.'

"'Are there really big trout in here?' says Cheerio to me.

"'Sometimes,' says I, which I bet is as much as Noah w'ud dare to say erbout the fishin' in heaven.

"Cheerio started fer his pack, aimin' to git his own equipment, I s'pose.

"'Wait a min-it,' I says. 'This hain't a very big place. Besides, maybe the show will be worth it.'

"An' I had no more'n got rid of that suggestion when we heard a big splash that sounded like maybe a beaver had split his tail from end to end. An' I see that Mak was fast to a trout that was bending his five-ounce rod like a reed shaken in the wind.

"We-ell, jist remember that we had been fishin' fer three days 'ithout a rise. Crotch, I felt all excited an' happy. In fact, hardly payin' attention, I waded out until the water was up to my knee. It didn't matter, of course. I was that much nearer the fun. Cheerio waded out too, but I reckon he did it so he c'ud make me hear what he wanted to say.

"Things was rippin' when Cheerio got hold of my arm. I paid e-nough attention to make out that he had sunthin' to say, but thar warn't no time to listen.

"'Got a good stout leader?' I yells at Mak.

"'Two X,' he says, tryin' to pole the raft eround 'ith one hand while the trout was pullin' off line like an old-fashioned retreat.

"'Look at him!' says Cheerio, smack in my right ear. He acts as if he had a trained seal on the end of the line, and as if he was afraid to hurt it. Why in thunder doesn't he give that fish a taste of the butt? He's holding his rod too low!'

"Somehow that made me mad. I taught Mak how to fly-fish myself. 'Cheerio,' says I, fergittin' that warn't his right name, 'if I was you, I w'ud stand eround 'ith my mouth shut. Even the best of men can learn sunthin' now an' then.'

"Ayah. Things began to happen. Away goes hunks of line. That trout was goin' places, fast an' powerful. In fact, he was plowin' straight up the flowage where me an' Cheerio was standin' like a couple of pie-eyed cranes that had swallowed their cuds. Crotch! I knew Mak didn't have more'n a hundred feet of line, backin' and all. An it was too early in the game to put the butt to that fish. If a feller sh'ud do that, sunthin' was goin' to bust between.

"Man, I legged it out of the water an' up the shore until I came to a rock as big as a muskmelon. By that time it was plain as the nose on an elephant's face that the trout was goin' to attempt to run the fust riffle. So I heaved that stone an' leaped in, splashing water all over myself—like a feller as old as I be, an' as crazy, sh'ud have done.

"Thar hain't a doubt but that Cheerio considered me a comical sight, but that w'udn't have bothered me none becuz I had turned the tide of the battle, fer a min-it er so anyway. In fact, Mak had to strip line 'ith his left hand, like a feller measurin' a red-hot wire.

"Cheerio j'ined me where I stood. 'Look at him now,' he says. 'Why doesn't he use his reel instead of tryin' to strip line that way? He'll get fouled.'

"By that time I w'ud not have listened to the prophet Obadiah, not if he was talkin' like that.

"'How,' I says, 'in the holy name of Sam Cook do yer expect a man to take in line fast e-nough on a reel with a fish comin' in like that one? Hain't he actin' just as unreasonable as a blinded b'ar? Can't yer see thar's nothin' else to do but strip line?'

"'But I've read—' begins Cheerio.

"I stopped him. 'By Jericho,' I says, 'never mind what ye've read!'

"Of course that trout reached the south end of Mak's line while we was talkin' that way. An' thar warn't nothin' I c'ud do erbout that, bein' that the flowage was too wide down thar. So the time had come to put the whole business to the issue. If anybudy doubted that the leader w'ud hold, er that the rod w'ud take the gaff, he only needed to wait an' see, fer it was sartinly time fer all thar was in that outfit to be held ag'inst that fish.

'Now he has come to his senses,' Cheerio says to me. 'He sh'ud of done that long ago.'

"It come to me that life was too short to waste talk on a man that needed to be drowned in six inches of water, which is the most humiliatin' death I can think erbout. But I did take time to say out of that corner of my mouth that warn't chewin' a pipestem:

"'A man like you, Cheerio, w'ud insult his own pallbearers.'

"It may be that sunthin' else w'ud have occurred to me, but jist then Mak's rod snapped back to idle an' I thought his fish had gone free.

"'May the Lord guard the parson's language,' I says, kinda reverent like.

"But b'crotch, that trout had only turned quick—mad at the braddin' the hook had given him. An' if Cheerio was still convinced that a man sh'ud use his reel at all times, he sartinly got a demonstration on how to strip line as fast as a live fish can run on you. It was nip an' tuck who'd git ahead. By gosh! What fun I had.

"'Is he dippin' his colors?' I sings out in a tone loud enough fer Nancy to hear me, sixty miles away.

"'I think so,' says Mak, between his teeth. 'But, Dud, I didn't bring a landin' net!'

"Crotch a'mighty, that meant hanging on till the last with all the untoward chances hangin' over Mak like a cloud of buzzards. Even Cheerio had stopped talkin'. We jist stood an' watched, like men who knew the Almighty don't have to answer what Doc Brownin' use to call impromptu prayers when they don't fit in 'ith the general scheme of things. Not that I thought erbout prayin', becuz it hain't easy to pray in cold water up to your knees.

"At last, Mak started to bend over to hook his finger inter that trout's gills. I was so impatient that it seemed to me a man 'ith a two-by-four fer a backbone might have bent double in half th' time Mak was takin'. But at last he got that fish, b'crotch.

"It was all over. Life is pee-culiar. It piles up mountains of trouble until a man can't see over the top. Then, puff—an' everythin' is as level as a pond.

"I started to fill my pipe until I remembered that my t'bacco was so wet it w'udn't have burned in a month of Sundays. Then I happened to look up inter the west. And, sir, by crotch, thar was as purty a rainbow as a man ever see.

"When we waded ashore Cheerio says, 'Do you know, I suspect that Mak has fergotten all about sellin' me that rod.'

"'Ayah,' I says, 'it w'udn't surprise me if the deal was off.'

The Trout of Standup Rips

When Dudley Barney, Dud's namesake, shows up, it is the occasion for the telling of Barney's mother's courtship. She was then Diana Deems and built like "a good fly rod" as Dud recalls. "The best lookin' gal King Solomon ever laid eyes on—maybe prettier."

And could she fly fish! A contest for her attentions was inevitable. The showdown, when it came, involved two amorous men, a big trout and a place called Standup Rips on the East Branch of the Kennebec.

We join Mak and young Dudley as Dud tells the story the way he says it should be told: properly. (See Appendix for notes on location.)

MAK, WHEN THE ALMIGHTY RESTED on the seventh day, He noticed that He had left sunthin' out of the pitchur. It was lookin' at Adam an' Eve that reminded Him of that. They was mighty plain-lookin' ancestors, I reckon. So He says to Hisself, says He, 'I reckon this won't ever do.' An' that's how He happened to put a half pint of magic stuff in humanity. Tharafter, every time the magic come to the top, a beautiful person like Nancy Dean, er Diana Deems, was born in a world that usually runs erlong purty commonplace, in spite of beauty parlors and sech vain attempts to alter what is.

The fust time I ever laid eyes on my Nancy was durin' a recess-time, down't the schoolhouse. She was out playin' games 'ith little folks. The news had got erbout thar was a new schoolmarm. That was how I happened to be drivin' by. The wind was kinda fussin' eround in her brown hair. An' I begun to feel jealous of the wind.

Yes, sir, by gum! An' that's the way love hit Lloyd Barney. Right smack a-tween the eyes. Him an' a college chum stopped at The Forks Hotel, on their way up to fish Parlin Pond. But after they'd discovered Diana Deems, they lost all interest in Parlin Pond, an' they never did git thar, I reckon.

Now, of course, I'm a teller of fishin' stories, when I ain't ruminatin' erbout huntin', so I can't do justice to the courtin' that went on after that. It w'ud be sort of pitiful if I sh'ud try. The best I can do is to abbreviate that part of it.

Them young fellers, Barney—an' let's call the other feller Bradey, becuz that warn't his name—went after Diana hammer an' tongs. Jericho, no matter where we went fishin', they'd follow as fast as time an' space permitted. Diana enjoyed it, but her father didn't. The old feller c'udn't seem to figger it out, at fust. It took him several days to see daylight on that situation.

"Dud," he says to me, "it has come, an' there's no use runnin' away from it. The vanguards of the biological hosts are upon us. Diana has grown up. An' the old days are in the back of the back."

"Yes, sir," I says, "an' the vanguard is Irish."

"I know," he says, "but let's go on with business as usual. Today we'll have a go at the big trout at Standup Rips."

So I got all packed to lunch out—grub fer the four of us. I mean, of course, Diana, her folks, an' myself. But lo an' behold, when the time came to start up the branch, the only one to appear was old man Deems.

"Diana an' her mother are going shopping at Bingham," he says to me.

"Then we'll take my canoe an' pole up the river. We can try the fishin' on the way, if that suits yer," says I.

"Fine!" he says. "Dud, it has been revealed to me that youth passed me some time back, and it wasn't going my way, either. So I've resolved, henceforth, to take my time. I'll loaf when it's pleasant to loaf, and when loafing gets tiresome, I'll work a spell until loafing invites me again. Do you know Walt Whitman, Dud?"

"No. Guess he never fished up here, did he?"

"Probably not, but he cast a long line. I just wondered if you would recall his declaration about loafing and inviting the soul. It suggests good medicine."

"Y'know," I says, feelin' a little troubled, "I w'udn't take Barney an' Bradey too seriously."

"God bless your soul," says he, while he stepped in the canoe. "I assure you that I will not, from now on. I've washed my hands. Diana's of age. We've done the best we c'ud fer her. From now on, she'll have to make her own decisions. Amen. Now, b'gosh, let's devote the rest of this day to fishing. Don't mention biology to me not once."

"I hardly ever talk erbout subjects I don't understand," says I, hitchin' a little mite of a brown an' gold bucktail that I had fixed myself to his leader.

"That goes for both of us," he says, whippin' out thirty er forty feet of line.

So I got hold of my pole an' started settin' the canoe up the river. Now . . . fer jist a min-it I want to talk erbout the river. Dang it all, I always liked the Bible story of Naaman, the captain of the king's hosts. Death had writ its name an' address on his hide, but when old Elisha said he'd have to wash seven times in the river Jordan to git rid of his plague, Naaman says, "Wash in that dirty water! Are not Abana an' Pharpar purtier rivers than all the waters of Israel?" Jumpin' horn pout, Scripture is generally too much fer me, but I c'ud have read that to the bottom when I was knee-high to a pie-eyed crane. Naaman knew his own rivers, and he loved 'em, so the Jordan looked like another man's mother-in-law to him.

Take the Kennebec, up here where it's the Kennebec an' not two-thirds man's filthiness as it is when it gits to Merrymeeting Bay. My heart goes out to the Kennebec, like a bride adorned to meet a photographer. An' best of it all is the East Branch, set to rights by the hills that ferever fence it in. All the way from Injun Pond to the place where the West Branch butts in, the East Branch is as wild as an untamed hoss an' as purty as a violet. And if that combination sounds impossible set to English, it ain't in geography.

An' the East Branch, twenty years ago, was the sort of water which a fisherman's heart pants fer, in spite of all the ruin log drives can work on a river. An' if that ain't good quotation, er poetry, it is the fact as I knew it. May my pipe go out in the midst of medi-tation, if I've stretched anything.

It was a pleasure to handle a canoe fer your grandfather Deems. He handled a nice line, like business. An' that's the way we went up the river that mornin'. The water was flat—no head guzzlin' down on us from Moosehead Lake—jist the natural pitch of the East Branch, like God made it in June.

We hooked as many as twenty trout, but only saved four small ones that was all silvered an' dotted 'ith the color of mayflowers that grow in the spring at the edge of old snow. Them was fer our dinner when we got to Stan'up Rips.

Sometimes it was nip an' tuck on the way up the river, an' I had to pole purty lively. But bine-by, like boys on a day off an' a ticket to the circus, we come to Stan'up Pool, where the hills push the East Branch to the right. The main current goes boomin' down the rips, but some of it swings back up eround the pool an' washes over gravel bottom that is as clean as a boy's neck after his ma has conducted Saturday night.

Thar's a flat rock, out purty nigh the middle, that is big enough fer comfortable fishin'. A man can stand on it an cast where he pleases. I paddled Deems up to it' an' he climbed out on it. Then I handed him his net an' collateral. That done, I went ashore; pulled the canoe up high an' dry an' begun to putter erbout gittin' dinner ready. It was a nice place to wait the issue.

Crotch, I loved it thar then, an' I do now. Lookin' up the river, from top the ledge, yer c'ud see half a mile of blue water. It was almost purple that day, an, it fell all over itself sweepin' down Stan'up Pool. Yer c'ud hear it talkin' erbout June in Maine. Of course, the black flies was thar to remind a man that life is no bed of nursery rhymes. But even at that, the birds disputed any notion that the earth warn't good e-nough fer even pessimists. Gentlemen, ye'll never know how lucky I've been in my time. I've been able to make my livin' at playin' hooky. An' Almighty never sent His truant officers after me!

Yes, sir! An' grandfather Deems c'ud fish. It was nice to watch him. But by gum, he didn't raise a fish before dinnertime. Ye'd have sworn that the branch was as empty of fish as a collection plate of dollar bills.

Bine-by, Deems allowed that he was ready fer some dinner; an' I had it fixed. I had a little tin of medium good biscuits that I baked, an' pink trout meat, done proper. Then I had set some tea to coolin' in a spring that was so cold it hurt your hands.

So we sot down an' sipped our tea. And to quote from my favorite book, we talked of cabbages an' kings. When I remember sech times, I feel it'll be all right if they don't let me inter heaven. I know what it's like.

Then we cleaned up an' embarked fer up the river. I poled up to the mouth of Moxie Stream. We fished thar a while. But it was more'n three o'clock when Mr. Deems hooked the fust trout. When we got it in the net, I see that it was one of them Moxie Lake trout that had been sluiced out on a head of water. It weighed 'bout two pounds an' was dark—almost bluish erlong the lateral line, an' spotted as red as the devil's diamonds.

"Dud," says Deems, 'it's time we got back to Standup Rips, becuz the trout are on the feed ag'in."

So we run down the current as easy as a b'ar cub slides down an old stub. But when we arrived, thar was them two young pups, Barney an' Bradey.

"What, didn't you fellers go to Bingham?" I says.

Guess they didn't appreciate that becuz, we found out later, they didn't know Diana had gone to Bingham. They had put their heads together an' figgered she'd gone upriver 'ith her father. So I reckon that we didn't look especially good to them—jist two old fishers an no Diana at all. Deems chuckled when he saw the look on their faces.

"What luck?" he says to them.

It was young Barney that told the truth. "Rotten," says he, but of course he warn't thinkin' erbout trout.

But they continued 'ith the fishin' becuz they c'udn't think what else to do, I guess. We fished at the foot of the rapids above them. An' it was more'n an hour a-fore we got any action. Then thar was a brief hatch of stone flies. The pool, the length of it, came to life with hungry fish. Now, thar's one sure way to catch trout, as likely ye've noticed: to be on hand when the fish begin to feed.

Both Barney an' Bradey woke up an' begun to fish in earnest. They warn't left-handed at it, either. So I s'pose that they had known summers when thar'd been more time to practice. Anyhow, they got some trout. How many I don't know, becuz we was busy ourselves. Jist at the last of it, we hooked the big trout of Stan'up Rips. But Deems took him on what ye'd call a 4X leader nowadays, which is a better thing to conjure 'ith than to hold a really big trout in fast water. So when that old slab-sided cuss wanted to go down river, we let him. That meant runnin' the rips.

Barney an' Bradey galloped after us, bein' int'rested in the sequel, I s'pose. But they was too late. That durn cuss of a trout busted that leader as easy as yer c'ud tell me from Simon Peter. So that was when them young fellers found out erbout the big trout of Stan'up Rips.

When we got back to the hotel, Diana an' her ma was home. They'd traveled on Will Whorf's stage. The boys gathered round, glad to have an excuse, an' told her ebout the big trout her father had lost. By the color in her cheeks, it was plain she enjoyed the attention.

A couple of days passed, during which Mr. Deems an' me did all the fishin' alone. Diana had acquired two guides of her own, an' her ma went erlong 'ith her to keep the guides comp'ny which pleased them, no end. Oh, they waited on Diana tooth an' nail. It was a comical sight, er chivalrous, accordin' to a man's philosophy. An' let me say, it has always seemed to me that the reach of any an' all the common philosophies is no more than an old-fashioned cubit, which I've been told was from the tip of a man's longest finger back to the end of his funny bone.

Be that as it is, if Diana's head warn't turned, she was smarter than Barney an' Bradey. Really, I'd like to dwell over this part of the report, but since I never courted but one woman, I ain't up to describin' the happenings in an' erbout The Forks Hotel. Due allowance sh'ud be made fer the season an' the weather.

Fer instance, it was a handsome sight to see the moon roll up from away over by Moxie, till the reflection of its face laid on the water that flowed out from under the old covered bridge at The Forks. The sight of it made a spell upon the impressionable, apparently.

On the second night after we'd lost the big trout at Stan'up, I was settin out on the porch, feet on the rail, an' meditatin' on trout fishin' in general, when young Bradey joined me.

"Good evening, sir," he says, an' sot down in a chair, near

enough to borrow a match.

Of course I knew as well as he did that Barney had beat his time in that heat, an' that he was out walkin' with Diana in the moonlight. Thar was a misery on Bradey's face that was as old as a triangle, an' I cal'late that a triangle is older than mathematics. I felt sorry fer Bradey, in a comfortable way.

But he jist sot thar an' never said a word fer ten min-its er so.

"We-ell, son," I says, "time runs on, eh?"

"Don't let me keep you up," says he, missin' my p'int.

"No. No, I won't," I says, "becuz I'm jist settin'—that's all. We had a great day. Got four extra nice trout. How'd yer do yourself?"

Blast it, he c'udn't seem to remember, er he didn't try. Jist what gits inter a man's head when he thinks the world is as thinly populated as the Garden of Eden? Crotch!

"Look," he says, sudden, "I want to ask you something. Suppose two men love the same girl?"

"We-ell," says I, "it's ag'inst the law fer both of 'em to marry her, an' I guess that it usually ends up that the law ain't vi'lated."

"In this case," he says, ignorin' my flippancy, "the men in question are friends."

"In heaven," I says, "that might make some difference."

"To stop beating around the bush," says he, "it's us."

"Yer surprise me," says I.

He grinned. But it was a sick grin—at least as I made it out under the piazza roof.

"You're not surprised," he says. An' then, after a min-it, he added, "Lloyd an' I have a plan to settle it. The man who catches the big trout, on a fly, any pattern, wins the right to court Diana—"

He c'udn't go on becuz his throat seemed to stick fast.

"Crotch," I says, "what if somebudy else catches that trout?"

"That wouldn't count," says he, tryin' his best to grin ag'in. All of a sudden, I see that he was in dead earnest, an' I felt flabbergasted at sech dummed nonsense.

"Are yer actually in earnest?" I asks him.

"Just that," says he. "The man who gets that trout wins. The other fellow packs his baggage and leaves."

"But what if Diana don't like the idea?"

"Please," he says. "The affair is already too complicated. Don't suggest more difficulties."

"An' has Barney gone out 'ith Diana to try to explain this cockeye plan to her?"

"No," he says, scowlin' up at the moon. "No. Of course he didn't. She isn't to know. What do you think we are? But he has agreed. We have given our word to each other, in the name of our alma mater."

"Who is Elmer Marter?" I says. An' he acted as though I was thickheaded, er blasphemous, becuz he got to his feet an' walked inside the hotel. But he came back in a min-it.

"Please do not mention this matter to a soul," he says. "I should not have spoken about it, but somehow I was lonely."

"Trust me," says I, "that never a word will escape my lips. I w'udn't repeat it to a pie-eyed crane."

Yes, sir. That was the plot. So help me, the next mornin' them two Irishmen struck out fer Stan'up Rips. An' thar was what is often called a mark of determination on their faces. The while, the young lady slept on, undisturbed by the turn of events, I reckon.

Nothin' happened that day. An' that night Bradey strolled 'ith Diana in the moonlight. Barney walked the hotel piazza, back an' forth, until I guess he wore a trail in the spruce boards. Finally, he got tired, I reckon, becuz he sot down beside me.

"Got a match to spare?" he says to me.

I was prepared. He lit his pipe an' puffed like an adder. I jist waited. Finally, he says:

"Look, what happens when two men fall in love with the same girl? Friends, mind you."

"We-ell," says I, "it don't happen very often, prob'ly, but usually the girl straightens it out in the long run. One er t'other gits the worst of it. I mean, he marries her."

"Hump," he says, an' puffed some more. The idea seemed to be to make a smoke screen. He'd been in the navy an' maybe got the idea thar.

After another min-it er so, he added, "It's a devil of a situation."

"So I gathered," says I.

"What! How did you know?"

"Oh, I'm smart at guessin'."

"Look," he says, "to change the subject, what do you suppose become of that big trout that Mr. Deems lost? We fished for him all day and never saw a sign."

"We-ell," I says, "maybe somebudy else has caught him, by this time. I don't think he's very smart either."

"Gorry! I hope not!" says Barney.

"I've always heard that thar was plenty of fish in the sea, as good as ever was caught. That goes even fer trout an' women, son."

"It's a damned lie, then. Look— No. Never mind. Well, good

night, Dud. I've got to get up early."

"Don't fergit to call Bradey," I says.

"What? Say, who has been talking? What do you mean?"

"Me? Nothin' at all. I jist thought Bradey might be sleepy."

"Oh. Sure. I'll wake him up."

"If it was me," I calls after him, "I'd let Bradey concentrate on the trout, an' I'd put in my own time to better advantage."

"If you were I," says he, "you would do the same as I do."

Ayah. I bet he didn't git to sleep until Bradey come in. 'Long toward mornin' sunthin' waked me up. So I shoved my legs in my britches. It was a Sunday, which in them days meant a day off, if a man was guidin' the right folks, an' Mr. Deems was. So it was my day to do as I pleased. I went downstairs an' out on the porch. It was a chilly, foggy mornin'. It made me grin a little when I thought how hard it was to fit the weather tergether—moonlight nights an' foggy mornings.

Jist then my eyes caught sight of Barney an' Bradey goin' up the road. I watched them turn through the barway to the meadows erlong the west side of the Branch. Thar they goes, side by side an' not sayin' a word, as near as I c'ud make out.

"By gum," I says to myself, "here's your chance to have a ringside seat at the tournament where Ireland fights it out." I went back to the kitchen an' got a snack to eat. After which, I struck out up the trail to Stan'up Rips. That pair of tracks was plain enough in the wet June grass. An' I felt like young Saul who went in search of his father's jackasses.

And I hurried erlong, intendin' to overtake them, but I had to give it up. They warn't lingerin' erlong the way, an' they was a pair of able fellers. Then I begun to wonder if they w'ud welcome my comp'ny. They sartinly hadn't invited me. That made me feel a little sneaky. Still, I c'udn't see any harm in it. An' I felt a sort of left-handed responsibility, like most everybudy else when a thing ain't any of their business. So I kept on.

Fog hung heavy over the river, like smoke over a town when the weather is goin' to rain. Thar was no black flies to bother a feller, but the mosquitoes was substituting. All in all, I wondered why I hadn't stayed in bed that Sunday morning. Bine-by, I was goin' down the drivers' path that comes to Stan'up Rips. An' in a min-it er so, I heard voices.

Somehow, I thought it might be more fun if I didn't interduce myself right off. So I stood behind a big yeller birch an' watched them. Maybe a half hour passed. Then Bradey hooked a fish, but it was only a two-pounder. An' Bradey swore erbout it.

Finally Barney said, "It's my guess that trout never came back here at all. He's downriver somewhere. And I'm going to fish down a ways—at least to the pool below the first bend. Are you?"

Bradey considered. At last he says, "No. I'll stick around here, today anyway."

"You know," says Barney with a kinda uneasy grin, "Diana's mother wouldn't approve of our fishin' on Sunday."

"Can't help it," says Bradey. "Besides, I don't exactly approve of her. She's too contented with things as they are."

Barney grinned. "So long," he says, "keep a tight line, but this time I don't wish you luck."

"That's mutual," says Bradey, an' he kept on castin'.

We-ell, if I kept incognito, as Doc Brownin'useter say, I had to keep Bradey comp'ny. An' in a way, I've always been glad I did, fer I saw justice done, which is more than happens every Sunday, by crotch.

Now we've come to the hoptoad an' the trout that et him. Some folks will tell yer, sober as deacons, that toads rain down all becuz they migrate from where they're hatched when it's damp, as a man w'ud expect them to do if he knew his toads.

While Bradey was fishin', his eyes spotted sunthin'. He bent over an' grabbed, but evidently missed. Then he laid down his rod an' made a business of catchin' the thing. It was a little mite of a toad. He put it in his pocket an' looked up an' down the river, like his conscience was uneasy. Then he took a knife an' cut the wings an' hackle off a nice Parm' Belle that was tied on a number eight hook. Yer can figger the rest out fer yourself.

I watched him wade out in the pool until the water was half up to his armpits. Then he fed down his line, until the current caught it an' sucked it down some more. The danged cuss was no novice at that sort of thing, er if he was, inheritance is turrible. The current did the rest—all but what the trout did.

Crotch, that trout dum near yanked the rod out of Bradey's hand. It ripped out yards of line on a run across current, then dropped down the river. Bradey fought it all the way, an had a bite an' leverage that was wicked becuz that fish had swallowed the little toad. Oh, the young feller played a cool game. He reeled line, as he worked down, step at a time. An' at last was able to beach his trout, which was as beaten out as a smoked mackerel.

Even a feller behind a birch tree c'ud see that it was Deems's fish. But I made up my mind that I w'ud swear it warn't so big as the fish we had lost, although, of course, I still had in mind that they hadn't dealt with Diana Deems, not yit, b'gosh. An' I knew she w'udn't be had fer the flip of a coin, as yer might say.

Bradey had ruined his rod, as I saw later on. An' he was breathin' fast when he came back. Fellers, it was the trout, no mistake. Ag'in, like the fish we had taken at the mouth of Moxie, this warn't no regular river trout, which are long an' light-colored, like the water. This fish was dark, an' as thick as the blade of a canoe paddle. It warn't as big as I had thought it was when Mr. Deems had it on, but then that warn't to be expected. Anyhow, it was a fish that w'ud weigh a good five pounds, I'd say, although it's hard to guess the weight of a big trout unless yer caught it yourself, an' then it's apt to be improbable.

Fust thing I knew I was standin' out in plain sight, but Bradey was so intent on his own luck that he never looked my way, an' so I stepped behind the tree ag'in. I watched him lay that trout out in the grass between the woods an' the gravel. I saw the grin on his

face, but his hands was still shaky.

Then he took off the denuded fly an' put back a good one. He looked eround ag'in. Nobudy in sight. So he sot down on a rock where the warm light of the sun, which was jist pullin' up over the hills, w'ud fall on him. Prob'ly he was chilly becuz he'd been in the cold water up to his arms. It was in my mind that everythin' was over, an' I was jist goin' to step out an' make myself known when I caught sight of sun-thin' runnin' erlong the bank by the ledge that yer have to climb eround when ye're goin' up the river afoot. When I saw the critter ag'in, I made out that it was an almighty big mink. The old feller was runnin' in an' out of places, huntin' as he came. I've watched 'em many a time. This old feller was black as sin, an' as lanky. He looked like he'd been up late of nights.

Yep. Ye've guessed it. His nose led him to the trout, where Bradey had laid it out in state while he waited fer Barney to come back. An' I watched that mink drag it down to the edge of the river. W'ud yer guess that he c'udn't drag so big a fish? He did. An' it all happened behind Bradey's back, while he warmed hisself in the sun.

After that, Bradey sot some more. Purty soon, Barney come eround the bend, fishin' as he came. When he got thar he said, "Well, no luck down there, either. We should have brought dinner."

Bradey grinned. "I've got our dinner," he says. "Come have a look."

"What?" says Barney, his voice a little louder'n common.

"I caught the trout."

"Go on!" exclaims Barney moppin' his for'head an' pushin' back his red hair.

Bradey led the way. An' when he got thar, he c'udn't believe his eyes. He knelt down an' pawed eround in the grass. Then he hunted the length of that little patch. Barney watched him, 'ith a puzzled look on his face. At last Bradey stood up straight.

"He's gone!" he says.

Barney got down an' felt of the grass where Bradey was p'intin'. "There is slime on this spot," he said, lookin' up at Bradey. "I can feel it with my hands."

"But that's all," says Bradey, an' his face was black as thunder at two o'clock in the mornin'.

They looked up in the trees as if they thought that a hawk er eagle had swiped the fish.

"Damn it!" says Bradey. "I quit. I'm goin' back to the hotel. Damn it all!"

"Wait a minute," says Barney. "We haven't looked everywhere."

But Bradey never stopped. Barney looked more puzzled, began to search all over ag'in. It's funny how honest an' serious men can be erbout foolishness. I thought it was my turn. An' walked out in plain sight.

Barney looked up at me. "Oh, I thought it was Bradey," he says. Then a funny look spread over his face, an' he says, down in his throat, "Did you hide Bradey's trout?"

It made me feel out of patience, but I tried to be gentle becuz I warn't hankerin' fer no row, an' circumstantial evidence was ag'in me.

"No," I says to Barney, "I never touched Bradey's trout. But I know exactly what did become of it. A mink took it."

"A mink?" says he, not believin' me at all, an' makin' the fact plain that he didn't.

B'crotch, I'd had e-nough. "Come here," I says to him.

The trail of slime an' wet was still discernible on the rocks—
that is, here an' thar. Moreover, at the edge of the water where the
old cuss had braced hisself fer a last heave, I found a set of mink
tracks. An' by gum, I made Barney stick his city nose in those
tracks until he saw them, too.

"Thar's the story," says I.

"Was it the big trout, I mean the big feller?" he asks, lookin' in
my face where he knelt.

"Yes," says I, "to be honest, I w'ud say it was."

"That settles it then," says he. "It's over. Bradey wins."

"No, it don't," I says. "It don't settle a thing, by crotch!"

"Why not?" he asks. An' his face brightened up, which showed
his blood pressure was more intelligent than he acted.

"That," I says, "is your question. Answer it yourself. But let me
tell yer sunthin' a-fore I go home. Diana Deems is too good fer a
danged idgit like you. A lot of sprawl ye've got, both of yer. Bah!"

An' I left him thar. I hadn't gone a half mile, seems as though,
when I overtook Bradey shamblin' erlong like a lost soul in
Jericho. He looked glum but he made out to speak.

"Hello," says he, "I didn't know you were upriver this morning."

"I know yer didn't," I says, "but I was."

A Duplicious Incident

This story first appeared in the Dud Dean collection Where Flows the Kennebec *published by Coward-McCann in 1947. It was selected for the anthology* White Pine and Blue Water—A State of Maine Reader *edited by Henry Beston. It may not be what the chamber of commerce would choose to depict local characters, but, of course, this story only shows a certain variety of Maine character. It does so with a marvelous touch of accuracy and with abundant humor. Those who have read "Dead Water Doings" have already met Bill X. Dud and Mak are in the shiretown of Skowhegan when they encounter his wife, Mrs. X.*

THIS IS BILL X'S STORY. IT ISN'T MINE. I do not think that proves anything, except that I was five or ten dollars ahead of my economic incompetency.

Dud and I were at the county seat. Turning the corner of Madison Avenue and Water Street, we met Mrs. X. You observe that I am omitting the last name. Mrs. X is a large women. She is a mountain of protoplasm and a molehill of virtue.

Wasting no more than a glance at Dud, who squandered no more on her, she began a puffing, tearful story. Them nincompoop wardens had gone and put her Bill in jail ag'in. Jist what did they think she and Bill's misfortunate children could live on while they had their vile revenge? Here it was, near to Christmus, the birthday of Him who said suffer the little children to come unto Him and consider the lilies of the field. And not a cent! Not a cent did she have to her name. And Pansy—that was the baby—was the cutest little angel! And Bill Junior, and Don, and Philander, and Frankie, and Narcissus, who was the next youngest girl, and Bob, and Georgie—they were all good children, even if their father warn't religious. And what was she (their mother) to do? Christmus was goin' to be like somebudy's funeral at their house instead of a Christian holiday. But there! She could stand all that, if she knew where the next meal was coming from. And she wished that I had been there at the court to hear them game wardens lie about poor, helpless, innersent Bill, who had been the victim of their evil, connivin' plot. She knew that I was not the man to watch justice miscarry. And, finally, would I lend her ten dollars to keep her dear ones alive a little while longer?

I knew Mrs. X. I knew Bill X. But there were the children, Pansy, Narcissus, and all the rest. Furthermore, they always looked half-clad and partially starved. Also, I did have ten dollars.

Mrs. X saw me weakening. Her hand was half out for the money, which, by the way, I had determined would be five dollars instead of the suggested ten.

"Jist a min-it," interposed Dud, anticipating my charity. "Did yer say Bill was in jail, Malty?"

"I certainly did. Don't you read the papers?"

"Sometimes I do. Then ag'in I have spells when I rely on my neighbors. All I was comin' at was that maybe Mak an' me c'ud go over to the jail, where Bill's boardin' at the taxpayers' expense, an' have a good talk with him. Then if Mak figgered yer needed money worse'n he does hisself, he c'ud see yer later."

Mrs. X was not pleased with Dud. Dabbling a last week's hanky at her eyes, she said, "I'd be awful glad to have our minister call on poor Bill, and Bill w'ud be, too. But I don't see what that has got to do with the fact that I hain't had no breakfast myself, an' I'm in a delicate condition and all."

Dud addressed me. "Mak, let's go call on this feller townsman of ours. As fer Malty's breakfast, the town has to look after Bill's family while he's incarcerated."

Dud was right. When we had walked away from Bill's missus, Dud said to me, "I thought if yer had a few min-its to invest on your eddication, it w'ud be a good idea."

The Sheriff led us into the town's "boardinghouse" where Bill was "doing time."

"Howareyer, Bill?" said Dud. "The last time I seen yer, you was gang-hookin' trout off the spawnin' bed at East Carry Pond."

Bill replied that he was feelin' as well as c'ud be expected under the circumstances, but that he was as unhappy as a houn'-dorg tied to a manicure-spreader.

"How did it happen to yer?" asked Dud.

"I am good an' sick of rehashin' it," grunted Bill. "Every time I open my mouth down here, somebudy puts his foot in it. I told that cornseated jedge zactly how it happened, an' the durn cuss acted as if he figgered I was lying. When I git free, thar's a man that don't want to cross my path, becuz if he does I'll kill him with my two hands."

"Bill always was a vicious talker," Dud said to me.

"See here, Dud, I wounded that buck erbout three o'clock in the afternoon. What man, except a lounge lizard in a red shirt w'ud leave a deer to die a lingerin' death an' be et up by varments? Of course it got dark. It always does after the sun goes down. Was I to blame that I had a devil of a time comin' up with that buck? W'ud it have been kind to dumb animals if I had gone home, leavin' the poor innersent critter to bleed away his life a half inch at a time?

"Natcherly I had a flashlight. Nobudy but a tender-toed city-ite w'ud git catched out after dark without some sort of a light. Do they expect a man to hedgehorg back in the pitch dark!

"'Sunrise to sunset,' says that jedge. Don't the poor idgit know that them lawmakers down to Augusty can't regulate daylight an' dark? Now, see here, Dud, don't you always figger to have a light in your pocket when ye're huntin' ten er fifteen miles from home?"

"Ayah, I do," agreed Dud, "but I don't ordinarily tote a six-cell light. Two batteries make plenty of light when the weary hunter homeward plods, as the poet says."

"Huh. Them smart-faced lawyers tried to make a p'int of that; said that a six-celled flashlight looked s'picious. But I told 'em, and that ornery jedge, too. Says I, 'One of them ten-cent flashlights hain't no more use to a man in the dark than a firefly crawled under the Lord's bushel basket.' That's the very words I told them!"

"How much did they soak yer?" asked Dud.

Bill's eyes blazed. "They tried to collect a hundred dollars an' the costs of court. 'I won't pay it,' I told them. So here I be."

"Sure as preachin' yer are," said Dud. "Didjer ever hear erbout the time the game wardens tried to catch Elijah Dole?"

"Naw, an' I don't want to hear it," said Bill.

"The int'restin' part of it was that they didn't catch 'Lijah. He was too smart for them."

"Be yer tryin' to incinderate that I hain't smart?"

"Elijah shot a moose," drawled Dud, ignoring Bill's question. "It was in closed season. The wardens got wind of it, but they c'udn't pin it on 'Lijah. So they schemed with a taxidermist. The feller wrote Elijah, saying that he understood of confidential parties that 'Lijah had a-quired a moose, an' that he, the taxidermist, wanted to buy a head an' was prepared to pay well for it.

"Elijah was lumberin' on the lower Enchanted. It happened that he had jist lost a roan hoss. It was out in back of the hovel, froze as stiff as an old maid at the North Pole. Elijah went out an' sawed off the roan's head, boxed it up, an' shipped it to the taxidermist—express collect. But, of course, 'Lijah was a smart one."

It was obvious that Bill did not enjoy the implications. In fact, he scowled at Dud over ten days' growth of fertile whiskers.

"Dud," he said, "yer don't understand my case. 'Lijah Dole has been dead a good many years. Time has changed some things in a way that don't seem possible. When 'Lijah was cuttin' big punkin pine, they didn't put a man in jail fer followin' a bad-hit deer a lee-tle mite beyont sunset. In fact, thar warn't no fool sunset law in his day. Why, nowadays, they've got jurisdiction to put a man behind the bars fer jist spittin' on a sidewalk. I'm tellin' you that if 'Lijah was alive today, they'd have him down here permanently."

"Accordin' to the paper," drawled Dud, "you did your shootin' nearer to sunrise than sunset."

"Oh, so that's what they printed? Wa-al, let me tell yer, that this town is so full of prebaricators that thar's only room in this jail fer folks that tell the truth. Is a man supposed to keep lookin' at his watch every two er three min-its? How do they know a man owns a watch? Be they givin' them away with huntin' licenses?"

"The paper allowed that yer didn't even have a huntin' license," remarked Dud.

"Why them cussed two-faced prebaricators! That editor had better leave this country before I git free."

"Did yer have a license, Bill?"

"Huh? Wa-al, I sorta spoke fer one; told the town clerk I'd be after one. Then it slipped my mind. But that hain't the p'int. The p'int is that I wounded a buck. He was bleedin' at every jump an' blattin' in awful pain."

"I never happened to hear a buck blat, exactly," said Dud.

"Is that so? Wa-al, yer sh'ud have been with me. An' if yer was, I know that yer w'ud have said that it w'ud be turrible cruelty to leave that critter to die in the dark. But what does the law say? The law says that I sh'ud have gone home an' let that buck die by inches of misery becuz the sun had set offish'ly down in Augusty!"

Bill's voice had attained the edge of tears, but Dud, whose expression never changed, was not moved.

"The paper didn't mention a buck," he said.

"Oh! It didn't, eh? Wa-al, that proves how far they was willin' to go to cover up them triflin' game wardens."

"The paper said they worked a trick on yer, Bill. Didn't say jist what it was, an' I wondered if it was sunthin' like they tried to pull on Elijah Dole, years ago."

The guise of noble tenderness fell from Bill's face like a derby hat struck by a brick. His eyes grew black with indignation. And his teeth were grinding-angry when he spoke.

"So that's what they're telling—is it? They're backin' up them psychopathetic wardens—are they? By goshamighty, I'm a-goin' to sue that paper fer slanderous character. Can't I do it?"

"We-ell, I guess yer c'ud sue," said Dud, cautiously, "but it might turn out expensive and embarrassin'."

The suggestion of more expense sobered Bill. And he nodded solemnly at Dud. Then he said, "I guess it w'ud be cheaper to shoot the editor."

Dud chuckled. "Some public cemeteries," he said to me, "are a lot more crowded than Bill's private buryin' ground."

Bill sought refuge in a chew of tobacco. Then he said, "In a way, that's a fact becuz I've always been too damned tender-hearted. Live an' let live has always been my principle, except when I got mad. But from now on, things is goin' to be differunt."

Dud shook his head in feigned seriousness. "It's no use, Bill. Y'll have to take it. But if yer was as smart as 'Lijah was, or even some game wardens—"

"By tarnel," snarled Bill, kicking over a substantial bench, "I hain't goin' to let yer stay here an' call me a fool. I won't stand it from an illiterated feller like you, Dud Dean. I won't put up with it, not even in this place. All yer know erbout my case is what ye've read in the papers—"

"You been readin' the papers, Bill?"

"My glasses is broke. I can't see a thing, that is, near to."

Dud turned again to me. "Bill can't read a word er write his own name down."

"Don't believe a word of that," cautioned Bill. "I don't lay claims to an eddication equal to some lawyers, but mine amounts to more than most guides has got."

"Seems to me," said Dud, "that it w'ud do yer good to tell us the truth erbout this case, after all the effort ye've made to tell everythin' but the truth."

"Bah. Wa-al, I don't mind tellin' you fellers becuz yer can warn folks of the skulduggery that has been worked on honest men like me. *Prima facie*, I never wounded no buck—that is, not that I know of."

"Sounds pee-culiar to hear yer confess that," said Dud.

Bill continued. "Earning a living hain't like pickin' up quail the Lord has dropped in your lap. Times is hard. I can remember when a man c'ud git twenty-five dollars apiece fer all—take taxes. Nowadays, a man is like a poked sheep bein' led to the slaughter. Er look at it this way. If a man must work from sunup to sundown to git a livin' fer hisself an' his family, how is he goin' git his deer legal? By geeprus, I had rather let the Almighty answer that 'un than them fellers that makes laws fer other folk to mind. Them fellers hain't got no more sense 'n a houn'-dorg with his head blowed off his neck. Gol-durn it, I can remember when a common man had some rights, but not now. Why, them lawmakers hain't fit to 'sociate with mortality.

"I tell yer that's jist how it stands! So, one night, when the weather was on the edge of raining, thinks I, 'None of them tender-toed wardens will be outdoors tonight, an' therefore now is the time to exercise the natural-born rights of a man bred in a free country.' Yer see, I had been gittin' madder fer weeks at a time. An' when I git mad, sunthin' has got to give way."

"Wait a min-it," Dud said, "did you issue that warnin' to them game wardens, er how did they git wind of it?"

"Them fellers! Look here, I'd thank yer to understand that I don't 'sociate with no pinions of the law, not with sech game laws as we've got in this state, anyhow. Not me! Wa-al, I cleaned up old Bertha an' made sure I had plenty of ammunition. Then I oozes down to the old Ball place. As a matter of fact, I warn't too sure that I'd find anythin' down thar becuz after ye've shot up a field three er four times, the deer git smartish. An' I had already killed— It was an awful black night. Somehow, the air felt wet, like bad luck, but I didn't pay much attention. Natcherly, I know better than to barge inter a place like that before I've looked over the lay of the land. A man always has to make sure that none of them stinkers is sneakin' around. I thought that the coast was clear, near as I c'ud tell. But I listened some more.

"Ever notice how much a man can hear on a night like that? Maybe ye'll hear an owl away off in the woods, er somebudy shootin' a gun, but most of the sounds come a-whisperin' and a-rustlin'. The night feels like silk. Geeprus, when a man has been married as long as I have he can appreciate quiet, when it ain't too noisy. Then, by tarnel, here come them lawmakers, durn their shrunken hides. An' what do they cook up? They forbid a man to go huntin' when he wants to go hunting. What next? Next, they hire a gang of sneakin' wardens. Consider the dupliciousness of them creepin' wardens. They cal'late to deceive the very elected."

"Wait a min-it," interposed Dud, "be yer tryin' to say that a warden w'ud try to outwit a politician?"

"No! Confound it. Don't the Book read erbout them that

cal'lates to deceive the very elected? Yer a purty one to incinderate that somebudy else is illiterated. Wa-al, listen to me. I say them fellers in their reedick'lus fan-wing britches an' cowboy hats hain't got no right to hinder freeborn citizens in the persuit of life, liberty, an' deer meat. So as soon as I felt reasonably sure that none of them sisters was thereabouts, I eased on my light. An' that light is a sweetheart. I can throw light clear across a hundred-acre lot. So I swung it around, slow an' methodistical. Jist when I was ready to give it up as a bad job, smack-o, a set of eyes burned back at me.

"Damn it, I warn't long erbout correspondin' to sech insolation. Bung! goes a flock of double-O buckshot. An' out goes them eyes. But that deer begun to let out the most unreasonable blats yer ever heard. Thinks I, 'Now ye've done it. They can hear that critter fer miles.' But I got my legs under me an' made a run fer it. When I got thar, she was kickin' like a hay tedder. I warn't long erbout slittin' her throat, let me tell yer."

"Her?" questioned Dud.

"Yeh. It was a big doe. After I fired at her, up jumps two of her lambs. Dang it, I had fergot to reload old Bertha. But fer that I w'ud have had one of them."

"And that w'ud have made two," said Dud.

"Sure. An' I might have got the other one. But if yer want to hear this, don't keep buttin' in on me. Maybe yer don't know but night huntin' is sunthin' like murder in a book. Ye're in head over heels. Thar hain't nothin' to be done that yer ain't already done, so yer might's well see it through. I dressed off the doe in the pitch dark—a trick them wardens c'udn't do to their souls, if they had any, which they hain't. Then I loaded her inter the back seat of the old flivver. After that, I waited some. Then I eased her out to the main road without any headlights.

"So far, so good, as the preacher said after the wedding. An' if I had only gone home then an' thar, I w'udn't be here, durn their hides. But of course it felt to me as if the night was young an' auspacious. So I thought I'd like to go down the road to the old Owens place. With me a thought like that is the same as done. Thank the good Lord, Parson, I had sense e-nough to take that doe out of the car an' to hide her back in the bushes."

Dud interrupted Bill. "Allowin' that we sh'ud fergit that yer was night huntin' ag'inst the law, didn't it come to your mind that the law only allows a man one deer in this state? Er did yer think that deer tags was hitched to a huntin' license like coupons on a gilt-edged bond?"

"Wa-al, I was goin to mention the fact that my memory hain't so long as a miskeeter wiggler when I git to shootin' at deer. I can't help it, no more'n a person can go without food. However, if I had give the matter more thought that night, I w'ud have been a sorrier but happier man. But I didn't. I went down to the Owens place, backed the Ford inter the bushes out of sight, covered up the brass with a blanket, an' soft-footed up towards the old apple orchard. Jist beyond the bridge, over the brook from the beaver bog, it seemed to me I heard a noise. Of course I waited and listened careful. After maybe as much as ten minutes, I snuck on the light. An' thar he was, maybe five er six rods away. Seems to me, now, that them eyes didn't look jist right. But the way a deer's eyes look under a light depends on the night air. I've seen them when they looked almost pink-red. Then ag'in, they'll look almost green, er white, like a star. But anyhow, I thought it was one of my nights. I must of been excited. Anyhow, I pulled."

"Can yer hold a light, an' shoot at the same time?" asked Dud. "I always heard it took two fellers to jack deer."

"Hah, some more of your ignorance. As I was saying, I let her go. Down goes them eyes. Sunthin' rattled in the bushes an' went thump on the ground. Natcherly, I run up to cut my deer's throat. Imagine how I felt! It was jist a moth-eaten buck's head them sneakin' critters had tied up in the bushes. The plaster of Paris was tricklin' out of them buckshot holes an' runnin' away in leetle streams of dust. Crotchidy, I was took by surprise, an' it might have been as much as five seconds a-fore I jumped an' run—which didn't do me any good becuz I landed in a game warden's arms.

"Jist try to imagine how I felt. I w'ud as soon be on the bosom of hell. He was a powerful cuss. I did all I c'ud to make him think that he had catched hold of a she-bobcat, but thar was two of them, an' only one of me. So it come to me that I w'ud have to do some stratifying. So I begun to laugh like it was all a joke. 'Ha, ha,' I says. 'You boys has had your fun, an' I've had mine. Be yer foolish enough to think that yer c'ud fool me with that old trick? Why, I seen yer when yer put it up thar. An' thar sartinly hain't no law ag'inst shootin' a stuffed deer head."

" 'There's a law ag'inst huntin' in the dark with a jack light," says the big feller, who was still huggin' me like a she-b'ar.

" 'Yesss,' says the other feller, soft an' calm as sunthin' on ice. 'Yesss,' he says. An' before I knew it, he had clicked a pair of them handcuffs on me.

" 'He threw his flashlight over there in the alders,' says the feller.

"'Yesss, I know,' says the second stinker, 'I found it.'"

"Crotch," exclaimed Dud, "so they worked that old stunt on yer? I knew that yer warn't so smart as some presidents we had, but I didn't realize that yer was as foolish as a porcupine. Crotch, an' they've been all these years at catchin' yer!"

"By tarnelnation," said Bill, scowling at Dud, "if that's all ye've to say when a neighbor is in affliction an' trouble, I w'ud thank yer to remove yerself outer my sight. Go hobnob them deceivin' wardens."

"We-ell, guess we might's well. But Bill, what became of that doe yer hid in the bushes before yer went down't the Owens place?"

"None of your business, Dud Dean, you duplicious turncoat."

"Too bad if it went to waste."

"Ask the old lady," said Bill, and he began to laugh as if that was the only pleasant angle. "She tells me that the meat is jist as prime an' tender as a defrosted rooster. Geeprus, how I'd like a fry of it. They feed a man down here like a hoss. But don't worry erbout that doe goin' to waste. My folks ain't starving, thanks to me an' no one else!"

When we walked away from the county jail, Dud said, "Now we can hunt up Malty, an' you can give her the ten dollars."

"It was only five," I said. "And thanks for the object lesson. Bill is an intriguing character, eh?"

Dud laughed. "Sech fellers are conundrums, but it beats me who thought them up in the fust place. Seems to me, sometimes, that life is a long parade. Them in the front gits tired of luggin' the banners, an' them in back hain't got the faintest notion what it's all erbout."

A Dud Dean Photo Album

The Dud Dean stories were the creation of Arthur "Mak" Macdougall, shown fishing from a string of boom logs on the Kennebec River. His wife, Leah Parks Macdougall, below right, was his chief critic and proofreader. Bottom, the study camp on Wyman Lake where the stories were put down on paper.

Center, with canoe pole in hand, Arthur Macdougall gazes up the West Branch of the Kennebec River toward Bigelow Mountain. At left, he chats with dam keeper Lawny Durgin at a Dead River camp. Bottom, Mak (right) and friends on a fishing expedition.

"Go fishin' now! and then later on if you git a chance."

The Dud Dean stories take place in and around the town of Bingham, Maine, shown above circa 1931. The stories' characters, as well as Dud himself, were inspired by many of Arthur Macdougall's friends and neighbors.

People constitute Dud's chief inter-est. Well, people and trout fishing, for as Dud tells us in his stories, it's hard to separate the two.

At right, Jack Owens, one of Arthur Macdougall's best friends and the man who introduced him to fly fishing. Below, Mak nets a trout.

"A fish like that knows more'n some folks that wanted to run fer president."

"Crotch, I needed to think like a genius, but I was only a hunter."

Top, left: A glimpse of "dug-out road." Top, right: Gathering around a camp fire where many of the Dud Dean stories came to life. Bottom, the Kennebec River sweeps past a log boom.

In all, Arthur Macdougall (upper right, center) wrote fifty-six Dud Dean stories, most of which were featured in FIELD & STREAM magazine. Below, Mrs. Chief Stanwood, who appears in the stories, holds a 19-pound landlocked salmon from Tunk Lake. Right, Mak's beloved East Branch of the Kennebec.

Now, of course, I'm a teller of fishin' stories, when I ain't ruminatin' erbout huntin'...

One of Arthur Macdougall's good friends and fishing companions, the Reverend George A. Humphries of Meutchen, New Jersey.

'Long About Morning

Published in Field & Stream *in January 1938, this story appeared the next year in the Dud Dean anthology* The Sun Stood Still. *In 1947 it was included in* Where Flows the Kennebec.

From the first paragraph the reader is aware that this fishing yarn is about catching two fishes, as Thoreau put it. Michael McIntosh, who edited Classics of American Sporting Fiction *(which , by the way, includes three Dud Dean stories) emphasizes the change in material found in most outdoor magazines. "Interest," he writes, "[has] shifted from the more philosophical aspects of sport toward a concern with obtaining bag limits and trophies." Reflecting on what he terms the "legacy of the Golden Age" of outdoor writing, McIntosh concludes that the aim was once ". . . to show us how we might be better human beings."*

This story speaks from that "Golden Age," and its setting is fittingly grand. Dud's paddle noiselessly enters the water, and we glide out upon Moosehead Lake—that forty-mile-long, shining king of mountain lakes.

"SOMETIMES," SAID DUD DEAN, "it seems to me that thar's a perversity mixed up in the charity of events. Of course, now an' then the cussedest matters git ironed out as slick as a b'iled shirt.

An' that's the long, long justice. But it's hard to remember that. An' thar's times when the powers that be seem to delight in addin' more an' more grief, until the only way out is to laugh yourself out, which almost amounts to liftin' yourself by the ears.

"It helps some if a man can git hold of some sort of a yardstick. If he can, life, as it wakes him up every morning, ain't as bad as takin' raw castor oil.

"I mean . . . well, take the Reverend Thomas Tomkins. Thar's a name fer yer. It's hard to guess what his parents had in mind when they hitched him to that fer life. Ye're right if yer guess this parson didn't have any money. As a matter of fact, thar hain't much sense in puttin' pockets in a parson's trousers. Seems to me the extra cloth sh'ud be put on the seat. But ye're wrong if yer think that I guided him out of the goodness of Nancy's heart. I was well paid fer every min-it. Old Jeremy Holt paid the wages. In fact, the dicker was made the summer before.

"'Dud,' says Jeremy, 'my conscience is botherin' me like an ingrowin' toenail. Here I set, a man that has broke the Ten Commandments uphill and down. Of course, I never robbed no widders an' orphans, but I plucked their men ahead of time. I'm a skinflint, Dud—jist a miserable old trader. But look at me. Here I set, pockets full of nice cigars, the sun a-cookin' my p'isoned hide, the wind sorta layin' cool hands on me, an' the purtiest lake all eround me. I can't think of anythin' that I really want which I hain't got.'

"When he stopped talking, I never said a word—jist kept on paddlin' up the lake. So bine-by he come to the p'int. 'Never met my wife—did yer Dud?'

"He knew crotchly well I had never met his wife. 'No, sir,' I says, 'Never had the pleasure.'

"Fer some reason that amused him some. 'My wife,' he goes on 'is an old-fashioned person. She gits up Sunday mornings an' gives me hell, et cetera. When she has worked herself up inter the right frame of mind, she goes to church.'

"An' I never made no comment on that.

"'I've been goin' to church, lately, myself,' he says, lookin' at me in the stern.

"'That so?' says I.

"'Yes. But it hain't done a mite of good. Nevertheless, our young preacher kinda gits under my skin. I'll be damned, Dud, if he don't act like a man! Somehow, he found out that I am a fishin' fool. An' he kinda played that up to me. Fust off, I was suspicious. It hain't exactly a new idea to use a can opener. I figgered he was tryin' to catch me off my guard, when he w'ud let me have the works between the eyes. Thinks I, "I'm too old a buck, boy. Yer can't catch me by puttin' salt on my tail."

"'But do yer know, Dud, that warn't his game. I found out easy enough that the poor cuss does fish, when he can steal time off to commit sech a sin—fishes near home, of course. All he catches is now and then a liverling. Know what I mean?

"'Bah, I can't stomach talkin' about it. He works fer a damned charitable bunch of fourflushers. They make me sick. 'Tween you an' me, I've accumulated considerable bad stock in the last few years. An' I figger to unload some of it on that bunch, although the chances are that they've already got plenty. But a little more won't hurt them. Leave it to your Uncle Jeremy. On the other hand, maybe I won't do it. They'd likely bellyache to my wife.

"'All I'm comin' at is that this young preacher of ours is comin' up here next summer, if I can figger how to pay the bills without hurtin' his pride.'

"We-ell, old Jeremy rattled on like that most of the afternoon while he was fishin' up the lake. But I never paid much attention. Jeremy warn't one to tilt at windmills, if yer rec'lect what I think I mean. Howsomever, that's how the Reverend Thomas Tomkins happened to git up here the next summer.

"He come early, before Jeremy was due. When I met the Reverend, I jedged that Jeremy warn't far off on his estimation. I liked that preacher from the start to the finish, which is more'n I c'ud say— Let that go.

"To begin with, he had a little boy's capacity to enjoy fishing. Rememberin' what old Jeremy had grumbled erbout this preacher's congregation, I thought that if they was that bad the young feller hadn't let it git him down. I marveled at his enjoyment of everythin' he saw.

"It was a wholesome experience fer me. All the yarns I've told yer, Mak, reflect some things I've learned from folks who came up here to fish in our country. Nancy an' them account fer all the eddication I ever had beyond a few winter terms in the early days.

"I've known guides who practiced a dumb scorn of cityfolks an' what they knew from books. To me, that always seemed a mistake. One time Sim Cates told me that he had lived in the woods all his life, but that he learned sunthin' new every day. 'An' that's why I like it,' says Sim. That's the right spirit, seems to me, but to that I w'ud add that I've also learned from books which other folks had read.

"Now this was back in the days when sea gulls begun to appear inland, on account of the protection they was gittin' at the coast maybe. I w'udn't go so far as to say that a sea gull is as purty as a little chippin' sparrow in the fust day of spring, but they look washed an' white when they're flyin' over a blue lake.

"'Kinda beautiful,' I says to the Reverend, on that fust day we went out.

"'So is the devil,' says he.

"'Any pitchurs I ever see of him didn't present him in that light,' says I. 'He had a long tail, p'inted at the end, an' some horns on his head'

"'Tommyrot,' says he. 'The devil is a very handsome character. What do these gulls eat, back here in the wilderness?'

"That question had me becuz I'd never given the matter a thought. 'Why, this an' that,' says I.

"'Do you happen to know where they nest?'

"'Yes,' I says.

"'Let's go visit them at home. They've got to change their habits to survive up here in this environment.'

"So I paddled him to a little mite of an island of broken ledges, piled upwards. As a matter of fact, I had never taken time to land on that place before, although I had noticed that the gulls nested thar.

"Our visit sartinly opened my eyes. We found eggshells that was never laid by a gull. Also, thar was evidence that them gulls had been eatin' little ducks. That was a lesson.

"And the Reverend had a powerful little magnifyin' glass. He was always lookin' at things with it. He showed me bunches of stuff that I called moss, but under that glass a bit of it looked like one of Nancy's flower beds. That opened my mind and eyes to the beauty we don't ordinarily see er hear. Us men are dull two-legged critters on an earth where the cup runs over, an' we don't know it.

"By crotch, I bought me one of them pocket-sized magnifiers jist as soon as I c'ud. Fer awhile, I was ashamed to let anyone see me usin' it, but I got over that foolishness. I'll never fergit the look on Mat Markham's face when he seen me lookin' through it at some nymphs. 'Huh,' says he, 'next thing ye'll be wearin' silk drawers.' Dang it, I give Mat a good, stiff talkin'-to. I warn't goin' to let Mat Markham patronize me an' my magnifier.

"The parson c'ud tell how old a salmon was by the spawnin' rings on its scales. I was skeptical until I see that he was right at least nine times out of ten, near's I c'ud tell. That is a common place now, but in them days I had never heard tell of it, er of a microscope fer that matter.

"Ayah. He was an int'restin cuss, that preacher. An' among all them things, he was jist erbout the fust feller I ever knew who tied his own flies. Up to that time, I'd always supposed that the flies in the world was tied by women becuz their hands wer smaller an' smarter, maybe. But he had rigged a pair of pinchers to serve fer a vice, an' c'ud do a nice job.

"The fust night after he come, he had me over to his camp. An' how he put the questions to me erbout natural flies. In no time I realized how little I knew erbout them things which trout et. Y'see, trout was nice an' plentiful in them days. An' they was usually hungry. We gen'rally got them 'ith one fly er another. A man didn't need to know why.

"The parson had the fust imitations of mayflies I had ever seen. Only, I called 'em caddis flies becuz I always heard 'em called that an' didn't know any better. We called the real caddis a what-chur-call-it. When I learned the difference, I felt like two cents at the World's Fair. But he told me erbout a little book with all them things in it. Yer can bet I bought it, an' read it when it come—read it a good many times.

"That night the Reverend talked 'bout old Jeremy. 'At heart,' he says, 'Mr. Holt is a gentleman.'

"'Yes,' I says, feelin' a little doubtful.

"And he laughed at me. 'We have this treasure in frail earthen vessels, you know,' he says.

"'Yes,' says I, 'sometimes in brass kettles.'

"Did I mention that the young feller was to be thar only a week? That was all. I know well enough that Jeremy cussed erbout that. But that was as long as the parson would accept of Jeremy. Now a week, Mak, is a danged short time, unless ye're spendin' it in a jail. Yer keep thinking tomorrow I'll do so an' so, and the fust thing yer know, ye've come to the last day, an' it's time to go. That's partly what I had in mind when I made them openin' remarks, as Doc Brownin' said the time he was givin' the Grangers a talk on the difference between patent medicines an' straight whisky.

"I think this parson wanted to git a big fish. Most folks had jist as soon. So at one time er another, we tried every fly from Jock Scott to great Scott. An' small good it done us! The fish warn't feeding. It was what w'ud be called in these days a set-down strike, er maybe a misbegotten solunar period. Under my breath I called it sunthin' else. It w'ud have tickled me to see him git a bigger fish than Jeremy had ever catched. An' what's more, yer know it would have pleased Jeremy too.

"But night after night Moosehead was as calm as a dead prophet. Maybe ye'd see a pindlin' ring away off somewhere, but by the time yer got thar, the fish, er whatever, w'ud be nowhere in sight. However, the Reverend kept fishing an' assurin' me that each day's end was the most glorious since the night Noah's ark grounded on Mount Ararat. But I kept feelin' worse an' worse, an' more an' more down at the heels. To make matters sadder, the live-bait fishermen were bringin' in a few nice fish.

"Finally, on Saturday morning, a beautiful trout rose clear out of the water at a little Cahill fly. It was one of them crotchly per-vokin' strikes that ain't aimed at the fly at all, but is executed becuz sunthin' in a trout's head says, 'Let's play leapfrog!' Suppose we remind ourselves once more jist how good a really big trout looks. It may be that this old cuss warn't rigged out like Solomon in all his glory, but he was arrayed in better taste! The side of him was as wide as a proper paddle blade. An' I never seen a pink that 'ud beat that on him, unless it was the color of a girl's cheeks when she has been out countin' the stars on a sharp winter night 'ith some young sprout.

"Ayah. It was one of them trout. I was consid'ably excited. But did he come ag'in? Did the best Christmus ever come ag'in? Did the downright hottest an' most hilarious Fourth of July ever come ag'in? Yer know it didn't, Mak. An' neither did that trout. I c'ud imagine the cuss cruisin' this way an' that, an' agrinnin' out of the corner of his mouth at the thought of the excitement he had caused up in that canoe. But we stuck eround until the sun was so high that thar warn't no sense in it.

"'Another perfect day,' says the Reverend, puttin' down his rod an' stretchin' his arms.

"'And as poor a day to fish as c'ud be picked out,' says I. But neither of us mentioned that it was his last day, an' half of it gone already.

"We-ell, we did locate a few small trout. As I remember, he took six er seven that 'ud go erbout half pound apiece. That sort of betokened that the jinx was asleep, er sleepy. Evidently the big trout we had seen in the forenoon was a good omen. But mind yer, the half-dozen trout we had were all we'd caught fer the week.

"Crotch, I felt sorry. In fact, I almost suggested, erlong about five o'clock in the afternoon, that we haul up, git out on a flat rock, an' hold prayers fer a hatch of sunthin' that w'ud start the big fellers a-feedin' on top. But I didn't becuz thar's some things that come erlong with a string of events er not at all. Thar's no sense at all, as I seen it, fer a sinner to pray the Lord that sunthin' will happen out of its turn, jist to please a fisherman. Ayah. But don't think I warn't serious.

"Anyhow, we decided to head down the lake in the direction of that cove where the big feller had made the pass at the little Cahill. Thar was a chance, and thar's nothin' like bein' on hand an' prepared, in case Providence does put the cards in your hands. On the way down, we fished some, here an' thar, but 'ithout any luck.

"When we got down to the cove, thar was a canoe in thar ahead of us. Thar they was, right where we sh'ud have been. I made out that it was Tom Collins an' a sporter. It had been a week of tough breaks.

"We-ell, since Tom was square where we sh'ud be, thar warn't much else fer us to do but to cruise eround. The young preacher cast in 'bout every likely place. An' all that time thar warn't a fish that showed, ner a sign of an insect on the water.

"'This,' I says, rememberin' sunthin' all of a sudden, 'reminds me of the time Chandler Cates an' his boys went fishin' in at Chase Pond. They got in thar late, on account of finishin' up their haying. But they rigged up a lean-to, made a fire, an' had some hot supper. Then they went to bed, intendin' to be up at the crack of day fer their fishin'. Chandler went right off to sleep, but the boys, bein' boys, c'udn't sleep. They kept hearin' noises in the woods an' out on the pond, an' guessin' what they was. Finally Forest Cates woke up his father.

"'Pa,' he says, 'what time does it git daylight?'

"'Huh?' says Chandler. 'Keep still an' go to sleep.'

"'But yer c'udn't put off Forest that easy. 'Pa, I said what time does it git daylight?'

"'Oh,' grunts Chandler, 'I s'pose erlong 'bout morning.'

"That made the Reverend laugh. 'By which, I take it,' he says, 'that you intend to imply that affairs are never so bad that we may not look forward to the morning. Well said. And amen!'

"That was as good as I c'ud have explained it. An' bine-by comes the still of the day, when it's really neither day er night but what I call the recess. Off down the lake a loon laughed at a joke he'd heard a year er two ago, an' then it was stiller, like everythin' had been hushed up and told to git ready fer bed.

"It was Tom Collins' voice that interrupted. We c'ud hear him jist as plain as though he'd been talkin in our ears.

"'Geeprus!' says Tom.

"We watched them, an' purty soon we saw what they was

int'rested in. A big fish was puddlin' within fifty feet of their canoe. Now, don't fail to use your imagination on this. Remember that we had been fishin' all that week an' hadn't seen nothin' like that. And, mark yer, so far as we c'ud tell, that was the only fish that warn't settin' on his bottom, on the bottom of Moosehead Lake. If yer take that inter consideration, ye'll comprehend how int'rested we was.

"I suggested, right from the shoulder, that we git over an' do some fishin' on our own, but do yer think that young parson w'ud do it? No, sir! It aggravated me, I'm afraid. Tom's fisherman kept castin' a nice long line every time the fish b'iled, an' between rises. They changed flies purty often while we sot thar an' watched them. When I c'udn't stand it no longer, we paddled over. I mean, I did the paddlin'.

"'Hello, Dud,' says Tom. 'Maybe ye've got sunthin' this fish will take.'

"See? That was our chance—a gentleman's chance, too. But I warn't usin' the rod, so thar warn't any castin' done from my canoe. Instid, we watched that sporter, who didn't seem to be the least anxious to have us show him how to hook that fish. Whichever it was, it was feedin' two er three inches under the surface. Thar'd come a big swirl like he had turned a complete circle, the length of him. An' not once did he make a sign that he c'ud see the various wet-fly patterns which Tom's man was castin' right over him.

"I guess that the Reverend had been hunting in his kit fer some time when he whispered to me, 'I have a hunch one of those mayflies of mine would work, but I am afraid that I haven't any— I left the box in the camp.'

"I came to life in a hurry. 'Fer crotch's sake,' I says, 'look some more. They might be jist the checker.'

"At last, he got out that rig I spoke of an' tied a fly right then an' thar. Tom watched him out of the corner of his eye an' was amused. Neither Tom er me had ever seen that done a-fore. My hand kept openin' and shuttin' so that yer might have thought that I wanted to tie that fly myself. Prob'ly he was only ten min-its er so gittin' done, but it seemed half an hour to me.

"When it was done, he said to me, 'Just paddle as close as you can without getting in their way.'

"That suited me fine. 'Put on a good stout leader,' I says, 'becuz ye'll need it if that old stager takes hold.'

"But what come next durn near floored me. 'I think,' says the parson, talkin' to Tom an' the other feller, 'that I have the fly you need. We'll come up and pass it to you.'

"Mak, that potbellied son-of-a-gun that Tom was guidin' took that fly.

"'Now,' says the Reverend lookin' at me, 'let's pull back an' watch the fun.'

"Crotch, I see that I hain't got over that business yit! Right now, I'm in the same frame of mind. Mak, that big fish took the fly. Not the min-it the feller cast it, but after it had set eround a while, an' he had twitched it a hair, like the preacher told him to do. Crotch! It was like lightin' strikin' sunthin'. An' he came out of the water like a prize fighter's right arm aimed at the other feller's chin—an uppercut.

"I was comforted a mite when I see that it warn't a trout. It was only an old-fashioned salmon. Me an' the preacher hung to the gunwales until that canoe shook like a poplar leaf at nighttime.

"'Watch out,' says Tom to his man, 'and I'll git out further where maybe we can handle this fish. The durn cuss will pull us ashore, er sunthin', if we stay in here.'

"Then the sporter tried to stand up. 'Don't do that,' says Tom, unless your legs can reach the bottom. We've got to go at this gentle, like we was catchin' flies with molasses. Let him run, but put on all the drag yer dare.'

"Ayah. Me an' the Reverend sot thar an' watched it all. We seen that salmon, which was durn near a yard long if he was an inch, shootin' up out of the water ten er twelve times. Crotch, it was a purty sight. At last, when the shadders all erlong the shore was as black as the end of a weasel's tail, we see Tom handlin' a big net. An' then we seen that salmon swung inter the canoe. All of a sudden it was night. Saturday night! We had three miles to paddle back to camp.

"I never trusted myself to say a word. But after we paddled over, an' the parson had admired the fish an' congratulated the fisherman, I headed out fer supper. Once er twice, down the lake, the Reverend w'ud stretch out his arms, a way he had of doin' when he was extra satisfied.

"'This,' he says to me, 'has been an unforgettable, happy week, Dud,' he says.

"Next morning, I went with him down't the railroad station. An' I stayed until his train had pulled out. He stopped to shake my hand for the third time, on the steps up inter the coach.

"'Dud,' he says, 'you've done me a lot of good. And I'll never forget that story—"It gets daylight 'long about morning!"'"

"When old Jeremy arrived—two er three weeks later—he was feelin' high an' handsome.

"'Dud,' he says, 'that was the best thing I ever did in my life. Thanks to you, our minister had himself a wonderful time. An' you sh'ud have heard the Sunday sermon he preached on the Chandler Cates story.

"'Was it a good sermon?' I asks Jeremy.

"'Good! Why it was the best damn sermon ever heard. Even my wife said that it was a hell of a good sermon.'

"'Did your wife say that?' I says.

"'No, she didn't,' says Jeremy, 'but that's what she meant.'"

Crazy Stiller Goes A-Fishing

It is with this story that the long association between Field & Stream *magazine and the Dud Dean yarns began. It appeared in April 1929 under the title "The Big Fish of Pierce Pond." Dud Dean himself, as painted by Arthur Fuller, was on the cover. The story was illustrated by the inimitable cartoons of Stanley Foss Bartlett. It was a grand start.*

Pierce Pond lies three miles west of Caratunk village which is situated just off Route 201 and fifteen miles north of Bingham, Maine. Nowadays the pond can be reached by road, but at the time of this story the trail left the Kennebec's west bank just above Caratunk, immediately climbed some four hundred feet, and then followed up the cascading course of Pierce Pond Stream. It was worth the climb and the tramp.

Pierce Pond is a beautiful body of water. In 1936, Arthur Macdougall wrote: ". . . most of us keep going back to Pierce Pond because its wild beauty haunts us . . . the shoreline is forever wild land and the green islands and the gray rocks are like old friends in a changing world." But what about those fabulous salmon and trout? Those stories were all true as well. Scrapbooks are filled with photographic proof: Anna Roosevelt Boettiger displaying a spectacular catch and Field &

Stream *editor Ray P. Holland's wife holding an eight-and-a-half-pound salmon and a four-pound squaretail. Of course that salmon wasn't anything compared to the eighteen pounders that Pierce Pond could produce. And then there was "Nemo," the giant salmon that anglers saw on the surface but never caught.*

This story is one of three Dud Dean yarns reprinted in Classics of American Sporting Fiction.

DUD DEAN AND I WERE AT PIERCE POND. Out in front were lisping waters, deeply inked with night shadows. On the western skyline the black softwoods, blunt and spire-like, stood against a faint wash of gray light. Over our heads were the vaguely whispering spruce and pine, and over all, the stars. There is, surely, something about the quiet of the wildlands that awakens the soul. The artificialities of life slough off, and the exacting rules of a man-made game are regulated to their own insignificance.

"Is thar sunthin' in the Bible erbout a fool shall lead them?" Dud asked, breaking the spell.

I pulled myself back from vagrant meditations and squinted at Dud. In the half-darkness I could just make out the lines of his face. He looked sober, but I suspected that there was a jocular vein in his question.

"Let's see," I mused, as though trying to recall something of the sort. "No, I don't remember anything just like that, but it sounds like one of the Proverbs. Doesn't it? Why?"

"Oh, nothin' much. I was jist thinkin' erbout how we come to find out that the biggest trout an' salmon in our section of woods was in this lake."

"What do you mean? Haven't they always been here? The trout, I mean."

"Now," said Dud, with a chuckle, "ye've raised what old Doc Brownin' w'ud call a controversial question. The answer is—maybe. Then ag'in, maybe not. All I know is that nobudy dreamed thar was anythin' in this pond but pickerel until erbout thirty-five years ago."

That was, to me, surprising information, since Pierce Pond is now famous for its nonmigratory salmon and big brook trout.

"Let's have the rest of the story," I suggested.

"We-el," drawled Dud, "I d'know's yer'd call it much of a story, but if yer don't mind a little hist'ry, I c'ud sort of pass the evenin' off."

I nodded encouragingly. And Dud began his story.

"Pierce Pond Stream is a hellion. From the dam, she tumbles almost straight down to the Kennebec River. This country had some mighty big punkin pine, not to mention such as spruce an' hemlock. So, erbout fifty years ago a bunch of lumbermen got together an' built a dam at the outlet of this lake—what's left of that dam is down thar now. Then they started drivin' logs outer the lake—big logs that w'ud run a thousand feet to the tree, more er less.

"I ain't a-doubtin' but that somebudy had fished here afore then, but that's erbout when the word went out that thar was nothin' in here but pickerel. Gosh! Some of them old-time pickerel w'ud remind yer of them pike we read erbout. Pickerel an' trout don't mix, as everybudy knows. The pickerel welcomes trout 'ith wide-open mouths. An' bine-by the pickerel is lonely. I think that thar may have been, now an' then, a trout in Pierce Pond in them days, but they was sartinly scarce. So folks sorta scratched this water off their fishin' list. In them days, it was considered low-

down to fish fer sech common fish as pickerel. You can understand that. Nobudy is goin' to fool 'ith pickerel as long as thar's
more trout than a man can lug home.

"Thar is a story—I've heard Dave Pooler tell it—that even the
pickerel was planted in this lake. If it ain't true, God only knows
how they got up here. Anyhow, 'bout the time they was lumberin'
in here, a group of men that was addicted to fishin', as Nancy w'ud
put it, took it inter their heads that they'd stock this big lake 'ith
salmon, becuz it is a proven fact that once salmon git big enough to
defend themselves, they hold their own ag'in all comers. 'N fact, it
is contended that salmon'll drive the pickerel out. Anyhow, only a
few folks knew anythin' erbout the plans since from time immemo-
rial it has been the habit of fishermen to keep sech private enterprise
to themselves. But them that did know was mostly of the mind that
puttin' small salmon in this water w'udn't amount to no more'n a
snowstorm on the last day of April. We figured that them salmon
w'ud disappear like molasses an' pancakes in a lumber camp.

"Now, consarnin' the actual plantin' of them fust Pierce Pond
salmon, thar are five er six different stories, an' all of 'em are more
er less apocryphal. Fer instance, it's claimed that the fust stockin'
was western Quinnat salmon. I happened to be one of them that
lugged them fust salmon up here, an' I know that they came from
the Sebago Lake hatchery. They was what the fish experts call
Salmo salar sebago, which is only to say that they was a sort of
Atlantic salmon that ran up Sebago way, in the dim ages, an' fergot the way back to the sea. Our state fellers been strippin' an'
rearin' them fish fer a good many years. An' they was the best of
all the nonmigratory salmon, by crotch.

"Gen'rally speakin', thar has been four different sorts of all closely related to the Atlantic species, pretty carelessly planted in our ponds. Fust, the federal gover'ment has been raisin' Grand Lake nonmigratories. They've been at that erbout fifty years, I understand. An' as near's I've been able to study it out, them little salmon is practically the same as the now famous Ouananiche of the St. John's waters. They never git mor'n five pounds heavy. Then the state ran some hatcheries at Green Lake, down in Washington County. Them Green Lake salmon useter run bigger'n the Schoodics did. In the third place, the regular sea-runners have been netted at the mouths of our rivers, stripped fer spawn. Yer'd s'pose that maybe them fish w'ud grow bigger than the nonmigratories in our inland lakes. But they don't.

"As a matter of fact, thar ain't no salmon that ever matched our Sebago strain in fresh water. An' these Sebago is the fourth sort that yer'll find in our ponds. Now, as a matter of fact, it takes some studyin' to tell these salmon apart. I've guided some fish experts in my day, an' that's how I come to know 'bout the situation. Size is erbout the only difference.

"Long's I've got this far on a lecture, I might add that the western Quinnat has been put in a few of our Maine lakes. He grows like a house on fire, but so far has failed to establish hisself spawnin', whereas the eastern fresh-water salmon will spawn successfully, if the inlets er outlets make it possible. Some years after we put the fust Sebago salmon in here, a few Quinnat salmon was planted. They grew wonderfully—thick an' pugnacious—but they never reached the weight of them Sebagos.

"That jist erbout wades through all the yarns consarnin' the big fish of Pierce Pond. The various local yarns is true, but the truth is mixed up, as lies sometimes are, and as the best shift at the truth us poor human critters can muster often is.

"We-ell, I've sort of paddled up the wrong brook in this yarn, I thought yer might be interested in the salmon puzzle. To git back an' on with the yarn I had in mind, we dumped the fust can of little Sebagos in at the dam. An' it was no sooner done, than we see a dart of motion in the water, lookin' like a small submarine was comin'. How them poor little salmon did scatter! An' we seen it warn't no use to dump any more in the pond proper; so we lugged the rest up two er three inlet streams, an' dumped 'em thar.

"Erbout five years run along, an' all that time nobudy caught a dog-goned salmon. Those that had a hand in plantin' them fust fish did a lot of tryin', but we had to give up an' admit that it looked like the pickerel had cleaned them salmon, bones an' all. The spectators, them that was in on the know, all said, 'We told yer so.'

"I guess it was only a year er so after that when a feller who went by the name of Crazy Stiller came to town. He was one of them knights of the sample case. I mean, he sold stuff, when he c'ud. He'd been comin' up this way fer two er three years, an' almost everybudy knew him well enough to call him by his popular nickname, which indicates better'n I can what he was like. Well, this time I'm gittin' at, he splashed inter town with a brand-new rod an' a fishin' outfit good enough to make Hiram of Tyre turn green 'ith envy, as Doc Brownin' useter say.

"'Where can I go to catch some real fish?' he asks Mark, who ran a general store.

"Mark was usually on the alert to put a joke over. 'C'ud yer stand a real hike, if yer was goin' to git some real fishin'?' he asks Crazy Stiller.

"Crazy 'lowed that he w'ud climb the mountains of the moon to git some real big fish.

"'Then,' says Mark, with a wink at his store clerk, 'if yer cross your heart that yer won't tell, I'll tip yer off to a real place where the biggest trout an' salmon in the universe is waitin' fer the ketchin'.'

"'Where is it?' says Crazy. 'My gosh, man, don't think I'd ever tell a soul.'

"Of course, Jack Owens—that was the clerk's name—was wonderin' what Mark was comin' at. An' when Mark says, in an impressive whisper, 'Pierce Pond,' Jack got down under the back-side of the counter, like he was after sunthin'. He told me after-ward that he had to stick 'bout two yards of towelin' into his mouth. 'Pierce Pond!' thinks Jack. 'That's rich! Nothin' but a pick-erel pond at the end of a three-mile climb up a mountain.'

"But Crazy Stiller was green at fishin', an' greener'n that erbout country 'round here, so he eagerly swallowed all the bunk Mark handed him.

"'I've got to git me a guide,' he says. 'Who'd yer recommend?'

"We-ell, Crazy's thinkin' that he needed a guide was how I come into the pitchur. Mark called me in. Crazy was hoverin' an Mark purty near had a fit tryin' to wise me up. Finally I got the idea. An' I agreed to go. I have never regretted it.

"Before we left on the Caratunk stage, 'bout half of the fellers in town was wise, an' so many of them come 'round to wish us luck that it seemed to me the cat w'ud fall through the bag. But Crazy jist got all preened up, an it never entered his head that erbout everybudy seemed to know all 'bout Mark's secret.

"At Caratunk the Kennebec was high an' we durn near upset the canoe gittin' across. I must say that Crazy s'prised me some when we started up the mountain to Pierce Pond. In them days thar warn't even so much of a trail as thar is now. In places yer had to hang on with your teeth, as yer might say. I was luggin' most everythin' but his new rod, which he w'udn't trust to me. He was excited as a kid goin' to his fust circus, an' finally he 'lowed that he'd go on ahead. Not bein' excited myself, I let him go it, an' took my own time. So, 'cordin' to his tell, he got to the pond a half hour b'fore I did.

"Anyway, when I got thar, I see him a-runnin' up an' down the shore by the dam, an' it was plain to see he was all worked up. When he see me, he waved his rod an' yelled, 'I've seen four jump already. Git that tackle box open.' Crotch, he was all pantin' and wheezy 'ith excitement.

"So I opens up his little tin trunk an' thar was the gol-darnedest mess of stuff yer ever see.

"'What'll I try fust?' he wanted to know. I said that I guessed it didn't make much of a difference. 'That's right,' he says. 'They'll take anything.'

"It was my opinion that pickerel w'udn't take flies, though I know now that ain't true. An' so I hitched on a small copper spoon 'ith a little silver tip on it.

"Crazy! Gosh, if ever a nickname fitted, it was his'n. When I'd got his riggin' ready, he fetched his castin' rod three er four times 'round his head, give a gosh awful heave, an' let her go in the general direction of the pond. Away went the spoon an' line like a bullet. But the spoon went faster'n the line an' fetched away out in the pond. An' by crotch, it no sooner hit the water than whang! Judgin' from the commotion out thar, yer'd have said that the spoon exploded. I had been settin' down, but yer can bet I got up an' stared at the place where that piece of junk had struck.

"'Did yer see that?' shouts Crazy. 'Didjer see that fish?' His questions kinda took me off guard an' I says, 'Crotch, but that must have been a big pickerel!'

"'Pickerel!' says Crazy Stiller, kinda scornful an' surperior. 'Pickerel? Say, I'm beginnin' to think that Mark Savage has put sunthin' over on me.'

"Bein' honest at heart, I nodded. But that warn't what he meant becuz he went on to say: 'Sendin' me off with a guide that don't know a pickerel from a salmon when he sees it. Here, give me another one of them shiny spoons. An' this time see that yer tie it on so it'll stay.'

"I pawed 'round in that tin casket of his'n, but nothin' like the spoon he'd lost had been buried in it. So I hitched up a tin fish, painted like one of them war transports. Crazy fetched three or four more circles 'round his head, an' I ducked fer cover. Honest, he knew so blamed little 'bout fishin' that he c'udn't have thrown an anchor overboard. But finally he let her go at the pond. That tin sucker went erbout six feet, an' he had one beauty of a backlash.

"Here," he says, 'you unfix this, an' I'll try the other rod.'

"But before he had begun on his new fly rod an idea stung him, an' he jumped an' shouts, 'I've got an idea.' An' away he races fer the woods.

"I went to unsnarlin' his castin' line, but it warn't more'n a min-it' when back he come with a big nightwalker squirmin' and wigglin' between his fingers. Usually, you know, a feller can't find a worm in the woods—not a regular angleworm, I mean—but he had happened on a place where somebudy had dumped some one time er another. Speakin' of luck, that feller was her adopted son.

"Naturally, I didn't pay much attention to him, bein' as I was unsnarlin' his last idea, but I see him strugglin' to git that worm on a big hook. Bine-by, he heaves it out with erbout a pound of lead—to make sure it w'udn't float, I s'pose. An' then was when I got the surprise of my life. Fer that bait no sooner hit the water than he got the durn-dest strike yer ever see. I tell yer that I fergot all erbout that backlash an' tried to take his fly rod away from him.

"'Let go of that!' he screams. 'Let go, I tell yer!'

"Thar was a kind of a wild light in his eyes, so I set down ag'in. No pickerel is worth fightin' over, an' I s'posed that was what he had hooked. But after pullin' an' pullin', an' it was nip an' tuck which w'ud bust the rod fust, by crotch if he didn't land the purtiest trout I ever laid my eyes on. Of course he busted his tip all to pieces.

"'Get your net,' he shouts at me.

"Net? I says. "You mean a baseball bat."

"I'm not lyin'. That same trout weighed nine pounds an' fourteen ounces, which is the biggest brook trout I ever see. My gosh! My gosh! An' that nitwit caught him with a nightwalker.

"After that, we hunted fer more worms. But the one Crazy had found must have been the last of his race. When he—I mean Crazy, not the worm—was convinced that thar warn't no more worms ter be had, he let me rig up a cast of flies. As a matter of fact, he had bought a sample of every fly that was invented an' some that was never invented, but was jist born of tremors an' plumb foolishness.

"The way that dub cast them flies was e-nough to make Napoleon cry like an old maid. I had to hold on to a tree to keep from hittin' him. But believe me er not, the fourth splash he made, I see a big streak of silver, like a stick of pulpwood in size, hit his fly. Bang! An' that was all.

"'He's gone,' sobs the big slob. 'He's g-g-gone!'

"'So's your leader,' I says.

"We-ell, I hitched up another leader. An' it was the same story over ag'in. *Whang! Bang!* Then he managed to hook a good one an' broke the second tip. But he had one left. An' after some bunglin', he managed to cast out another fly. Up come another salmon, like a jack-in-the-box. When that fish began to ask fer more line, Crazy Stiller jist hung back all the harder. His eyes bunged out like one of them dolls that says 'Mamma' when yer turn it upside down.

"I was half loony myself by that time. 'By crotch,' I says, 'let that fish go!' Up flopped the salmon ag'in. 'Let him go!' I hollers. 'Give him line! Ease up on him, yer durn idgit. Let him go! D'yer hear me?'

"'Let him go?' says the big tub of lard. 'Let him go? Why should I let him go? I want him.'

"By crotch, I was so plumb beside myself that I was standin' on one leg, like a pie-eyed crane. 'You crotchly lunkhead,' I shouts at him, 'if yer don't give that fish some line, I'll murder yer.'

"But it warn't no use. Jist then that salmon give a leap bigger an' better'n any hitherto, an' he was gone. Crazy started bawlin' like a two-year-old. 'He's, he's gone, too,' he blubbers.

"'Give me that rod,' I says, grabbin' it from him. Then I took a cast, guessin' that it warn't no use after all that commotion. But so help me Hannibal, as Doc Brownin' useter say, if I didn't git a strike that knocked the reel loose—anyway it dropped off inter the lake. That fish got plenty of line all right. An' off he run with it, an' didn't show hisself. Finally, I got that reel back on an' snubbed the old cuss. He went up in the air like a rocket. He kinda seemed to shake hisself all over, but I'd got a good tight line by that time. *Whish,* he goes. Then up he goes. Down deep he goes, like his watch had dropped out of his pocket an' gone to the bottom. I had to lift on him some becuz it ain't safe, ever, to let one of them old stagers go cruisin' around on the bottom. An' up he comes, like he'd found the watch an' was goin' to hang it on a Christmas tree.

"Gosh! No wonder I keep a-fishin' an' a-dreamin' to do that all over ag'in. Crazy had a good rod. Sometimes I was out in the pond, up to my belt er more. Sometimes I was runnin' up an' down the shore, an' at sech times, Crazy kept gittin' in my way, shoutin' directions at me an' tryin' to take his rod away from me. I got so mad I warn't a gentleman no longer. Next thing I knew he had fell down right in front of where I was goin'. Of course, I fell on top of him. He groaned, but I was so mad when I got up ag'in that I give him a kick where he'd mind it least. But I didn't have no time to stop an' see the effects the kick had on him becuz that fish was a-jumpin' ag'in.

"We was goin' through that sort of thing fer a good, long hour. But in spite of Crazy, an' everythin' else, I tuckered that fish. He was an old male with his under jaw curled up over his nose. He was the best landlocked salmon I ever see, an' he weighed twenty-two pounds, not to mention some odd ounces.

"We-ell, Crazy went at it ag'in, down nearer the dam, 'an got strikes enough to bust up the rest of his riggin'. So we struck out fer home. By that time, I had cooled off some, so I let Crazy have the salmon to go 'ith his nice squaretail. When we got down to Caratunk, he told, right in front of me, that he caught that big salmon on an angleworm, same's he did the trout.

"Ye've heard of the gold rush of '49," said Dud, winding up his tale. "Well, that's jist the way it was around here, an' it ain't all over yit. When we got to Bingham, Crazy showed his fish all over town. Of course yer never saw sech a foolish lookin' bunch as them fellers was that had spoofed him inter goin' to Pierce Pond. They was all set to kid the pants off'n him, so they was all flabbergasted when he showed up with them big fish.

"Yep, it started an exodus to Pierce Pond. Oh, well," concluded Dud, knocking the ashes out of his pipe, "if thar ain't sunthin' in the Bible erbout a fool shall lead them, thar sh'ud be."

Once in the Stilly Night

In 1934, when this story was written, the abandonment of farms that once dotted the hill country around Bingham was well underway. Most of the little schoolhouses were by then vacant, and already the scrub woods had crossed the stone walls and were filling the pastures. Route 16, then a dirt road, climbed up Babbit Ridge and, seven miles east of Bingham, intersected with the Old Lake Road, which once ran roughly north-northeast from Solon to Mayfield. People who know still call this Ben Adams Corner, and Ben and his neighbors sleep not far away in a cemetery guarded by a huge pine. Once one could have traveled the Old Lake Road and stopped for a drink of water at a dozen farms.

Arthur Macdougall's last book of poems, The Old Lake Road, *poignantly records a way of life and the stalwart independence that has ceased to be. This woods-invaded farming country was just the place for a rollicking adventure once on a stilly night.*

DUD DEAN HELD THE EMPTY FRYING PAN over the coals of our little fire. The fat caught, flared and burned out. After that burst of yellow light, the night seemed darker, blacker than before.

"Trout are middlin' fodder," said Dud, as he laid aside the pan and drew his pipe from his shirt pocket.

There was nothing to add to that; so I settled back against a tree and stretched my legs toward the little fire. Dud paused in the act of pouring a palmful of cut plug into the bowl of his pipe. We heard a distinct sniffing a few feet beyond the campfire's fringe of light.

"Porcupine," I guessed aloud.

In a moment I secured a flashlight from the pack at my side. And the light caught a half-grown raccoon sniffing at the fish bones we had lately thrown aside.

Dud chuckled. "Cunnin' little cuss. And that reminds me, all of a sudden, of the time I went rarecoon huntin'."

"Coon hunting?"

"Ayah. Thar's a sport we've neglected up this way, although coons ain't what yer'd call thick. Up to the time I was persuaded to enlist, I had occasionally read erbout it but had never partici- pated. It was a feller by the name of Shurtliff, who lived down to Lewiston, that talked me into goin'. He sold pickles, but mostly I guess he talked hounds an' rarecoons. He claimed that he sold fifty-seven sorts of pickles, an' had owned fifty-eight coon hounds, and that his last was the champion of the lot. This last hound's name was Vinegar.

"Shurtliff was interduced to me downtown. 'Well, well,' says he, 'so ye're Dud Dean? I've heard that yer know more erbout trout than Izaak Walton hisself. But what do yer know about coonhounds?'

"'I can tell 'em from pointers,' I says.

"'I sh'ud hope so!' he says. 'How w'ud yer like to go coon huntin' with me some night?'

"We-ell, it really didn't appeal to me, but I c'udn't put that feller off. In due time I went. And it turned out to be the most crotchly night I ever put in o'er land er sea. If that was a sample of coon huntin', a feller has to take events jist as they come, an' nobudy is so much subjected to the caprice an' damp humor of circumstances as the coon hunter is apt to be. Still, it's a grand sport, if yer can take it.

"Shurtliff brung two other fellers from his town. One was named Joseph and the other Louis. But Shurtliff talked, mostly, erbout his dog. Accordin' to his talk, an ordinary coonhound sometimes strayed from the straight and narrow path, but not Vinegar. Vinegar never chased anythin' but coons.

"I'm afraid that put an idea in my head. I really didn't know where to look for rarecoons, but I felt purty sure I c'ud find Vinegar a skunk. An' it kinda tickled my perversity to think erbout sech an adventure. Y'see, back in the summer I had been 'tendin' to some fishin' down on the Old Lake Road. On my way out, I had to haul up while a she-skunk as big as Rhode Island sort of saun-tered across the road. She was proudly followed by six duplicates in smaller calibers. That made seven, as I thought it over, an' it didn't seem too farfetched to imagine thar was one more in the neighborhood. That made eight. So I suggested that we try the rarecoon huntin' erlong the Old Lake Road.

"It was a purty night when we started out. The moon was as big as an Irishman's heart, an' the road over Babbit Ridge was as plain as day. When we reached the fields around the Ben Adams place, everythin' looked mighty purty in the silver light. 'Let's leave the car here,' I suggested, when we came to the corners. 'Maybe we'll pick up a coon track while we're walkin' up the old road.'

"'Are they that thick?' says Joseph.

"'Thicker,' I says, thinkin' of them skunks.

"But b'crotch, that Vinegar acted like he was one dog that was purty near as good as his owner claimed. If he winded any skunks, he never paid any attention. Fust, he got out of the car, tail in the air, an' sniffed and snuffed. Next he galloped off like he'd got the situation in hand. We hustled to git all our trappings tergether. It seems that yer always want to take all yer can lug on a coon hunt becuz the more yer start with, the less ye'll git back 'ith.

"Shurtliff an' Joe took the lanterns. Louis pulled out a little rifle that he declared had an ivory bead on it which c'ud be seen in the dark. Well, he sure needed it before that night was done. The moon got off her trail and never got back on it. The sky got black as the inside of a felt hat, an' a damp wind begun to blow from the south.

"'Listen,' I says to Shurtliff, when we'd gone erbout ten rods.

"All hands stopped and listened. Lo an' b'hold, Vinegar was jist a-tearin' pages out of his music book—*rip, rippity, rip.* An' whatever it was that he was chasin', it was headed 'bout opposite the little white schoolhouse.

"'That's him,' says Shurtliff.

"I c'ud have told him that the verb 'to be' never takes an object, as I've heard Nancy say more'n a thousand times, but what is the use of a feller talkin' what he don't believe hisself? I let it pass. What was puzzlin' me was how we was ever goin' to git to that rarecoon if that Vinegar hound kept on chasin' him out of the country.

"At fust, we didn't hurry any to speak of, but bine-by that dog begun to bark treed. By that time, we was jist opposite the Vigue place, and Shurtliff an' Joe jist left me an' Louis. I was lank an' fit in them days but those two fellers had been trained in a sport that turns out supermen in the legs. They lit out like the devil had 'em by the tail an' was twistin it at every jump. Of course, they had the lanterns which was some advantage. Louis an' me w'ud have made better time if we had been able see where we was going.

"As it was, I kept busy tryin' to keep up with Louis, whose feet was faster'n his jedgment. The fust thing I really see, after we left the road, was a big pine tree right in front of me. I thought it looked sort of familiar, but when ye're all out of wind even an old acquaintance is apt to be fergot. I see that Louis dodged the pine, but in a few steps he fetched up ag'in sunthin' else. It laid him out flat like he'd been punched in the chin. Up he got an' ducked to the left. An' down he went ag'in. That time he lay where he'd fallen.

"'Where am I?' he says to me, when I helped him to get to his feet.

"'Ye're in a graveyard,' I says. 'Ye've run plum down the middle of it and fetched up ag'in the back fence.'

"Yer see, the old front gate had been wide open, an' since it was built plenty wide we got in all easy. But the way out warn't so easy, which is typical of sech places.

"After Louis got his wind, he was satisfied to let me lead the way. When we got to the spot where Vinegar was barkin', I see that he'd apparently run his game up a thunderin' big basswood. Fust he'd put his paws up as far as he c'ud reach, then throw back his head an' let her roll. Then he'd go around the tree an' repeat. Joe had broken his lantern an' was riggin' up a little carbide light, which he had all the time. It looked like them guys either thought me an' Louis c'ud see in the dark, er didn't care a dang.

"As near as I c'ud make out this was a big occasion. I certainly admired Vinegar's voice. The yowls run out of him like buckshot out of a tin horn. Bine-by, Joe got so he c'ud train his light on the tree. It was as empty of rarecoons as a prayer meetin' is of hoss traders. But one of them basswoods is sure to be as hollow as a blue heron; so we looked the old tree over. It was perfectly plain that a man c'udn't climb a tree like that, not even if Paul Bunyan hisself had been thar to boost him.

"'Well, thar's jist one thing to do,' says Shurtliff, 'an' that is to smoke 'em out.'

"'But thar hain't no hole to build a fire in,' says Joe.

"'If we had only brought erlong an ax,' says Louis, 'we c'ud chop a hole.'

"'Yes,' says Shurtliff, kinda scornful, 'if we had an ax, we c'ud cut this durned tree down flat.'

"I must say that it looked like a purty pickle, as Shurtliff wu'd have said hisself in a more rational moment. But Vinegar solved the problem by racin' off to another tree. In erbout two jerks of a buck's tail, he was barkin' up, like the basswood had been a sorry mistake. To this day, I d'know whether he had made an error, er that the woods was full of rarecoons. Of course Shurtliff an' his pal Joe left everythin'—but the lantern. However it was a short go, an' me an' Louis warn't far behind at the finish. That time, Vinegar had picked out a rock maple. Joe's light found a pair of eyes that was lookin' down on us like they hated the sight of us. Shurtliff insisted that he had better do the shootin', but Louis was stubborn an' w'udn't give in.

"If Louis got that ivory bead on that coon, he must have aimed at the wrong end of the critter. That was my fust experience 'ith a peeved coon. When it lit in our midst, it was fightin' mad. I took a kick at it with the toe of my right boot, but missed, an' hit

Vinegar in the jaws. Crotch, but warn't I ashamed of myself. Vinegar let a bellow out of him like it didn't feel none too good, but seemed to think that the coon had done it.

"For a little while it looked to me like that rarecoon was goin' to be too much fer Vinegar, but at last the old hound got a grip on the coon an' never let go. I felt kinda sorry. It's too bad when a good fight has to end that way. I always like to see it a draw.

"Vinegar hadn't a mite of int'rest in a dead coon. Jist went off inter the night, an' left it with us to skin-out number one. Joe produced a business-like knife. 'Number one,' says Shurtliff, with jist as much satisfaction as though he'd licked the coon hisself. It was a good chance fer me to git the lantern, an' I laid hold on it in case Vinegar sh'ud find some more coons. It warn't more'n three minits until I knew I'd done a smart thing. Ag'in, Vinegar begun to bellow as loud as it was dark. Shurtliff jist dove with the other light, an' we left Joe a-skinnin' his coon in the dark.

"That time, I was ahead all of the way, until I busted out in a piece of pasture an' dang-near ran inter proof a-plenty that I was in the vanguard. By crotch, if thar warn't the same skunk I'd seen in the summer, it was her spittin' image. She looked as big as a dead hoss to me, an' I put on the breaks so fast yer c'ud have heard me skid in the wet grass. While I stood thar, on the fringe of things, Shurtliff and Louis went by me like the wind on a pond. Purty soon thar was a mighty thrashin' in the brush an' out came Joe a-wavin' that skinnin' knife in his right hand. But he warn't the least mad. 'This place,' he sings out at me, 'must be full of coons.' Of course none of 'em paid any attention to me. If they had, they'd have heard what I said becuz I didn't whisper it. If the place was full of rarecoons, thar was an almighty skunk wedged in between.

"When them fellers from Lewiston had taken in the situation, we all gathered round with considerable caution. Vinegar did a lot of growlin' and threatenin' but kept it in mind that he weren't dealin' with no coon. While we was considerin', Louis stepped forward an' said that he was goin' to shoot her head off. I backed up some more. But Shurtliff jist waved Louis to the rear like he was David bein' offered Saul's armor.

"'I'll pick her up by the tail,' he says. 'They can't atomize when their feet is off the ground.'

"'Then what'll yer do,' demands Louis.

"'Then you crack her in the head with a club, an' thar won't be any mess at all.'

"'A skunk like that hain't worth the risk,' says Louis.

"'Every last one of them critters sh'ud be exterminated,' says Shurtliff, glaring at the old girl, who had her head in a pile of rocks but her battery facin' the foe. 'We have got to do it in the int'rest of sport, but thar ain't no sense in stirrin' up a cyclone. It can be done neatly and with dispatch. If yer was to shoot at her, like enough ye'd jist nick her.'

"'Is that so!' says Louis. 'Well, I'd rather have a nicked skunk in the bush than a live one in my hands.'

"Nobudy laughed at that. Finally Joe says, 'I'll crack her, if ye'll hold her high an' dry.' So Shurtliff told Vinegar to go in an' get at her—the idea bein' to take the skunk's mind off'n him an' Joe. But shucks, a skunk ain't got a mind. Old Vinegar knew that an' walked stiff legged around his victim. But when she warn't lookin', Shurtliff walked in on tiptoe an' jerked her free an' clear at arm's length. I must say that he struck me like a man 'ith more courage than precaution. But by crotch nothin' happened. Even Vinegar acted like he c'uldn't believe his eyes or nose.

"Joe walked in 'ith his stick.

"'Steady now,' says Shurtliff.

"'All set?' says Joe.

"'Let her have it,' says Shurtliff, purty tight lipped.

"I guess that skunk thought Shurtliff was talkin' to her becuz she let them have it!

"Shurtliff dropped the critter. Vinegar got so excited that he rushed in an' grappled with her. I'd have laughed if it had choked me. An' it durn near did.

"Vinegar finished the skunk without assistance. An' all I c'ud think of as we went along out of thar was the line erbout a vase in which roses has once been distilled—how if yer break an' shatter it, the scent of the roses remains 'ith it still. But by the time we come out to the road ag'in, Shurtliff's spirits had so far revived that he c'ud whistle, 'Thar'll be a hot time in the town tonight.' I don't think that anythin' ever kept him down fer long. The world was his brine, as yer might say.

"We left Vinegar behind. When I see him last, he was plowin' his nose through the grass an' foamin' at the mouth. But he an' Shurtliff was erbout alike as a dog an' master sh'ud be, an' when we stepped inter the road, Vinegar bounded out after us like nothin' at all had happened—but not smellin' that way. Louis said that we might's well go home becuz the hound wu'dn't be able to smell anythin' fer a week, which didn't sound probable to me.

"'Cheer up,' says Joe, 'we've got one— Say! Where is that coon?'

"That was one of them rhetorical questions becuz he knew durn well that he'd left that coon right where we left him skinnin' it.

"'Well,' says Louis purty disgusted, 'I must say that this a damned fine beginnin'.'

"Up to the old Brown place thar's an old side road to the west that leads off to some more old, fergotten farms. We took that. In places it was full of alders, which ain't the easiest to git through in the dark. But we had to take it becuz Vinegar was barkin' in thar. Shurtliff got his shoe caught in the crotch of an alder and fell on his face. He talked sunthin' fierce, but it didn't have any effect on the alders. To help matters out, Joe had to fall down, too, an' the lantern he was carryin' went out. But we lit her up ag'in an' went on. Thar's that eternal principle erbout coon huntin'—to go on, an' let the dead bury their dead.

"Finally, from away up on top the hill, we heard Vinegar announcin' to the tall night that he'd treed his game. Gittin' to a dog that's barkin' up ain't so much of a picnic as yer'd suppose. Every bush an' branch in the woods reaches out an' takes a hunk out of your clothes, an' now an' then, ye'll lose a patch of hide. The woods don't seem friendly in the dark.

"When we did reach Vinegar, he set up a tarnation of a noise around a birch as big as a barrel, an' taller'n a tree ought to be. When we got the carbide light on the object of our chase, it was plain that Vinegar hadn't made no mistake this time. But the eyes that glared back at us looked shifty an' too far apart to me. Louis drew a bead on 'em that looked to be as careless as a kid shootin' a robin.

"'Hold on,' I says, 'sunthin' tells me that it w'ud be a mistake to hit that critter where yer hit that coon. I w'ud a whole lot rather have Shurtliff pick it up by the tail.'

" 'Aw, hurry up,' says Shurtliff lookin' scornful at me, 'we hain't got all night to spend in this place.'

"It looked like Louis did hurry up becuz I don't believe he nicked that bobcat. It slid out of the tree from the back like a chap 'ith skis on his feet. Nobudy ever called Dud Dean a coward— twice—an' I rushed around with the rest of 'em. Vinegar muckled that bobcat right where he lit on the ground. Fer a moment, it was quite a fight. I got too close one spell, an' if that cat didn't make a pass at me, I was in a high state of excitment. 'Bout then, the cat walloped Vinegar so hard that he let a howl out of him a yard long. Joe had to drop the lantern. Of course the danged thing went out ag'in which left it 50 percent darker.

All through it, Vinegar displayed more courage than jedgment. Him an' the bobcat was jist a confusion. Louis hopped around with his gun pointed fust at the hound and then at the cat. Finally, I yanked the weapon out of his hands. But by that time the bobcat was gone, like the night had reached out an' taken him off. Even Vinegar c'udn't believe it fer as much as twenty seconds. When he did, he raced off like the soldier he was. An' we all took after the noise Vinegar was makin'. But crotch, we never did catch up 'ith them ag'in. They treed four or five times, but the durn cat w'udn't stay treed. It was tarnation goin'. I believe that we actually went through growths of young firs that the wind c'udn't have blown through. All in all, we was up an' down—tripped down, knocked down, an' jist plain down, causes unaccounted fer— more than a hundred times.

"Bine-by I begun to wonder where we was, anyway. But Shurtliff didn't seem to think that was at all important. He seemed to think that as long as we followed that bobcat we'd come out on the main street of Lewiston in the end. But I had begun to feel sure that we was as good as lost—turned 'round—right then. Finally I said so. Say, them fellers was scornful. Even Louis was indignant an' declared that he had never been lost in his life. Meantime, Vinegar had gone out of hearin'.

"So I give it up. I knew an awful good cure fer what ailed them rarecoon hunters, an' decided to let it work. I let them have their own way. Gosh, it was fun! We tramped 'round and 'round like little children playin' ring around the rosy—only thar warn't no rosy, jist us hunters lost out in the Almighty's black night. At least, I was sure that I didn't have no more idea where I was than Larb Blare had the time he got pifficated an' wandered into the Methodist church.

"Bine-by, danged if we didn't cross a road with thick alders in it. Thinks I, 'Shurtliff will recognize this place.' But he didn't. So we circled 'round some more, until we crossed that road ag'in. I had to laugh out loud—struck me that way, yer know.

"'What yer laughin' at?' says Shurtliff in a provoked voice.

"I never bothered to answer him. A man don't need to answer sech questions' in the long run. Finally, we struck off ag'in, but didn't come back to the road no more. After Shurtliff had fallen over the same windfall a half dozen times in half an hour, he admitted that the woods was full of blowdowns. I sat down. I was tired, tired as a dog on the Fourth of July.

"'What's the matter?' says Shurtliff, sort of teeterin' on his feet.

"'Nothin',' I says, 'except that I'm kinda dizzy.'

"It was Joe's turn, so he seemed to think. 'Ye're damned right,' he says, 'condemn it! We've been travelin' in a circle fer the last ten min-its. Now what'll we do?'

"'Well,' I says, 'I've always heard that the thing to do, when lost, is to sit down an' act calm. If that don't appeal to fellers, we can keep on followin' Shurtliff until he drops dead.'

"Somehow, I guess Shurtliff didn't like that, but of course he'd known fer a long time that he didn't know where he was. So we sot. It was still in them woods. And it was as dark as underground. It made a man feel unimportant without anybudy's help. Nobudy said anythin'. I watched our lantern burnin' low, and when it sputtered out, it struck me that it was a little tin symbol of all man's efforts to git along in the Almighty's night of all time. 'Long erbout that time, I fell to thinkin' how good my own bed w'ud feel, if I was in it. I tried to think of sunthin' that was softer than a feather bed, but I c'udn't. 'Bout then, I went to sleep.

When I woke up, it was rainin' a little. The other rarecoon hunters was sleepin'. It's kinda funny to watch the rain fall on a face that don't know it. When I got up an' looked around, I swear that I c'udn't see nothin' that looked familiar. But I seen a stunpile, which indicated that we was in some grown-up farmin' land.

"In a min-it Joe woke up. He got to his feet an' looked about in considerable bewilderment. Then he says, 'What's that backend of a little white buildin' over thar?'

"I looked over where he was p'intin', an' I was some surprised myself. 'That,' I says, like I'd known it all the time, 'is the little old schoolhouse we come by last night.'

"By crotch, if we hadn't put in the tag end of the night, after

Vinegar had gone out of hearin', wanderin' eround an' finally sleepin' within a few rods of Shurtliff's car. Joe woke up the other two in a hurry, an' we legged it fer the automobile. When we got to it, thar was Vinegar, curled up in the back seat. An' the scent of the roses hung 'round him still."

Men and Mice

Erratic gusts pelt a bone-chilling rain across the gray surface of upper Pierce Pond. There is no shelter in the rowboat where Mak and Dud are fishing without the slightest luck. Mak has begun to shiver, and it doesn't help his mood when Dud suggests that the next time he writes a story he does so in a leaky woodshed with his feet in a tub of water just to see if he can describe the type of weather that tests a man's grit and true affability, rather than the usual pretty sunset and mayfly setting. The hours drip by. Dud tells about seeing a big trout nail a mouse that had fallen into the water. Perhaps there is a reason for what seems like a random bit of conversation. Dud stuffs a box of pop-bugs back into his pack and rather mysteriously produces another small container.

WHEN HE REMOVED THE COVER of the second box, I saw three objects about an inch long. One was white, one was black, and the third was brown.

"Holy Moses, Dud, those are mice!"

"Micers," corrected Dud. "Take your pick. They're fittin' fer a time like this."

"How have the mighty fallen," I muttered.

"No sech thing!"

I picked the little brown mouse as being, perhaps, the most lifelike of the lot.

"If it works," said Dud, "let me have a turn. We might's well be hung fer hoss thieves as jackasses."

I cast about thirty feet of line, dropping the bait close to the ledge that walls in the north end of the big island. After a few moments I began to strip in line. The creation moved toward us, very much like a live mouse on an aquatic migration. Dud watched intently.

When the trout struck, I was in the midst of a shiver that involved every muscle in my body. The strike, which was slow, startled me, and I jerked the lure away. The mouse hopped out of the water and came to rest about a yard ahead of the fish. It did not offer to strike again.

"Hold on, Mak!" chuckled Dud. "That's a mouse, not a bat. I'm afraid that leap fer freedom put that fish down fer keeps. An' that looked like a real trout. Why not fetch in that micer an' give it a rest? It don't seem logical to have mice as thick an' fast as a hatch of mayflies."

I recovered the bait.

"Anyhow, that trout made me feel warmer," I said.

"Now try 'im ag'in."

I cast again, but there was no response.

"Crotch," muttered Dud in a frankly disappointed voice. "Try another hatch. Try this black 'un. Nobody ever saw a black mouse up in this neck of woods, but—"

"Let's try the white one," I suggested, "because it looks colder."

"Yer don't mean ye're feelin' cold ag'in!"

I continued casting the brown mouse. Nothing at all happened.

"Wait about ten min-its," said Dud. "Let's have us a smoke."

"Let's go ashore and build a fire."

"Crotch, we ain't got no time fer a fire now. Jist think how warm an' dry ye'll be when Gabriel blows his horn."

"All right, you take a turn at micing," I suggested.

"By godfreys I will, but I'm goin' to try one of them nine-foot leaders. As fer them mice, guess I'll try the black 'un. Jist as soon, I guess. No, it's too black. An' that white 'un looks too white, seems so."

"Then why not try this brown one? It's too brown."

In a moment Dud stood up and cast the brown mouse out into the narrow strip of water between the island and the mainland. "Jist like an owl had dropped it," he explained. "Mm, my pipe's gone out. Got a match?"

I offered my match case. Dud reached for it. *Bang!* The mouse shot up into the air. Dud reeled in several feet of line. *Bang* again.

"An' I hooked him that time, Mak."

A great salmon, nearly a yard long and thicker than any I had ever seen, leaped straight up over the gray water. I uttered a mean- ingless ejaculation and gripped the gunwales tightly.

"How heavy is that leader?" I gasped.

"Ayah," drawled Dud, "I had about the same idea myself. It tapers from b'gosh to I-guess."

As I grunted, "Good-bye mouse," the salmon sailed out and down the channel toward the northwest.

"Ye mean good-bye micers," corrected Dud, and as he spoke his pipe fell from his lips into the water.

Hardly looking at it, I scooped it in with the landing net. The salmon had out more than twenty-five yards of line and was apparently plowing ahead to the bitter end. "He's on his way," I said disappointedly.

"You fiddle while Rome burns an' let's see what kind of a fireman I be. A fish ain't lost until he's throwed the hook; an by crotch, that's a good-sized hook."

And at that remark the big fish slid upward, like a bright lance hurled aloft.

Dud chuckled. "Look at that old cuss shake hisself. Ain't that a fish? Ain't that a fish!"

"It's the best nonmigratory salmon I ever saw," I said.

"I w'udn't go that far," drawled Dud, "but if I sh'ud happen to git him in near the boat, draw a pitchur of him, Mak, becuz I'm beginnin' to be a little a-feared that we ain't never goin—Thar! What did I tell ye? By crotch a-mighty—"

"Is he—is he gone?"

"No, he ain't, becuz I read his mind an' had that slack ready."

"Read his mind!"

"Sartinly. A fish like that knows more'n some folks that wanted to run fer president. Thar! Jist look at that."

It was only one more wild and splendid leap, high and clear of the lake.

I exclaimed, "That fish will weigh fifteen pounds—at least!"

"He w'ud if a feller c'ud ever git hold of him long enough."

To my surprise, Dud began to reel in line.

"Guess he's takin' a deep breath," he said by way of explanation. "Seems to be easin' up a little. Don't hang no part of yer over the edge of the boat, Mak. A fish like this is dangerous. I ain't had so much fun since the time Doc Brownin' fell off the boomlog.

'Stead of swimmin' ashore, he tried to git back on the log. Every time he got most of his heft on it, it w'ud roll an' he'd pitch in on the other side. But he kept tryin' until he done it. Doc had a stubborn streak. An' what he called the boom warn't professional. Right now that fish is a-diggin' fer bottom an' shakin' his head like a young pup that has his first skunk. Thar he goes. Watch him now. Don't let him git away!"

The salmon was surging straight for the ledge again. The line cut the water. Dud's face was again a-gallop with grins. "If he don't stop before he hits that ledge, maybe we can pull him out of the hole he's goin' to make."

It was a moment of crisis, and Dud put more strain upon his splendid rod than he had previously ventured. It bent like a gray birch with a small boy at its terminal.

"Crotch, Mak," muttered Dud, "now I am afraid that this leader is goin' to hold an' I'll bust my best rod instead. That fish intends to lick me. He's—"

Up came the salmon in response to the lift of Dud's rod. And it fell back into the water like an inert thing. "No, yer don't!" cried Dud in a tone of pure delight. "No, yer don't, mister. I never hooked a good salmon in my life that didn't try that trick before we was done. A little bit of slack line helps when a feller like you tries to fall smack on a leader."

Of course, the fish kept moving after the futile attempt to fall on the leader. In fact, once started, it came at us about as slowly as cat out of a burning woodshed. And as it came abreast of the boat, it pulled a brand-new stunt, so far as my fishing experience went. I suppose that it actually jumped about four times in rapid succession, but it appeared to be standing on its tail and to be propelling itself by churning that extremity much more rapidly than the eye could see.

It was, in fact, a most astonishing performance. And when it was over, Dud was standing with about eighty feet of line at his feet. For a moment we both stared at each other. It was a tense moment. Anyone who thinks that it is easy to hang to a fish like that for about thirty minutes, only to lose him, is a . . . I had every reason to expect a hearty chuckle, for I had often seen Dud laugh off events like that. But the laugh somehow didn't materialize. Instead, Dud's fine old face seemed to be set in lines which I interpreted as meaning that it had hurt to lose that salmon.

But my emotion of compassion was a gentle thing compared with my feeling when I beheld Dud clap his right hand to the vicinity of his heart.

"Take it easy," I urged in consternation.

"Huh?"

And he slapped both hands to the back of his hips. By that time I was sure that this was worse than the day when a good friend of mine actually sobbed on a like occasion. Dud's hand went back to his heart and he looked off into the distance. There was no mistaking the utter gravity of his face.

"What," I managed to say, "in God's name is the matter?"

"Matter? By crotch a-mighty, I've lost my pipe!"

"Pipe?"

At that Dud stared at me for a long moment, and then, like a sun over January hills, a laugh burst from his lips. "Oh, Judas, I see what yer thought! Mak, I'm ashamed of yer."

"Well," I said recovering, "there's your pipe. I netted it when you dropped it into the lake during that salmon battle."

"Good! It seemed to me that I could remember puttin' that pipe in my shirt pocket."

A few moments passed, during which Dud soberly wiped out the bowl of his pipe with a white handkerchief and filled and lighted it. Then, assuming a tone of mock solemnity, he said, "Mak, the brown micer is gone ferever."

I nodded with equal solemnity.

"Ayah, it's gone. Mak, I don't believe even some presidents c'ud have landed that fish when it took to cakewalkin'. He caught me short, the old stager. The leader busted,"

"We ought to try that white mouse in the morning," I said.

"Jist at daylight," agreed Dud.

Dud Guides a Lady

From Indian Pond southward, the East Branch of the Kennebec twists and turns between the ledge-walled hills. In some fourteen and a half miles, it falls three hundred and fifty-seven feet in a series of falls, rips, and rapids. Today, thrill seekers in rubber rafts get sluiced down the river in one of the East's best-known white-water rides. But that is now and not in the days when Dud finds himself in an unexpected predicament.

Back then, Indian Pond was smaller than it is at present. Its headwater was maintained by a wooden dam rather than today's huge concrete barrier and hydroelectric station. The Somerset line of the Maine Central Railroad crossed the East Branch just below Indian Pond and in a short distance reached Indian Pond Station, set nearby the dam and the old river-driving quarters. It is on this station's plank platform that Dud first meets B. N. Turner.

"SOME DAY," SAID DAN NYE, "git Dud Dean to tell you 'bout the time he guided a flapper down the East Branch. But don't tell him that I put you wise. Jist break it easy-like. It'll be worth a thousand."

So one night, when we were camping at Foley Pond, I broached the subject. I was comfortably arranged, and Dud's pipe was going nicely.

"Let's see, Dud," I began, "didn't you guide a lady or something down the East Branch one time?"

It was dark but I could feel Dud's shrewd eyes turned on me.

"What d'yer mean by that, er sunthin'?"

I had got off on the wrong foot. "Why, why, you did, didn't you?"

A half-moment passed, then I heard Dud's inimitable chuckle.

"Maybe," he said, "I'll tell yer that adventure, if that's what ye're fishin' fer. But git this straight: she was a lady. By time! I've had trouble e-nough settlin' that."

Then Dud went on with his story. Hereafter, Dud is speaking.

Let's see, time's draggin', an' you never did know enough to turn in. We-ell, I'll begin it this way. That must of been the spring of 1913. Money warn't comin' in faster'n I c'ud use it; so I was pickin' up most any job that come my way. Erlong 'bout the fust of June, I got a crisp, short letter that said a friend had recommended me as a guide who knew the East Branch, some. An' w'ud I hire out to guide a party of one? It was signed, B. N. Turner.

Well, I read it over three-four times, an' showed it to Nancy. The letter was typewritten, by the way. Then I went down to Bingham station an' got Pearl Woodard to fix me up a telegram sayin' the prop'sition looked all right to me. Next day, back comes an answer, tellin' me to be at Indian Pond, June fifth without fail.

"I hope Mr. Turner will be agreeable," says Nancy, when I was startin' out the day before the fifth, which w'ud be the fourth, like enough. By Jericho! If she'd known what I found out later, she w'ud have been real serious erbout Mister Turner bein' agreeable.

We-ell, nothin' waits fer a man but trouble, as old Doc Brownin' useter say. I got everythin' fixed early the mornin' of the fifth. An' I had a nice, trappy little canoe I was real proud erbout. Of course I was feelin' purty good, becuz a party of one is easy guiding.

The train come in 'bout two o'clock. Fer a min-it er so, nobudy got off, but I see a colored feller a-pilin' off a lot of duffle; so I sorta eased up in that direction. Then off gits a woman, 'bout twenty-five, I'd say. Crotch! Come to think of it, she might be almost a grandmother now. She had on long yeller britches an' a green huntin' shirt. She was a sight—a sight, I mean! Upon my word, that colored feller blushed when he see me lookin' at the both of 'em. She gave him a bill. An' the conductor waved his hands. Thar we was, the flapper an' me a-standin' all alone on Injun Pond platform. It warn't none of my business, as I see it, jist then, so I started to go over to the dam where thar was some fellers workin' that I knew.

But she held up her hand. "Are you the guide, Dud Dean?" she asks me.

"Sometimes," I says.

"I am B. N. Turner."

Crotch, yer c'ud have used me fer log-chinkin'.

"But I was expectin' a man," I says, becuz it seemed like some explanation was necessary. Then I went on to say, "Instead of—"

She cut me off short, like a kid that was speakin' out of turn at a Christmas exercise.

"I can't see that the fact I am a woman makes any difference. My money is jist as good. And you have been hired to guide me down the East Branch. This is the East Branch, isn't it?" she says, wavin' her hand at the river.

"It is the East Branch," I says, "but it w'ud sartinly take us more'n the rest of this day to make The Forks."

She kinda screwed up her face at that, like I had wandered from the subject an' she c'udn't foller me. So I started in to clear up the situation, as Jim Perkins useter say, tellin' erbout some fight he'd jist got licked in.

"It w'ud mean campin' out two nights," I says.

"Oh," she says, sorta smilin'. I rec'lect that she was real purty when she smiled, but that warn't often. Most of the time her face was like a starched shirt. "I brought my own tent," she says.

I had been lookin' at her baggage. It looked like a small circus outfit I once seen down to Bingham. So by way of bein' pleasant, I says to her, "Where's the wild animals?"

We-ell, yer sh'ud have seen her scowl at me. "I find this banter silly," she snaps at me. "The question is: Are you going to guide me down the East Branch, as you agreed by wire to do?"

"I am not," I says. An' I meant it. Why, gosh all-hemlock. It was the dumdest prop'sition fer them careful-goin' days. Ye got to remember, Mak, that this was in 1913. Thar's a cool wind been blowin' sech foolishness out of the air since then, an' I must say the air smells cleaner to me.

"Why not?" she shot back at me, 'ith her eyes lookin' through me. "Is it ag'inst the law to guide a decent woman down the Kennebec?"

"Not if her husband—" I begins.

"Bosh!" she says. "Just because you live in the woods, don't think that there are stumps on Broadway. Rot! And tommy-rot!"

"Madam," I says, "speakin' of Broadway, didjer ever hear of the Straight an' Narrow Way?"

We-ell, thar ain't no sense in draggin' that out. Between you an' me, I was young an' reckless in them days. So I stored most of her junk in the drivers' shack, an' we got inter my canoe. Fust off, she was bound to string up a nice little rod.

You know the East Branch. Thar's some mean water in it. Fer one place, thar's the Hullin' Machine, an' a dozen more slipp'ry places. I had to carry 'round some. Then we'd ease down inter some of them nice pools. About two 'clock that mornin' they had shut down the gates at Injun Pond, an' the pulpwood drive was away ahead of us. Conditions was ideal fer fishin'. Thar was a chance fer squaretails, salmon, an' what not, as Doc Brownin' useter say when he was called out in the middle of the night.

When it come to fishin' that woman had everythin' I ever see hooked by the ear. More'n once she durn near hooked one of mine. But in them days good fly-men warn't so common, an' I was purty good at dodgin'. Fust off I tried to teach her sunthin' erbout the gentle art, but she w'udn't listen to me. A dozen times I had to yell at her, like the referee of a dog fight, to keep my canoe right side up. She was worse'n a monkey fer ballast.

An' mind yer, I never saw a better day fer fishin' on the East Branch. Thar was plenty of fish—plenty. Yer see a head of water slushes 'em out of Injun Pond.

Lots of 'em are Mooseheaders. It was strange that she c'udn't hook one. They'd roll up slow an' dignified. Then she'd fetch a squeal, an' a heave; yankin' the fly right out of their reach. I c'ud hear their teeth click.

We-ell, along 'bout then she begun to drop some of her know-it-all an' own-it-all ways.

"Oh, darn," she says, "what shall I do?"

"Yer might stop yankin' your fly out of their reach," I says. But that jist froze her up, an' she turned her back on me. I never see sech a person. It took me all the afternoon to figger out jist what ailed her.

Bine-by, while we was loafin' through a purty stretch of water a nice little salmon, that w'ud go three pounds, maybe, lashed out at her fly. She done her best to yank it away from him but warn't quick e-nough. He nailed that Jock Scott good an' tight. It s'prised her so, she durn near dropped her rod in the river. That's all that saved the rod at the start, I reckon.

Soon's she seed her line a-swishin' through the water, she begin to pull back, but that didn't do no harm becuz she never touched her line er reel. Gor-ry, but that salmon warn't long in heading fer the next pool below us.

Anyone that knows me, knows I ain't ever been able to take my fly fishin' like a drink of cold tea, an' I useter git excited in them days.

"Git a hold on that line," I yells at her, an' at the same time I headed my canoe fer the rips.

That fish had some start on us, an he was in the next pool when we got thar. Then the fun begun, but all that flapper c'ud do was to squeal an' pull back on her rod. Thar was somewhere near ten turns of line 'round the bow, an' hanged if thar any tellin' where the rest of it was, although that girl looked like a bobbin half unwound.

It was jist at that stage of the confusion in general that the fish begin to stand right up on his hind legs. "Oo-o-ooo," she squeals.

"Tarnation!" I busts out. "Give me that rod! D'yer hear?"

It has always been my intention to be a gentleman, wherever, an' whenever, but I guess I fergot that I had a lady aboard. I purty nigh upset the canoe, myself, a-reachin' fer that rod. Fust thing I knew, I had it in my hands. I'd a looked less foolish if I had known e-nough to let her finish what she'd begun. With them turns, bowlines, hangman's knots, sheep-shanks, an' what not, I had erbout as much chance of landin' that salmon as a deacon at a Democratic rally.

He fetched one er two jumps an' was gone. It took me half an hour to untangle that line. While I was workin' away on the line, I heard a funny noise an' looked up quick. By gum if that flapper warn't bawlin'. I felt meaner'n a rabbit 'ith fleas, but I c'udn't think of nothin' to say.

Someone oughter write a book fer all young guides to study. Thar ain't nothin' from fust aid to funeral services that they don't need to be ready fer. We-ell, bine-by she slowed down some an' seemed to change. I think she must have seen the pity in my eyes becuz she got madder'n a set-on bumble bee, an' says with a voice that was shaky but mean, "You're discharged!"

I was so dumfounded, I jist set an' stared at her. It was the fust anybudy had ever tried to fire me.

"What?" I says.

"Don't you understand American?" she says, slow an' careful. "You are fired!"

I set out to laugh, but finally I says, gentle as I c'ud, "Now see here. I don't blame yer, Mrs. Turner. Naturally yer don't feel very good, but it's a long walk back to Injun Pond, an' I happen to be headed downriver. Call it fired if yer want to, but I suggest that yer ride erlong 'ith me."

We-ell that woman had some brains, of course. Fer a min-it, she sot an' looked at me like I was the missin' link, an' turned what I had said over an' over in her mind.

"Very well," says she, short, an' her voice under control ag'in.

I finished reelin' up her line, threw her rod in the bottom of the canoe, an' dug the paddle deep. As I remember, I had some fool idea of reachin' The Forks b'fore sunset, which w'ud have busted a mallard's record, an' then some.

"Keep in the middle," I told her. "Don't throw your weight on the one side. An' git your underpinnin' under yer."

Maybe that made her mad, I don't know. Anyway, jist as we hit the white water an' I was diggin' to miss a nasty rock, she put her heft where it w'ud do the most good, from her point of view. All I c'ud remember, afterwards, was that I see the river comin' up inter my face, an' then it got dark an' so still that I stopped hearin' anythin'.

The next I knew, I was layin' on some almighty hard-feelin' rocks. Fust off, I figgered that it was the bottom of the river somewheres between where I'd gone down an' the Atlantic Ocean. But I put out my hands an' the rocks felt sorta dry. Then I begin to hear someone cryin'. "Can't be my funeral," thinks I, "becuz I can't smell no flowers."

Next I heard a voice, way off an' distant, sayin', "Are you dead, Mister Dean?"

I made out to answer, "No, marm, I don't think so becuz I feel kinda chilly."

Yer see, I was gittin' some of my senses back. Fust thing I saw, when I opened my eyes, was a tree. It warn't much of a tree, but it had some sky behind it. So I set up. My head was sorer than a bobtailed pup. I s'pose likely I'd bumped it on the bottom of the river. Then I see her settin' thar—wet an' with most of the starch gone out of her, by the looks of it.

"Where's the canoe?" I says.

"I hung onto that," she says. "It's d-down below here a little bit."

"Well," I says, "how'd I git here? Did I bounce here?"

"No-o-o."

I kinda felt all over myself; an' got up on my feet Thar didn't seem to be nothin' gone, an' I was all in one piece. Well, two an' two is four, most gen'rally. She'd pulled me out, somehow. I took a squint at the sun an' decided it was 'bout five. That gave us three hours, er so, of light. But we was in a pickle, jist the same. The grub I had brought along was in the bottom of the river.

We kept goin' till darkness had set in, an' then went ashore to fix up some sort of a camp. Nights git chilly 'long in June up this country, 'specially if ye're damp. I had a knife, an' managed ter strip off some bark fer a lean-to roof. Then it came to me that my matches was all wet. Jumpin' hornpouts, talk erbout a gone feelin'.

I'm hanged, though, if that flapper, er flipper, didn't produce a dinky little watertight matchbox. I've never been 'ithout one since. In fact, the one I've carried fer years— No, never mind that. I got a nice fire goin'. But we had nothin' to eat. Which was tough. I made two birch-bark cups, an' a bigger dish ter heat water in. Yer can do it, easy enough, if yer don't let the fire git up above the water line. It tasted hot an' comfortin'.

Then we sot down and settled in fer a long night. After a while she begun to talk.

"I suppose that you consider me all kinds of a fool," she says.

"No," I says, "I don't, but I wish yer w'ud tell me jist what your idea was in takin' this trip."

We-ell, she jist wanted to git out an' see places like she read erbout. That was all thar was to it. She was one of them females that had done too much thinkin' erbout the terrible injustices of a man-made world. One of them sort that thinks men w'ud still insist that their women wear veils an' stay indoors, if they had their way. Never stoppin' to think that the days when women did wear veils an' stay indoors was the days when veils an' doors was purty essential. B. N. Turner, anyhow, had an ingrown idea that a woman was jist as good as any man an' had set out to prove it. Which a min-it's reflection shows up to be a plumb foolish notion. I ain't never seen much diff'rence 'tween a female an' a male. A mean woman's as mean as a mean man, an' a good woman is as good as a good man, if not better.

She told me that she didn't intend to give up her independence jist becuz she was married to a man. That was the only funny thing I see er heard durin' that trip. I've never noticed any of Nancy's independence oozin' away. We've shared an' shared alike. What we've got, we've got together. What we had take on the jaw, as yer might say, we took together. If I wanted to go fishin', I went fishin', in spite of criticism. If Nancy wanted to go to a W.C.T.U. meetin', she went. An' I told B. N. Turner so. That seemed to interest her. She 'lowed that Nancy must be a woman with the modern point of view.

"Well," I says, "Nancy has always run her own affairs 'ithout borrowin' my britches. An' that, young woman, is a text fer meditation."

Oh, I preached her a durn good sermon, if I do say so.

"If yer want to be a whale of a success, ye've got to work sech material as comes to hand," I says. "Wearin' yeller britches may be comfortable, an' sensible, but it don't fool nobudy—t'wouldn't if yer c'ud make your husband wear dresses. Most men ain't worth imitatin'. When women recognize that, they may git somewhere. Independence ain't a matter of yeller britches an' hard-boiled airs. Jist take dumpin' me in the Branch, which I don't blame yer fer doin'. To do that, yer had to dump yourself an' your comforts. Strikes me," I says— Oh, well, I've forgotten jist what I did say after that. Never mind.

We set thar, an' shivered, an' dried out, fust in front an' then back. The fire got real warm, an' bine-by I sorta dropped off to sleep. I dreamed that I saw Nancy comin' up the river in a canoe, an' she was lookin' fer me. After that I lay thar, kinda awake an' half asleep.

Bine-by B. N. Turner give me a shake.

"Wake up!" she whispers. "There's a puppy, or some dog, trying to come in through the back of this lean-to."

I set up straight. Ye've heard a wood pig, out in the night, kinda cryin' an' pleadin', like he'd lost his soul mate. "Scat out of here!" I says, throwin' a stick.

An' the last thread of that mask she wore fell off her face. She had only sold herself on the idea that she was hard-boiled. She was jist a scared kid. Seems she'd been listenin' to that porcupine fer a long time. Thought it was a wolf er sunthin'. Take almost any person, put 'em out in the deep woods at night, an' the veneer of civilization's assurances falls off. The night has a voice of its own, an' it has done me a heap of good to listen.

Jist to git her mind back to normal, I told her what I knew 'bout porcupines, which, if I do say so, is a lot more'n the average woodsman, becuz I'm one of the few that has taken the trouble to notice them. Most folks call 'em stupid critters, an' let it go at that.

They do a lot of aggravatin' damage, like chewin' camp floors an' doors. Almost anythin' around a camp is splinters fer them. They damage an' kill some growin' trees. Our state paid a bounty on porcupines fer several years. I ain't sayin' the money was wasted. They do git purty numerous, by spells. But I do say that I c'ud have spent that money wiser—on house cats that have gone wild, an' half wild in the woods, fer instance. But never mind that. What I told B. N. Turner was erbout amusin' tricks I'd seen porcupines do. Nobudy, nor no thing is as foolish as we're apt to assume.

Anyhow, I didn't sleep no more, an' I c'ud see that she appreciated it. So we got started down the river with the light of mornin'. It's a nice ride down the East Branch. By crotch, it's beautiful! B. N. had washed in the river afore we started, an' blamed if she didn't look kinda human-sweet in mornin' light. I drove the canoe fer all I c'ud. When we got down to The Forks, she asked me to find someone to take her right over to Moxie Station. Said that she c'udn't wait to git back home. Um . . . don't it beat all how I run on when I git at a yarn?

I got Dan Nye to take her over to Moxie Station. When she left, out goes her hand.

"Good-bye, Mr. Dean," she says, 'ith sunshine in her face. "You'll never forget this trip, will you? Neither shall I. Thank you."

I put my canoe in the Kennebec an' went along down the river to Bingham. An' I'll bet ye're wonderin' how I squared all this 'ith Nancy. I'll tell yer 'bout that. Somehow, I c'udn't make up my mind to tell her, though I've always practiced bein' open an' above. Yer see, folks was awful set, in them days, on what is called conventionalities. It was jist erbout as bad to ignore them as to bust the Ten Commandments wide open. So I made up my mind to keep the whole business to myself. An' I'd already sworn Dan Nye to keep his mouth shut.

When I got home, Nancy says, "Well, how'd yer like Mr. Turner?"

"We-ell," I says, "he was kinda s'prisin' in some ways."

Right then I see Nancy was eyin' my clothes, which was wrinkled. Anybudy c'ud see that I'd been in the water all over. An' Nancy knew it hadn't rained none.

"I sh'ud say that he was surprising," she says. "Can't you go fishin' without fallin' in?"

"I c'ud, but—"

"I know all erbout it, Dudley Dean," she snaps out. "You poor spineless thing."

Crotch, I thought I was in a box, if she knew all erbout it.

"Well, Ma," I begins, but she w'udn't let me finish.

"How much did he pay you?

"Who?" I says, kinda blank like.

"Who w'ud I mean, but this man, B. N. Turner?"

"Oh," I says, "twenty dollars."

We-ell, that kinda salved Nancy.

"That," she admits, "is good pay for two days, if only you had backbone e-nough to leave liquor alone."

That smarted me some becuz I ain't never messed 'round with booze, but if she wanted to think that I'd fallen into the river in that way, I decided it was all right.

Maybe ye're wonderin' if Nancy ever did find out the difference. We-ell . . . you know Nancy.

Zoromaster Sayeth

The great problem in producing an anthology lies in the leaving out. This is especially true when there exists so much that deserves inclusion. The compiler is confronted constantly with the question: why this and not that?

"Zoromaster Sayeth" does not have the rollicking punch of many Dud Dean stories, but it enunciates a belief and a way of life that increasingly gave (and gives) substance to the Dud Dean stories. While the title is more than reminiscent of the Persian wiseman Zarathustra, the story concerns the questionable values of cults, creeds, packaged wisdom, and "psychic vibrations" in general. It enters the valley of the shadow where even doctors die, and it emerges beyond and in communion with the fundamental—and with courage.

This yarn appears in the last Dud Dean book, Dud Dean and the Enchanted, *published in 1954.*

DUD DEAN AND I WERE TALKING—or perhaps I had been expounding my conviction that there is prospective and therefore healing in the wilderness.

"We-ell, I think that ye're right in the main," said Dud, "but jist the same, I've known of folks to die of consumption who never worked anywhere than in the woods. What's more, I've known of folks to come down 'ith ulcers of the stomach from camp cooking. Howsoever, I've taken notice that a man can straighten out what's gone crooked, if he's willin' to git down to brass tacks.

"It all makes me think of my old friend, Ruel Cates. When Ruel was a little mite of a feller, the Cateses had a family reunion. The house was full of grown-up talkin' folks. Ruel was thar, but no one paid attention to him. He kept tryin' to tell erbout sunthin' wonderful, but each time he begun, some older person w'ud ignore him an' start talking. So he waited an' waited for a chance. Bine-by, thar was a lull, an' Ruel piped up in high, shrill, boyish voice: 'Pa planted some cu-cumpickles. An' he took a bottle, an' he put a little cu-cumpickle inside. An' it grew and grew, till it busted the damned thing.'

"I mean, thar's one of our troubles. We git our mind sot on one thing, fixed on it, an' it grows an' grows till it busts us.

"I've heard that we only use a small part of our brains, an' that seems probable. Mind and health is related. Good sense and brass tacks can do a lot for a man, when his mind threatens to git in a rut. I s'pose that ye've heard of Lyman Ford. Mat Markham guided him some. An' so did I at odd times. He was born in high gear. He was always jumpin' inter the collar. He made a lot of money by spreadin' hisself like a green bay tree. So he warn't uncommon smart, as I sized him up, but he was bound to work twice as hard and twice as long every day and inter the night. Sech folks hain't as common as lazy folks, but they're by no means uncommon.

"When Lyman took to trout fishing, he done it becuz it was done among his associates in business. An' Lyman went at his fishin' hell-bent-fer-election, same's he went at everythin' else. He acted like he had to do it er it w'udn't git done.

"I met him the fust time at Moxie Lake. The next time, he was at Pierce Pond. That time, he was in better comp'ny—like Doctor Wade, fer one. I often saw him in the years that intervened, as the old maid said, but the last time he come up to Bingham in a limousine full of blankets, hot-water-bottles, an' smellin' salts. It made my heart give a hitch an' a skip to see that one time up-and-git-at-it feller all huddled up an' caved in.

"But in a way, Doc Wade had warned me, although his letter was what Nancy called cryptic, which I reckon means short fer short. As I read it, the letter only said that Lyman warn't up to his old self. The fires was banked, steam low, er sunthin' like that. The plain part of it was that Doc Wade wanted me to help Lyman git a grip on hisself—however that was to be done. 'What he needs most,' the letter said, 'is to catch up with his fishing.'

"I was to meet Lyman at the post office at two forty-five P.M., the next Thursday. I smiled when I read that. Lyman had always lived that way. If he said quarter to three, he'd bust to make it at two forty-five. An' sure e-nough thar he was—only they had parked in front of Ervin Moore's drugstore. An' as I've indicated, Lyman was a sick man. The poor cuss looked like sunthin' moth an' rust had corrupted.

"'Well,' he says, 'don't stand there and gape forever. You see what's left of me. And if you're wondering why I am here, it's because of that ass of a Dr. Wade. He thinks that it should do me good to go trout fishing. It never did. Why should it now?'

"Crotch, to make it worse, Lyman had developed one of

them slow, sad smiles. Havin' proved it, he went on erbout Doc Wade. 'I have pointed out to Dr. Wade that the heart specialist, whom we have consulted, said that any exposure would kill me. And what did Dr. Wade say? He said, "Maine is a better place to die in than Chicago."'

"I was a mite nettled erbout the way he referred to Dr. Wade. An' I told him straight that I'd as soon listen to Doc Wade as any specialist that ever lived."

"'Huh! Huh!' says Lyman. An' then he sank back in his pillows an' blankets. Then in a woeful tone, he says, 'We shall wait for Mrs. Ford. She is in that drugstore.'

"I thought maybe I sh'ud go inside to meet the lady since I had never laid eyes on her. We-ell, yer know how it is. Yer guess what a person looks like, but most generally they don't. That time, I was right. She did. I mean that she had a sad, sweet face, like an old-fashioned pansy pressed in a copy of *The Best Loved Poems*.

"I told her who I was.

"'How do you do?' she says. But she didn't wait to find out. Jist blew off into a zephyr of words.

"'First,' she says to me, 'I want you to read Dr. Alexander Infinitude's letter of instructions, which he so kindly prepared, when I failed to persuade Lyman to remain in Chicago. I presume that you have noticed the grave condition of Lyman's health?'

"To save time, I did not answer. The specialist's 'instructions' were marked 1, 2, 3, 4, and so on to 49. It was full of words like caution, precautions, care, careful, exposure, an' so on. A good many para-graphs be-gun with 'By no means.' Fer example, 'By no means per-mit the patient to cast a fly in the usual manner.' And, 'By no means submit the patient to any intense emotional stimuli whatsoever.'

"'Madam,' says I, 'Lyman always was erbout as excitable as a cucumber in an icebox, but jist suppose he sh'ud hook on a really big trout that was bound to go all the ways to Sunday. W'ud a heart like his stand sech a strain?'

"The lady's smile was sad to behold when she replied, 'I don't perceive why anyone should become excited about a trout, big or otherwise, but we must avoid all risks. And for that reason, we must employ a guide who can be relied upon.'

"'How d'yer mean?' I says. 'Fer instance, what do yer mean?'

"'Why, if catching fish is violent exertion, then it is your duty to avoid fish. If you know where there are fish, you should also know where there are no fish.'

"'Yer mean that we're to play tiddlywinks er sun-thing?'

"'No. Lyman would not play tiddlywinks. On the other hand, he may insist upon fishing because Dr. Wade has suggested fishing—most unwisely, we think. But we must avoid excitement or undue exertion. You must see to it that Lyman does not catch fish.'

"The way she kept saying fish bothered me. 'Mad-am,' I says, 'up here they ain't fish becuz they're *trout*. An' I am sorry to tell yer that I am the last guide in all creation that yer w'ud want to hire. All my life I've been takin' folks where they c'ud catch trout, an' skippin' places where they warn't apt to catch trout. Besides, I'm excitable myself. I enjoy gittin' excited more than anythin' else in the world. Yer c'udn't trust me fer one min-it. Besides, I am not, never was, an' don't want to be a wet nurse.'

"Danged if she didn't shake her head an' smile at me slow an' sad. Says she, 'You are not that sort of a man at all. Even Dr. Wade described you as calm, controlled, and moderate in all things. Furthermore, that is the way you vibrate. I am particularly sensitive to vibrations. And, furthermore, Lyman is depending on you. He is not the demonstrative kind, but Lyman has his own appreciations of men and friendship.'

"We-ell, dang her little hide. She warn't so dull. Jist when I had cleared myself, she worked in that touch. An' I knew it. But danged if I warn't softened jist the same. I did feel bad erbout Lyman.

"She was still buyin' things when I went out. Lyman opened up his eyes. 'Well,' he said, 'are you going with us?' Blamed if I didn't say I was. So Lyman reached out a hand that was blue veined an' too weak to shake anythin' but an angel's wing.

"Of course the water we was goin' to fish had to jibe with Mrs. Ford's stipulations. Also, she wanted hot an' cold water. Water is a real simple element. An' I know where thar's plenty of cold water. Hot water is sunthin' else—I mean, where the fishin' is good. After figgering, I decided Attean Pond w'ud be the place. We c'ud drive to the shore of it, step inter a boat, an' git out of the boat inter a bedroom. Once we got thar, we c'ud boat eround from Moose River to Big Wood Pond.

"So off we goes with Nancy's blessing. 'Remember, Dudley,' she says, 'that you are to be a missionary, sort of.' Then she talked more'n that. Between Mrs. Ford's vibrations and Nancy's prohibitions, I was in a purty pickle. Off we goes, headed fer Jackman an' Attean Pond. All the way, up hill an' down, Mrs. Ford talked. I got the complete hist'ry of Lyman's case from murmurin' spark plugs to angina pee-tick-lus. She said that it had all come erbout becuz Lyman was too ambitious for gain and power.

"Lyman did rouse up long enough to protest. He said that hard work never killed a man, but thar warn't no punch in his speech—no more than thar is in a quotation. An' speakin' of quotation, that was Mrs. Ford's worst habit. She turned loose sunthin' from a feller she called Zoromaster at every turn in the conversation. Zoromaster sayeth, 'Human ambitions are lamentable follies, and man is his own taskmaster.'

"She asked me if I was familiar with the wisdom of Zoromaster, but after that fer a sample, I didn't mind admittin' that I warn't.

"'Zoromaster sayeth, "The ambitions of men are nonsense to the stars, and the body hath no more need of vestment than vestment hath need of the body."'

"It occurred to me that if this Zoromaster had waded eround in a January snowdrift, he might have changed his idea on vestment. Crotch, in real good winter weather even the vestment needs a body to keep it warm. I've seen long-legged underwear hung out in February that was frozen so stiff yer c'udn't help pityin' it.

"We-ell, I hired that boat of the Holdens which is almost as big as a steamboat. I took my own canoe aboard with the idea Lyman an' me might want to go fishing, but I hadn't taken inter account how far gone he was. Best he c'ud do was to troll off the end of the big boat, which he must have known was foolish-hopeless.

"Even in the old days, Lyman never impressed me as bein' much of a fly fisherman. It was only a routine 'ith him. Anyhow, we trolled with the assistance of Zoromaster. That was jist as much fun as playin' ringeround-the-rosey. Crotch, the prospect stretched ahead until life disappeared into nothingness, as Zoromaster w'ud have said, an' prob'ly did.

"One thing that irritated me, as much as anything, was that condemned chauffeur, whose name was Tony sunthin' er other. I never met a mortal who c'ud give up carin' a dang erbout anythin' so easy as he did. The young saphead had been completely lost since the day they left Chicago, an' he had no more idea where he was at Attean than a south sea island cannibal w'ud have had. If I c'ud have talked with him it w'udn't have been so danged melancholy.

"When I'd watched Lyman a while, I seen that it was a fact the life had gone out of him. The way I studied it out, it never had occurred to him that Lyman Ford w'ud ever be sick. Not him! Now that he was, more er less, he was ready to lay down like a goat and die. No fight. Jist uncomprehending dismay. The only real positive move I saw him make durin' the fust day was to duck a little when a gull flew over the boat. Incidently, that gull was the only livin' thing that Tony the chauffeur recognized all the time we was at Attean. 'A gull!' he says. 'Well what d'yer know! A gull!'

"Fer the rest of it, Mrs. Ford talked. After a while, I got to feelin' awful strange. I c'udn't tell to save me whether we was fishin' er jist floatin' eround in a suspended state of Zoromasterianism. Talk erbout gittin' excited! How I wished that I c'ud. Mrs. Ford was the life of the party, accordin' to her lights, an' I seen that she was gently de-termined to be.

"That Zoromaster had said sunthin' unpleasant fer every occasion. 'Zoromaster sayeth, "No man can ever possess so little as an atom of this world. We but journey from daylight to dark, and in the end we pitch our tents beyond the edge of our knowledge."'

"Lyman did wake up a little when she quoted that. 'That reminds me,' he said. 'Does anyone know what's happened to the stock market?' But his wife came back with, 'Better to be anxious about the morrow than to fret thyself about to-day, for do not all our days add up to the morrow?'

"It was no wonder to me, after that, when Lyman began to discuss cremation versus lettin' nature take its course. It was so durn cheerful all day long that I mentioned the fact to Tony when we went back to camp.

"'I sh'ud worry,' he says, 'so long as they pay me good, and I eat good, even if this place is so back in the sticks that it stinks like it was brand new. Say, do you believe that thar's bears up in these mountains?'

"'Thar's b'ars in any mountain,' I says. 'How much does Lyman pay yer?'

"'That's my business,' he says. 'But them bears ain't dangerous—would you say?'

"'That's the b'ar's business,' I says. And I left him lookin' off across the lake to the mountains. I was lonely fer some human comp'ny. The way I felt an' the way everythin' looked didn't jibe. The July sun was setting, an' it looked like an army of gypsies on the march, leading yeller wagons an' red hosses all across the sky!

"Then who sh'ud I come across but Mrs. Ford on her way to supper. 'It's mighty purty in the west,' I says to her.

"She spread on one of them sweet, sad smiles. 'Zoromaster sayeth, "In nature man has no abode. While nature is in travail to produce a greener grasshopper, man must pray his way to a higher destiny."'

"Then she sighed. An' I sighed.

Gol durn it all, that Zoromaster made me sad. I don't know how

I c'ud be so de-pressed, but I was. Afore I went to bed that night, I sot down an' wrote Nancy a letter—tellin' her how it had always seemed to me a good old-fashioned custom to bury a man facin' the east, even if he didn't know it.

"So when I got up, afore daylight the next morning, I felt jist the same way—like a porcupine at the tip-top of a hackmatack at the end of a day in January, forty below, an' the wind blowin' like the devil was in it. Of course, Lyman didn't git up until dinner time, so I had that time on my hands. After I et, I borrowed an outboard motor an' a boat to go with it, an' I headed straight for the mouth of Moose River and Attean Rips. I got thar before real sunup.

"That's the time your streamer comes in handy, Mak—the one made of white bucktail and lime green, silver body, red throat, an' red tail. In ten min-its, I had turned loose a three-pound trout. What fun! I got rid of Zoromaster, condemn him. In another ten min-its I had a fat four-pounder. Crotch, I felt real good!

"When I got back to camp, several normal fellers came out to admire my trout. Then I met Tony. He asked me what kind of a fish that was. So I told him that it was a *Salvelinus fontinalis*. An' he said 'Who do you think yer kiddin'?'

"Then I got dinner packed an' ready, so we c'ud eat out if Lyman felt like it. I took special pains to pick out some prime steaks an' all that. When Lyman appeared, he was all wrapped up but shiverin' chilly. We boarded the big boat. When we had gone erbout half a mile, he broke the silence. 'I remember,' he says, an' stopped. Jist like that. He c'udn't remember what he had remembered. I knew well enough that he had been goin' to say he remembered a mornin' like that at Moosehead, er Spencer, er

Pierce Pond. Judus Priest, it was a sorry thing to watch him.

"Then we trolled. What a way to spend a day. The Lord fergive us! At noon, we put ashore on one of them purty little islands in Attean, an' et our dinner. Then we got back in the boat to cruise all the afternoon. Nothin' happened except two er three little half-pound trout, an' what Zoromaster sayeth. Except, of course, Lyman had to drink some hot milk now an' then.

"'Bout five o'clock Mrs. Ford smiled an' said, 'Slowly the plowman ploddeth down the lea, and leaves the world to darkness and to me.' That was some better than Zoromaster, an' I begun to wonder if things was goin' to improve.

"'That reminds me,' said Lyman, 'that I heard someone in the dining room say you caught a nice trout this morning.'

"'That is right,' says I. 'A real purty feller, too.'

"Lyman nodded. Then he said, 'We are not going to camp for supper tonight. You and Tony can get a lunch later. I want to be out here when the night comes on.'

"Mrs. Ford looked troubled, but if her Zoromaster ever said anythin' that fitted sech a turn of events she kept it to herself. Anyhow, of course that's how we happened to be out until the mayflies begun to hatch. Crotch, it was nice to watch them gray an' yeller flies fumble up from the mud, lay still a moment, an' then flutter off—only some of them didn't becuz the trout begun to smash at them.

"Who has got the words to describe a hatch of mayflies in a trout pond! It's a queer experience. All at once the nature of things takes wing. It's a mystery. It's all of life manifest in the hatch.

"The little thrushes was singin', and away up Moose River,

jist this side of out-a-hearing, an owl called *t'whoo, t'whoo.* Tony shivered. The poor cuss didn't know what it was.

"And while we watched, a bigger trout began to feed among the hungry little fellers. 'That trout,' says Lyman, 'reminds me of one I caught at Pierce Pond years ago.' Crotch, it done me good to hear him say it!

"Mrs. Ford ventured, 'Zoromaster sayeth, "Though man must make his bed in the house of uncertainty, let him say to his soul, I have another destiny."'

"Crotch! What did that have to do with a hatch of mayflies?

"'In the old days,' says Lyman, 'I would try a dry fly—something big and yellow, or grayish. We caught nice trout, and salmon too, in Lindsley Cove and down around Gull Rock . . . in the old days.'

"Zoromaster was stumped.

"All the time, Lyman had fergotten the Warden's Worry on the end of his line. Of course it had sunk to the bottom while we idled, a-watchin' the mayflies hatch. Bine-by, I s'pose, he must have given it a hitch. Anyhow, thar was a mighty thrashin' at it. Lyman made a grab at his rod butt, an' thar was a queer look on his face, but he didn't say anything. Prob'ly Mrs. Ford an' Tony never noticed.

"It was gittin' later. The water over under the mountain was black. The thrushes sounded sleepy. The owl got an answer, a ways off. Then a Sphinx moth came blunderin' over the boat. It flew so close to Tony that it scared him, so he swung at it. Off it goes, staggerin' and losing altitude until it was real low over the water. *Woosh!* goes a big trout.

"Do yer remember how yer felt at school, when all of a sudden the ball game swung your way, an' it was your turn at the bat? Gosh almighty, I was excited. And the fust fly I laid hold of was no fly at all, but one of them bass bugs with buck hair fer wings that was two inches an' a half long. The head was red, the body black, but the wings an' tail was yeller all over. Sun-thin' said to me, put it on! An' I did.

"'Don't git excited,' I says to Lyman. 'Jist drop it overboard an' let it drift.'

"Mrs. Ford stood up, full of alarm. 'You mustn't use your arm, Lyman dear. Dr. Alexan—'

"Twarn't much of a cast. But up comes that trout. Beautiful! All alive, savage, an' hungry as Nebuchadrezzar. That trout an' that bass bug landed a yard away from the rise.

"Mrs. Ford grabbed my arm, 'Take the pole! Take it away from him. This will be his death.'

"I looked at Lyman, an' his face looked blue, but I knew that it sartinly w'ud be the death of him if I took that rod away from him. And so far as I'm concerned, I'd rather die playin' a big trout than huggin' a hot water bottle. So I didn't admit that I was worried.

"That trout ripped off eighty yards of line. Lyman was sweatin'. It dripped off his nose an' chin. 'Take it easy,' I says.

"'Shut up!' he says.

"Mrs. Ford was weeping. Tony jist smoked cigarettes.

"Lyman reeled in a lot of line, and then he lost it all to the trout. The dang thing went down the contours. It had weight. And it used it. It tried to rush under the boat. That's when I noticed that we had drifted ag'inst one of them little islands. The bushes was within easy reach. Sunthin' went *woosh!* Tony jumped up, white as a lily of the field, an' he fell overboard, or he jumped. I didn't have time to tell which. Instead, I grabbed a pickpole and shoved us off the shore.

"And jist then Lyman says in a weak voice, 'The net.' I laid hold of the long-handled net an' stretched fer Lyman's trout, but c'udn't reach him. W'udn't have done any good becuz that trout went off like a muzzle-loadin' gun.

"Now it was dark, only yer c'ud see a little near the water. And it begun to rain; plunkin' on the dead calm of the water. I found a flashlight in my packbasket. Lyman worked that trout in ag'in. That time, I netted him. Dang it all, that was a handsome trout! Lyman an' me looked at it—glistenin' wet an' as purty as a flower garden—dang it, purtier!

"Lyman said, 'That trout is a dead ringer for one Dr. Wade caught in Grass Pond ten years ago. Who suggested trolling? Dud, you must have known better.'

"Where in crotch was Zoromaster? I looked eround. An' thar she was, right where she had crumbled down in a dead faint. Blazes, it took a turn out of me. An' I ran to the thermos jug fer some cold water. When I got back, Lyman had pushed her head down lower, an' she was comin' eround. In a min-it more, thar was that sweet, sad smile ag'in.

"Lyman says to her, 'Where's that blockhead of a chauffeur?'

"That was right e-nough. Where was the cuss? I shouted. An' back comes his voice from the other side of the island. An' do yer think we c'ud git him back? No.

When that little deer blew at us, just as the boat went ashore, Tony'd jumped out running—an' he hadn't stopped until he come to the water on the other side. So the durned idgit c'udn't find his way back ag'in. All the answer I c'ud git out of him was, 'Bears!'

"I told him to stay right where he was, if he valued his life, and I got the motor going an' we run eround the island, an' I pushed her in so he c'ud git aboard. Crotch, he'd aged.

"'Now I know what has made me ill,' says Lyman. 'Now I know. I've been afraid.'"

Dud filled his pipe.

I said, "Dr. Wade must have been pleased."

"Do you know," said Dud, "I intended to ask Doc how in creation Lyman ever got inter sech condition, but that next winter Doc died. Dropped dead in his own office."

Dud Dean and the Enchanted

This story appeared in the last Dud Dean collection, Dud Dean and the Enchanted, *published in 1954. The reader will quickly realize that this story does not have the artistry nor the lively pace we antici-pate in the beginning of a Dud Dean yarn. Still, it deserves not only inclusion in this anthology but the honor of being last. The piece is, in its way, a benediction. Here, spoken unashamedly, is what all the Dud Dean stories have been telling us. No matter how our lives may stum-ble we touch now and again what is truly real—the enchanted, which is not so much magically as mystically beautiful. Such momentary experiences may come anywhere, but no place so frequently as in the unspoiled out-of-doors. In this story, is a tender recollection of the old master guide who, in his later years, has embraced that spiritual sig-nificance for which we humans cast.*

It is interesting and perhaps notable that this is the only Dud Dean tale in which the "telling voice" is that of a woman.

Mak meets a lady in what he terms "modern Babylon" (New York), who inquires where she may find a guide who can cook, make a bough bed, and knows where to find trout and that rarest of Maine orchids, the white lady's slipper. As it turns out, the trout and the lady's slippers are but part of the agenda. The trip is to be a honeymoon and a quest. The lady and the man she is about to marry have "a hunger . . . to keep a tryst where . . . [the] triumph of the ancient earth survives."

Mak, of course, thinks of Dud Dean. Dud is retired, but he takes a party now and then when it suits him. Five weeks later Mak receives a letter from Mrs. Pendmaster (Pend) Davis reporting on their adventure.

DEAR MR. MACDOUGALL,

I am happy! Your friend was the most delightful and entrancing man! To that, we both agree. Pend and I have reviewed our honeymoon and the endless little delights that Dud contrived for us. We have them like a rosary to tell over and over, and I am not irreverent.

First thing. Dud asked us, "Which is most important—the lady's slippers er trout?"

I said trout because I knew how dearly Pend loves to fish for trout. And he has caught them in England, Scotland, and in the Pyrenees, as well as almost everywhere in North America.

But Pend said, "The lady's slippers. There is absolutely no question about that."

Honestly, I think that your old friend was pleased. But he almost insisted on giving us physical examinations. How careful and wise he is! When at last we convinced him that we really wanted to go afoot into a remote corner of the wilderness, and that I was prepared to undergo the torments of the blackfly and what else, he said:

"C'ud you even stand bein' lost? Reason I ask is that I've got a sartin place in mind which I hain't seen fer fifty years. Since then, thar's been a big fire in thar, an' since the fire it's been logged over.

So I might have to poke eround afore we got thar. But I am mortally sure that we can find your white moccasins, an' find them no end. And thar's bound to be some trout to catch. But to git thar, we'd have to go to Big Enchanted Pond, cross it, and then climb up inter Bulldog Mountain."

Enchanted! Did anyone ever have a honeymoon in a more fittingly named place? Of course we were enthusiastic. Pend said, "I have been lost with men in whom I had less confidence. And, by gosh, I managed to enjoy it. As for our lady, she has already risked more than that. Lead on, MacDuff."

Then the men bought our supplies. And your Mr. Dean loaned Pend one of his huge packbaskets. They carried fifty pounds each. All because Pend was determined that a honeymoon would be spoiled unless there was plenty to eat.

I do not believe that Dud Dean was even puzzled about where he was or where to go ahead. I know that Pend did not worry for a moment. He said to me, "This man is the genuine old guide. We need not fret." And yet, Dud had not gone that way for fifty years. Think of it, a lifetime!

We walked from the road that goes to Spencer Lake. What a breathless beauty there is in all that country! The Upper Enchanted! Verily. Dud told us about the terrible forest fire of 1895—the very year Pend was born. Dud showed us huge pine trunks that still lie where they fell after that fire. Pend cut into one with his ax. It was still sound under the outer gray shell. And Dud called to our attention the marine rock at the height of land—as one goes down to Enchanted Pond. That man is a matchless entertainer, because his own interests are so varied.

Dud told us about the legend that Enchanted Pond is bottomless beneath its deepest water. He pointed out the place at the lower end where some old lumberman had built a dam between those magnificent granite mountains.

And Pend caught three gloriously colored trout in that blue water, while Dud rowed us to the Bulldog Mountain shore. By the way, Pend did not keep those trout. I have had so much to learn about men and fishermen in these few weeks—things I might have learned years ago, if Pend had come into the store for a copy of your book years ago instead of a few months ago. *Dud Dean And His Country*! We'll never forget that man or his country—not ever.

The mountain was steep. Did you know that once there was a profile of a bulldog on the east end, until it slid off and away during a springtime deluge? What a savage name, Bulldog! Must there be a bulldog in the Enchanted Country? No. The Enchanted is rid of that. I am glad it is gone. But there is a great raw scar where the profile was.

Now we come to our weather. That old joke about the Maine man who said to the tourist who had complained about the weather, "What kind of weather do yer want? We've got all kinds," is no whimsy. There never was a lovelier day than when we started up the mountain. The sky was as blue as the ribbon that Alice wore into Wonderland. Then, as if by magic, the cumulus clouds grew forebodingly dark. It was as if the demons were angry because we had invaded their mountain. And how it rained!

Dud explained, with that solemn face he puts on, that it does not rain cats and dogs in the Enchanted—not even bulldogs. Instead, according to Dud, it rains rain, although sometimes it rains lady's slippers—white fer when she gets up in the morning, gold fer when she eats her dinner (at noon, of course) and pink fer when she goes to dance across the sunset. And then he added that he had known it to rain trout in the Enchanted, but that kind, he said, hardly ever take a fly, unless a fellow has the Pink Lady.

"I have a Pink Lady," said Pend. And I guess that I was, after such an interpolation!

Dud pretended not to comprehend the implication. He said, "Then I guess, maybe, yer c'ud git some trout if yer sh'ud try real hard. But yer know, thar was once a tribe of Indians that lived up an' down the Kennebec. And among them was a girl so purty that they called her 'Flower-of-the-Rising-Sun.' Of course, all the young fellers loved her. One of them was a big, tall chap who went by the name of Moxie, an' he courted her morning, noon, an' almost all night. So they were wed. Then the young man made a terrible mistake. Took his young wife with him when he went into the Enchanted to fish fer trout. Fer a little time they was happy an' contented until early one morning, when Moxie woke up. He looked fer his wife. She had left his side. He hurried outside the wigwam, and thar he saw her walkin' over the lake, where the risin' sun made a path.

"Moxie called to her, but she did not hear him. He ran to the lake and went after her in his birch canoe. No use. She jist went away, up the mountain, an' thar she vanished out of mortal sight. Poor Moxie! Not even a yeller leaf was turned upside down. Not even a twig had been rolled on its side. An' he never found her.

So after a while he left the Enchanted; wandered off, down country, an' where Moxie Mountain is he died of a broken heart.

Yer can see him any clear day, with his great shoulders an' chest heaved up ag'inst the sky.

"But what the Enchanted did with Flower-of-the-Rising-Sun, no man knows. Yer see, it ain't safe in here, but the trout don't know it. As fer fishermen, what do they know but trout?"

Of course, your old friend was talking to help us forget the drenching rain. Once he turned to look at us, and asked, "W'udn't you rather go back to the camps on the big lake? They're nice an comfortable. We c'ud sleep dry, an' then come up here tomorrow."

Pend looked to me. And I said, "No."

"Ye're sure?"

I was. But I was weary and very, very wet. At noontime we stopped at a little spring. And there Dud and Pend cooked our dinner. The rain continued. And once more Dud asked me, "Don't yer want to go back to the camps?"

I am so glad that I refused to turn back. So glad! When we went on, Dud said, "Mind now that I'm goin' it purty blind. Maybe I can't find that pond tonight. It's a small mark in this big country. And maybe it ain't thar anymore, like Flower-of-the-Rising-Sun. Queer things happen up here, an' ordinary things happen queerly. Even the trout, in this pond I'm lookin' fer, is strange. Some folks declare that thar ain't a trout in it to go over half a pound. An' some persons have fished in here to go back home vowin' that thar's no trout at all. And a few folks whisper erbout tremendous trout that haunt the place."

Pend asked, "But what do you say?"

"I say that it strikes me as odd that when I come in here fifty years ago, the weather was jist like it is this very afternoon. We was young fellers, Mat Markham an me. Thar was mighty heavy timber up here on the mountain. Take that an' the rainstorm, an' the light was dim. After a while, we both figgered that we was good an' lost. So we started settin' a line yer know, pickin' out a tree straight ahead of us, goin' to that, an' then pickin' another. Mat was kinda superstitious. He still is. I 'member that he said, 'If I ever git out of this god forsaken place, I'll never set foot on it ag'in.' And b'crotch, he was as good as his word, becuz he's never been in here since that time. I've always wanted to come in here, but until now this an' that has lured me elsewhere.

"When Mat an' me had gone over the divide, an' started down, the rain kinda piddled—good deal as it's doin' now. Mat kept on moaning, but I didn't pay much attention of course. All of a sud-den, I seen a big round raft of fog, like an old circus tent, but kinda moving, writhing, an' rolling. I scootched down so's I c'ud see under the fog, an' then I seen the pond, level, an' lookin' like an old kitchen floor that has been scoured with sand an' mopped an' mopped fer a hundred years by generations of peeticular women.

"'Look,' I says to Mat, who was still grumblin' erbout the rain an' foolish fools like us. 'Look,' I says. An' then I p'inted like this."

Mr. Macdougall, your Dud is a magician. When Pend and I looked where Dud had pointed, just as he had pointed for his friend fifty years ago, we saw a pond, or part of a pond. And there was a cloud of fog lying over it, like a circus tent!

"Great guns, man," exclaimed Pend. "You have an instinct for the abrupt. Is that the pond you were looking to find?"

"Don't know yit. Maybe. Anyhow, it's a pond. Or will it fold up in that cloud an' vanish away?"

Pend said, "We will soon find out!"

So he ran down to the shore of the pond, where he splashed his right hand in the water. "It's real," he said, while laughing back at us.

"C'ud be," said Dud.

But what a ghost of a pond it was, under that weird raft of mountain fog. It was gray and lonely. And for a moment, no more, I wished that I were back on Madison Avenue. And then I remembered how unearthly the skyscrapers look in fog and storm. One sees a few lower stories, but the rest are swallowed up, as if the building were immaterial or upside down in a vague, formless sea.

"Fust," said Dud, "good sense makes camp. Let's see . . . Ayah, over this way thar's a spring, er thar was fifty years ago."

We followed Dud.

"Here," he said. And I saw the sweetest little spring that came as by kindly magic from under a mound of soft moss. "And thar," said Dud. And I saw a single plant of *Cypripedium acaule* with ten blossoms on the one plant.

Dud smiled at me. "Ye'll have to excuse us becuz they're only pink ones. An' I don't mind if yer laugh at me when I tell yer that they was here fifty years ago."

Pend had brought that tent with the wonderfully light but water-proof material floor and all. And he and Dud were only a few moments setting it up.

"There is plenty of room for the three of us," I said.

Dud Dean laughed at me. "If yer don't mind," he said, "I will put up my own shelter—half where Mat an' me built us a lean-to so long ago. Now, when we're all shipshape, why not cook up sunthin' until it's real hot. I'll go explore to see if them cedars still grow near the south shore, where Mat an' me made our raft. Say, do yer know this is the most fun I've had since the day Mat fell inter a springhole on the shore of Middle Carry Pond? We was hedgehoggin' erlong the shore, lookin' fer a boat that had come up missing, as Mont Spinney said when his wife run off with the butter money. The shore, yer see, looked all firm an' trustworthy, but when Mat stepped in that place he jist went out of sight inter a deep springhole. An' the poor feller was so cold when he wallowed out that he kept saying, 'Colder'n hell, colder'n hell,' till Mak give him a lecture fer what he called apostasy.

"'What d'yer mean by that?' says Mat.

"'I mean that hell is not cold,' says Mak."

Pend and I began to unpack. And in a few moments, we heard Dud's ax. He had found the cedars. Pend explained to me that cedar was a light wood, and that it made a buoyant raft.

When Dud came back, he was poling a large raft. And he had a bundle of dry kindling wood tied and fastened on his shoulders. The fire was quickly kindled, and I am sure that mortals never ate more delicious food than our hot biscuits and beef stew. We went to bed and slept like small children—children in the Enchanted Country!

Dud awakened us. And I smelled bacon and coffee. "I figgered," he said, "that it w'ud be all right to wake yer up becuz the weather has improved Besides, the trout are puddlin' out front."

Did you ever try to dress in a sleeping-bag? There are difficulties. Dud called again. "I wish that ye'd hurry. Thar's an old she otter and her kits out in the pond. It's int'restin' to watch 'em cut up."

I just wrapped a blanket around me and went out. What a

handsomely graceful creature an otter is. There were four of them, diving, rising, and chasing each other in the water. How could one ever forget that strong, swift gracefulness!

At the farther end of the pond (it was shaped like a football) the trout continued to rise. "Puddling" Dud called it, "becuz they're only takin' nymphs near the surface."

Otters, trout, nymphs, and the earliest and most beautiful daylight in the Enchanted!

Of course, breakfast was delicious. "Coffee," said Dud, "must be part good spring water—none of your chemically diluted, polluted stuff that is as vile as bog-water! But, as Mat says, 'To make good coffee, fust take some coffee, put it in a coffee-pot full of b'ilin' water, an' then let it be so long as it takes to whistle, *Comin' Through the Rye.*'"

Pend and I decided to christen the pond "Ghost Lake." And then we embarked on Dud's raft. Of course I should have died if they had made me stay ashore, although I offered to do so, nevertheless. But the men insisted that I should go. Pend fished with flies. And I was so proud to observe that Dud Dean approved of Pend's skill.

It was all so beautifully done. The dry flies appeared to be so small and fragile—number twelves and fourteens, I think. Pend cast into the circles made by the feeding trout. Those vividly colored fish rose with astonishing savageness. And when hooked, they fought with all the grace of the otters.

When one went free, Pend would say, "Bully for you, mister." Then Dud Dean would chuckle. I counted all the fish that Dud actually netted to remove the flies. There were forty of them—

"none under half a pound, an' some of 'em almost big e-nough to scare a hot-house trout to death."

They saved one, an unimaginably beautiful thing. "Plenty fer three of us," said Dud. "An' now, let's go find the lady's slippers, if yer really meant what yer said."

The sun had risen. The pond was a strange pale green and warm with a golden light when we left the camp. It was amusing to me to witness Dud's apologetic way when the first lady's slippers that he found were a great bed of *Cypripedium calceolus pubescens*, the big yellow moccasin. "Y'know," he said, "I had fergotten all erbout them yeller slippers. Yer don't see 'em very often."

As a matter of fact, I had never seen them growing in the wild way. The large bed was mixed with ferns. The blossoms were like pure gold in that damp, dark setting of forest shadows. And there were so many of them! So amazingly abundant in that lavish place that I could not believe my eyes.

But all that was only to prepare us for the white slippers around the little lost bog, where like figments of utter beauty the enchanted white moccasins grew. When your rawboned old friend pushed a screen of ferns aside to show us the first patch, I loved him—that greatly simple man.

"Here they are," he said. "And to me, it seems as though I had only left them here a few hours ago. But it was fifty years ago. Ask Mat Markham." Then I detected an anxiety in his voice. "I s'pose that ye'll want to pick some?"

"Just one," I said.

I thought for a moment that he was going to hug me. "Glory be!" he said. "I reckon that the Indian girl c'ud spare yer more than that."

Pend and I took color photographs, as we had of the yellow moccasins. We have shown the slides to our friends. The question we always expect never fails to be asked:

"Where are they?" And I do not need to pretend vagueness to protect the stand, because I only know that they are somewhere on the other side of a mountain—somewhere in the Enchanted.

"B'fore we go back to camp," said Dud Dean, "I'd be pleased to have the lady try my little flyrod down here off the old beaver dam at the foot of this little bog. The trout in thar are little fellers, but the Lord has dressed 'em up real purty."

That was my first lesson in fly fishing. And the fly was a Red Ibis. I loved fly fishing in spite of the black-flies that beset us. Dud Dean was patient and cheerful when I tangled the line in cedars that grew too near the water. What fun it was to catch those handsome little trout.

And that was how our week began! We fell in love with your friend. He is a great soul and a charming gentleman. He is a mystic, but his big hands were made to hold an ax. He is a big, rawboned, weather-beaten man, but he can remember where he saw white lady's slippers growing fifty years ago.

Our days in that Enchanted Country were too swift, as I suppose days are sure to be when one is altogether happy and content. The last night was clear and lighted by a full moon. And is there a place on earth where the moonlight falls so magically as near a mountain top? Dud came to us where we sat looking out on the little lake. And he said, "If the idea sh'ud appeal to you folks, I w'ud like to show yer sunthin' strange and beautiful."

A pleasant sense of excitement filled me. Pend whispered to

me, "I have an intuition that we shall never forget this, whatever he has in mind."

We followed Dud along the west shore of the pond—no flashlights, because Dud said, "They'd be handy, but I w'udn't dare."

He led us to the strangest thing—an old dead pine (very ancient) that seemed to be fast in the soft soil of the shore, but lying its full length out in the pond.

"It's always been here," he said. "The water is real shallow, an' the bottom is hard shale and sand. So if anyone fell off, 'tw'udn't do 'em any harm. Matter of fact, we c'ud wade to the end of the log, if that was necessary. But the pine is as stidy as a boardwalk."

And then he walked out. I did not think that I could do it in that half-light, but with Pend's help I did. Dud was waiting for us at the end. And he whispered, "Look at the bottom."

The bottom was silver white.

"Sand," said Dud. "In the daytime yer can see it bubbling. Thar's a tremendous spring here, but it's always gentle—no gushing. Now, jist keep still an' watch."

As I watched, the water seemed to become clearer, or the moonlight brighter.

"Now," whispered Dud.

A school of little trout swam over the white sand, turned, and came back.

"Not yit," whispered Dud. "It hain't here yit."

Pend whispered in my ear, "I suspect that I know what he wants us to see. Watch."

Suddenly, as if they had been summoned from far away, the small trout were gone. And, without a visible approach, I saw a huge fish posed motionless over the sand. And I felt that queer excitement that is older than our race. And I saw the larger stripe of white-white on the creature's pectoral fins. I saw its eyes!

"Wait," whispered Dud.

And there, beside the first trout, lay another giant. They lay side by side, and I saw that they were perfectly matched.

"Wait," whispered Dud.

And there were three more, and then I saw another. There were six immense trout as if they had materialized from the clean water and the white sand. My eyes began to doubt, or I to doubt my eyes. I moved nearer to Pend, to touch him for assurance. And the trout were gone!

Dud chuckled. "It w'ud always be that way," he said.

We walked back to the camp in silence. Dud placed wood on the red coals. It caught fire, and the yellow light was welcome.

"Were they real?" I asked, feeling silly to do so, but unable to keep back the question.

"Of course they were real," said Pend.

But Dud Dean chuckled. "Speakin' fer myself, I'll have to say that I don't know. All I know is that's what I saw off that log when it was full moonlight fifty years ago. I was there to git a pail of water, but I went back after Mat Markham. And I know what Mat said. He says, 'Be you tryin' to fool me? Nobudy ever catched a trout that big. Nobudy ever heard of a big trout bein' catched in this pond. It's a crotchly lie, that's what it is!' And all the time, Mat stood thar lookin' at them trout jist the same as we did tonight.

"So much as I know, Mat was right when he said that no one ever claimed to git any really big trout in here. We didn't. And nor have we this time. In most waters, trout grow slow. I don't see any reason to think that trout grow fast in this little pond. It appears to be fair-to-middlin' trout water an' that's all.

"But if I was to let myself go, I w'ud take my oath that them big trout we saw tonight was the same trout that I saw fifty years ago. Yes sir, by crotch, I'll never forgit them trout. C'udn't. But yer may watch an' wait until kingdom-come an' ye'll never see them trout in the daylight. They don't even seem to be nearabouts in the daytime. So it figgers out this way: only time ye'll ever see 'em is late in a moonlight night. So I don't know. Sometimes I have wondered if it was a trick the moonlight played, but yer saw the smaller trout before the big ones come in tonight. W'ud yer say that it was a trick of the moonlight on the bottom, Pend?"

Pend replied, "No, it wasn't an illusion."

"We-ell, maybe it's the Enchanted—eh? Maybe it's like pink, and white, and yellow lady's slippers. All I know is that I've seen them trout twice. I guess I'm not apt to see them ever ag'in. But maybe you folks will. Yer know, I w'ud have been bad disapp'inted if storm er clouds had hidden the full moon tonight. We-ell, hope yer sleep sound. So goodnight."

When he had gone to his own camp, Pend and I sat together near the dying fire. And I said, "What do you really think, dear?"

"Think? Why I think that Dud Dean was like an old priest out there tonight. And deep in my heart, I think that the grand old fellow was passing something on to us, something he has loved, and that he wanted to share with us. God bless him."

Appendix I

Poems

POETIC EXPRESSIONS PLAY IN THE DUD DEAN yarns like light and shadow on the forest floor. It may be in the choice of a few remarkable words, as when Dud describes the coming of snow as having the sound of silence, or in the mystical sense, expressed in so many of the stories, that in nature there is a simple yet noble grandeur that gives character and courage to humankind.

Arthur Macdougall was at soul a poet. The selections that follow are a sample from his book of poems, *Far Enough For All The Years.*

THE NIGHT WE CAMPED ON MOXOS MOUNTAIN[1]

> The magic hatch of Caddis flies
> Was gone like afternoon;
> The twilight deepened round the lake,
> And day was done too soon.
>
> The moonlight fell on Moxos like
> A silver tide of prayer,
> And silence held a hand on us
> To keep us quiet there.

The hermit thrushes' singing was
An echo in our hearts;
The hoot owl's gossip hushed away
And so the long night starts.

The moonlight changed to rolling fog,
The black night bled to gray;
The little silver bells of dawn
Began to ring and play.

And thus the smile of morning came
Across the granite scars;
And sunrise towed a little wind
To sweep away the stars.

[1]Located ten miles north of Bingham, Moxie Mountain is the valley's signet. It is surrounded by ponds. Pleasant Pond lies to the north, while to the south is Heald Pond, where Moxie's scarred shoulders rise high above the reflecting water. Northeast of the mountain lie the Dimmick ponds. Above them is Mountain Pond, the site of this poem. It is cupped into the east side of Moxie at an elevation of nearly two thousand feet.

THE AUSTIN

We fished the upper Austin,
Where North and South unite
The black and lazy Austin
With meadows left and right.

We fished the winding Austin,
And trout a wild-rose red,
And green a-washed with gold dust,
Were where the Austin led.

We mocked a stolid pumper,
And whistled at a duck;

And knelt to kiss an orchid
To bring us better luck.

The ragged, tattered wildlands
The North branch plows between,
And pungent bluejoint meadows
The South branch washes clean

Were warm beneath the laughter
Of summer's golden sun,
And I, my heart kept wishing
Such days were never done.

SIMON PETER ON THE KENNEBEC

Where the river pushes through a mob of hills,
Day's end found me casting as an angler wills;
Casting line and leader where the river runs
Heedless of the sunset's iridescent puns.

Looking up, I saw him smiling down on me
Odd, how democratic fishermen can be!
Chief among us anglers, keeper of the Sign,
He who knew the Lord and drank the holy wine.

Simon Peter, asking why I fished with flies,
What I'd caught worth catching . . . fancy my surprise.
"Half a creel of teasing questions on Pale Duns,
Half a creel of answers, counting smaller ones."

"Friend," said Simon Peter, "try a longer cast."
So I cast for courage and achieved at last;
Cast my heart at courage . . . when it came, I struck.
"Lad," he said, "I'm going, but I wish you luck."

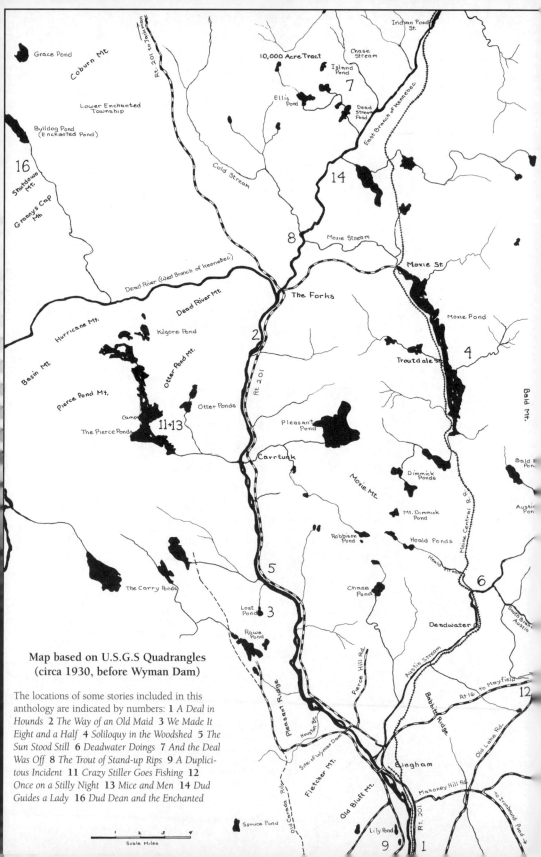

**Map based on U.S.G.S Quadrangles
(circa 1930, before Wyman Dam)**

The locations of some stories included in this
anthology are indicated by numbers: **1** *A Deal in
Hounds* **2** *The Way of an Old Maid* **3** *We Made It
Eight and a Half* **4** *Soliloquy in the Woodshed* **5** *The
Sun Stood Still* **6** *Deadwater Doings* **7** *And the Deal
Was Off* **8** *The Trout of Stand-up Rips* **9** *A Duplici-
tous Incident* **11** *Crazy Stiller Goes Fishing* **12**
Once on a Stilly Night **13** *Mice and Men* **14** *Dud
Guides a Lady* **16** *Dud Dean and the Enchanted*

Appendix II

Places and Characters

WITH A FEW EXCEPTIONS, the locations for Dud's adventures can be "pinned" on a map like the one presented here. The following notes add color and information for readers who have not had the joy of seeing these locations for themselves.

Villages

Bingham is a blessed village. It is held as in the hollow of a hand formed by hills and long-backed mountains, yet there is room for it to spread on level land. Bingham is also blessed by being situated on the banks of the Kennebec River, flowing black and silver against the steep bluff to the west and favored as a gateway to a land of lakes, ponds, streams, and forests.

To see the country of folding hills and great mountains surrounding Bingham, one needs to approach the village from the east, using Route 16. Down four miles, the road plunges from the top of Babbitt Ridge to the valley floor. A yellow sign warns of 10 percent grades, and woe to the vehicle that loses its brakes. Descending, one looks across the valley, its river and village still unseen, to the great mass of Fletcher Mountain and beyond to ranges of blue peaks—Bigelow, Sugarloaf, and Abraham.

If one uses Route 201 and approaches from the south, the introduction to Bingham is gentler and pastoral. Twelve miles to the north the scarred, blue shoulders of Moxie Mountain push against the sky. Much nearer at hand, just two miles above the village, Wyman Dam stretches from hill to hill, interrupting the free flow of the Kennebec and forming fourteen miles of lake.

When my father first came to Bingham, the dam did not exist, and the Kennebec flowed free from Caratunk to Bingham through a valley that, though walled with hills, contained intervening fields, islands, and farms. Much more has changed since my father came to preach, bury, marry—and fish. Then, before Route 201 entered the village or ran between the river and the hayfields of the Taylor farm, the road crossed the tracks of the Maine Central's Somerset Branch. That railroad brought a quiet prosperity to Bingham.

Still, when I was a boy in the late thirties and early forties, the village remained far closer to earlier times than to the present. The town's old snow roller (used before snowplows) was weathering away behind the fire hall, but the grading of our street was still done by a four-horse team pulling a road machine. There were electric lights at our house, but we still had a "refrigerator box," and the iceman gave us crystal slivers to suck on when he delivered ice. The days when herds of cattle were driven up the main street had passed, but there were photographs of that excitement.

The main street of my youth was much as it is described in the Dud Dean stories—an avenue for the breezes under the green arch of elms. There was the Bingham Hotel opposite Meadow Street (our street), then Ben Adams's small barbershop filled with a private collection of curios and antiques. Diagonally across the street was the substantial building shared by Preble and Robinson's grocery store and Frank Savage's dry-goods establishment. Covered stairs ran up the side of the building to the second floor and Kennebec Hall where the town's secular events took place—including moving pictures accompanied by one of the town's pianists.

The "town center" was just north of Preble and Robinson's store. There, the three-storied Hunnewell Block and Moore's drugstore were on the right, facing the Donigan Block, hardware store, and post office across Main Street. At the head of the street, nudged by the base of Flag Staff Hill, was Robie House's garage—a cement anomaly.

In those days, there was time to chat, which is what people did when they went uptown to get the mail and do errands. For longer confabs, the seats by the shoeboxes at the back of Bunny Pierce's clothing store were often used, or one leaned on the counter in Orin Hill's store under the glassy stare of a stuffed moose. Taking time to talk was worth it. My father met a well-known logger one morning on the sidewalk outside Erving Moore's drugstore. This man had been in the woods camp up in Enchanted Township when the blizzard-shrouded night was frozen even more solidly by hair-raising cries that filled the forest. The braver men lit lanterns and went out into the storm, but no explanation was ever found.

"What did the cries sound like?" my father asked.

Obligingly the old logger stepped out to the middle of the street and, with hands cupped around his mouth, let go with a rendition.

The village I remember, the Bingham of the Dud Dean stories, was an event as much as a place. It was people—colorful and just plain solid—stories, associations, the comfortably customary and interconnected, all woven through with the mysterious. Around all this the hills stood guard while season followed season, and the Kennebec, like a branch of eternity, swept by on its way to the ocean and the other world.

In the old days, **Caratunk** was an important stop for the stagecoach heading upriver. After tumbling down a mountainside, Pleasant Pond Stream runs through the village and sometimes, in a freshet, covers front lawns with rocks and small boulders. But events of such magnitude are rare in Caratunk. The houses on each side of the only street, which until fairly recently was also Route 201, are neat; a good bit of Yankee common sense and pride lives inside them. Clark's store still bears its sign, but when I was a boy, Albert Clark, himself, (see the story, "The Sun Stood Still") bagged the groceries and pumped the gas. I remember him as balding, tall, and wearing a bow tie.

Albert owned and operated his own telephone system, which served the summer people at Pleasant Pond. In his "Adventures in a Model T," Arthur Macdougall recounts:

"One day, during the summer, Albert received a call from New York City for a summer resident at The Pond, a broker by trade. Albert thought that the call was important. And he had just accomplished the involved maneuver of hitching New York City to Pleasant Pond, in Caratunk, Maine, when he heard a click on the line and then a noise like the ticking of a clock on a Sunday afternoon.

"And Albert said, 'By crotch, Hatty, you hang up, and if there's anything in Mr. Swan's call that you should know about, we'll tell you about it afterward.'"

Traveling some eight miles north on Route 201, one comes to **The Forks**. Its name is descriptive, for here the Kennebec splits into the East Branch and the Dead River. The East Branch pours out of Moosehead, while the Dead River flows from the mountain country of Bigelow and Coburn Gore.

The Forks was a crossroads, so to speak. Early on, its two rivers became highways for loggers and river drivers, and what is now Route 201 was the main road to Quebec. During the tense days when England and America nearly came to open war over the boundary between the United States and Canada (1840), there were troops encamped at The Forks. For years, supplies and an army of men left the village to fell the forest, thousands of immigrants passed through on their way to find new livelihoods, and cattle drives raised the dust of the village's street. There's a book to be written about The Forks—preferably a novel that could make full use of all the old raw and rollicking tales originating there.

In Dud's day, Route 201 crossed the East Branch through a long covered bridge. Just south of that span was one of two hotels. Its size—three and a half stories, with an equally high and lengthy ell—was an indication of the numbers of people who traveled through the village. Both the first and second stories had porches from which one could watch the moonlight dance on the moving surface of the East Branch (see "The Trout of Stand-up Rips").

Other Places, Not Located on the Map

Attean Pond—A lake-size body of water which lies southwest of Jackman on Route 201.

Basset Flats—A section of the old road to Caratunk. It lies approximately three-quarters of a mile north of Moscow village and the present site of Wyman Dam.

The Bunter Pool—My father favored the East Branch of the Kennebec River and especially this pool, which is situated perhaps three miles above The Forks, where Moxie and Cold Streams join the river. On many afternoons we drove to The Forks, crossed the bridge, turned right, and followed a hay-bordered track for a quarter of a mile till the alders closed in. Then the ceremony of cutting walking sticks was initiated. My father took great care to whittle the butt-end of his stick round and smooth. That ritual done, the trek would begin again, heading up the old log-drivers' trail.

We would fish till the sun bronzed the hillsides to the east and the twilight came in darkening shadows along the riverbank. Today, I close my eyes and see again the great sweep of the river as it comes down and turns in the bunter pool. I see my father's figure a quarter mile above me. He is up over his knees in water, which runs tinted by the final colors in the west. His perfect cast reaches out one last time, and then one last time again.

We always walked back to the car in the dark. Had he wanted to do so, I think my father would have remembered the flashlight at least once in while. There were times when it would have been handy—one place in particular, where the trail skirted ledges that dropped down to the sounding river. There, the river drivers had built walkways of logs to span the gullies, but these were no longer trustworthy.

"Remember, the word is diligence," my father warned on one such crossing. And I have remembered that admonition at different times and in places far from the East Branch.

There was another hazard on the driver's trail. The single wire of the old telephone line was up here and down there. At places it draped across the trail. There would come a warning *twang* when the metal tube of Dad's Thomas rod, held out before him, encountered the wire in the darkness.

Dimmick Siding—A railroad siding located about two and a half miles above Deadwater.

The "Dug-outs"—Narrow places where the road to Caratunk and The Forks had to be cut into the steep hillsides along the river.

The Gilroy and Gilroy Boom—Located approximately a mile below The Forks, where Gilroy Brook flows into the Kennebec from the west. Here the river sweeps around a group of islands.

The Gut—A section of the Kennebec near the Ed Burry place and close to where Carrying Place Brook flows into the bigger river.

Holden's Camps—Located on Attean Pond, southwest of Jackman.

The Hulling Machine—Once spectacular falls on the East Branch perhaps three-quarters of a mile below the old outlet of Indian Pond. These falls have since been flooded-out by a dam and power station.

The John Savage Place—A farm on the Mahoney Hill Road.

Lone Jack Pond—Its location is uncertain, but it is mentioned in connection with Robinson Pond, which is located on the map, south of Moxie Mountain.

The Old Ball Place—South of the Owens Place, this farm was settled by a veteran of the Revolution.

The Owens Place—A farm abutting the Kennebec in Concord,

Maine; it is below Lily Pond, which is shown at the bottom of the map.

Parlin Pond—Located on Route 201, approximately fifteen miles north of The Forks.

Stand-up Rips—The first strip of white water above The Forks, just below the Bunter Pool.

Withy Pond and Bog—Located just off the Old Lake Road, south of Ben Adams Corner.

People

In my father's day, the country of the upper Kennebec was filled with ready-made characters, many of whom appear undisguised in the Dud Dean stories. Others, for one good reason or another, appear incognito. Some characters—like Dud Dean, himself—are actually composite figures and therefore assume a rich humanness.

There were also the legions of men and women who, having read the Dud Dean yarns, came to Bing-

Left to right: Fellow outdoorsemen Jack Owens, Arthur Macdougall, and Robert Moore

ham to fish and meet Mak. One gentleman stopped his car in front of Thompson Restaurant, got out, and began calling "Hey, Mak!" It worked. He was quickly directed to the parsonage. Many came year after year, and some became my father's close friends. So Dick Lord in "The Sun Stood Still" and Lyman Ford in "Zoromaster Sayeth," while fictitious, are representative of the host of anglers who traveled to the upper Kennebec to fish in spirit with the master guide, Dud Dean.

Doc Browning—A melding of medical men who went in horse-drawn buggies or on snowshoes to wherever a lamp burned beside a sickbed, to use the old phrase. There was one Bingham physician who people said operated with a copy of *Gray's Anatomy* open on the table, but most of these men who served the upper Kennebec were skilled and respected physicians. They also practiced at being characters, which made them all the more endearing. Yearly it grows harder for us to feel the aura that surrounded these old-time medical men. No one should be surprised if erudition tumbles through Doc Browning's colorful expressions. After all, these doctors were well educated. Of course, a lot of ministers were educated, as well, but who would forgive a parson for being something of a rogue?

The Cateses of Cates Hill—This family lived above the Kennebec, some eight miles north of Bingham. Chandler was the patriarch and a master at telling humorous stories, often about himself or his boys. All the Cateses, even the youngest, "Little" Ruel, had a certain genius of expression. In "The Way of an Old Maid," Henry Gates, who maintains his soft voice, even when riled, is certainly a very thinly disguised Cates.

Tom Collins—Tom was one of the capable Bingham guides. His trim white house and attached barn still stand on the right-hand side of Route 201 as the road begins the ascent from Bingham to the village of Moscow.

Daniel Bean—The Beans were a large clan. Daniel was a Civil War veteran who lived on the west side of the river above Bingham.

Floyd Hunnewell—One way or another, the Kennebec River Hunnewells are descended from Israel Hunnewell, born in 1703 and a resident of Berwick and Wiscasset. Floyd was a man of many trades. Such versatility went along with making ends meet on the upper Kennebec. He farmed, ran a sawmill, did some blacksmithing, cut timber, and tended the boom that guided the logs past his farm. When Wyman Lake was created by the damming of the Kennebec at Moscow, Floyd waited as long as he could to abandon his set of buildings and move to higher ground. The day after they burned the house, water filled the cellar hole.

Erving and Robert Moore—One of Bingham's cultured men, Erving owned and operated Moore's Drugstore on Bingham's Main Street. Next door, shaded by elms, stood his home, which seemed to a small boy both big and exceptionally white. I remember visiting him only once. He was an old man with hair as white as his house. He was confined to bed, but he had brought to us artifacts that spoke of his varied interests: bullets found in Dead River, where one of Benedict Arnold's bateaus had overturned; an Indian adze mounted upon a handle with thongs; a door hinge from Pompeii.

Erving's son, Robert, eventually took over the business. Besides dispensing medicines, the store sold jewelry, cut glass, school supplies, photographic supplies, phonograph records, and more. From the back room, whose walls were lined with brown bottles and equipped with a druggist's apparatuses, came a number of unique preparations including an effective, pungent citronella fly dope.

Dan Nye—I have not been able to track down Dan but suspect that he was a real person. If so, he was certainly related to the author of the notable little book, *This is Where Mother Sat Down to Die*. Written by Belle Spaulding Nye, it describes life along the Kennebec above Bingham before construction of the Wyman Dam.

Jack Owens—When my father first came to Bingham, he was a worm fisherman (a fact we never discussed). His brother, Walter, had already discovered the art of fly fishing and urged a reformation, but it was Jack Owens who taught my father to fish with flies. He lived next door to the parsonage on Meadow Street in Bingham, and together Dad and Jack kept bees, talked away delightful hours, and went fishing whenever they could.

Jack was born in Moscow, Maine, in 1875. In his younger years he had guided and knew the country well. Later he became a tailor and for twenty-five years was connected with Mark Savage's dry goods company.

Jack was a source for many of the stories that are woven into the Dud Dean yarns, and his character and his code of life as a gentleman are there, as well. When he died in 1936, the notice in the newspaper read ". . . he was a kind man in his home and a good neighbor." Jack was much more than that to my father.

Dave Pooler—Dave was an "all-around" guide who knew Pierce Pond like the back of his hand. His brother, Bill Pooler, was also a woodsman and a friend of my father's. Bill died on the trail to Rock Pond.

Walter Robinson—Born on the Kennebec just above the site where Wyman Dam would be built, Walter was one of fourteen children. He was a man of fine qualities and became a prosperous store owner and successful operator of large woods operations at Deadwater and Indian Pond. He and several other prominent citizens formed the Bingham Improvement Society, which indicates the impact he had on his community. He was another Meadow Street neighbor and good friend to our family.

Mark Savage—Savage is a prominent Bingham name. Mark owned and operated a dry goods business.

Shurtliff—This inveterate coon hunter appears in "Once on a Stilly Night" and is identified as coming from Lewiston. I feel sure that he was a real person. However, I have not been able to find anyone who will admit to being his relative.

William Whorf—Will was one of the best-known characters in Bingham, and his stages carried passengers and mail from Skowhegan to The Forks. In 1893, when only nineteen, he bought a stage business and operated it for the next fifty years. For Will, the weather—as bad as the mud or the snowdrifts could be—was no excuse for staying home, nor was he above running errands for housewives along the way. Will Whorf thought a lot of his horses: Old Fred, Nigger, Maggie, and the spirited Switcher. It must have been a comedown when during his last years of service, he used an REO sedan.

Pearl Woodard—For years, Pearl was station agent in Bingham for the Somerset Railway and later for the Maine Central. He was a good man with the telegraph key, figures, and cards—not to mention his being a first-class storyteller.

The Youngs—Two massive mountains flank the Kennebec and Bingham to the west: Old Bluff and Fletcher. Between them is a narrow valley, which the Youngs called home. People used to say they lived "over behind Bluff."